REMIND ME TO SMILE

The Life and Times of
a Teenage Numanoid

Martin Downham

Hornet Books

First published 2016 by Hornet Books
Text © Martin Downham 2016
This work © Hornet Books Ltd
Paperback ISBN: 978-0-9955260-0-6

Editor: David Roberts
Proof reading: Suzannah Young
Front cover artwork is by Rob Monks. For further info please find him on his Facebook page, Roberica Monks, or on Twitter @roberica2010

Hornet Books
Ground Floor, 2B Vantage Park, Washingley Road,
Huntingdon, PE29 6SR

www.hornetbooks.com
info@hornetbooks.com

Printed and bound by CPI Group (UK) Ltd, Croydon

For Vicki,
Peter and Sam

Introduction

Music, as John Miles earnestly intoned on his 1976 single, was his first love, as well as being, quite probably, his last. That goes for me, too. Music is a wonderful, sensual, evocative, dynamic, multi-faceted spectrum of many-splendored things. It's happy and sad, light and dark. Music is a song that you can't get out of your head on the way to work; sometimes a song you wish you could get out of your head! Music is a song that you dance to at a party, the night of your first kiss. It's a song you heard at your first gig, or struggled to play along to on your guitar, desperately trying to fret that all-but-impossible F chord. It's a song that you remember from your first date and a song that reduced you to tears at a funeral. A tune will effortlessly take you back to earlier, younger, perhaps more innocent times and that is the essence of this book.

On the face of it, this has nothing to do with Gary Numan and Tubeway Army but bear with me. While this is no slavish, day-by-day biography of Numan, with full details of every album, single release, tour and event during his roller coaster of a career, it *IS* the story of the impact he had on my life.

My first exposure to music? Being born in the 1960s, I'd hear my Dad listening to Frank Sinatra crooning across the airwaves, emanating from our radiogram as *Worldwide Family Favourites* was broadcast each Sunday lunchtime. Mum was a bit more hip and would sing along to The Beatles but wasn't opposed to a crooner or two or maybe a bit of Petula Clark, Dusty Springfield and Dionne Warwick as well. We kids would hum along to the more popular songs in The Hit Parade, waiting for that one song to knock us flat and make us think, "THIS is what I've been waiting for, all my young life!"

Teenagers in the 1960s were spoilt by a plethora of new and exciting music and musicians, lead by The Beatles. John Lennon was famously quoted as saying that once he heard Elvis Presley for the very first time in the late 1950s, his life changed forever. That's how powerful music can be. In the literally hopeless, militant, strike-addled, three-day week of the 1970s, the Sex Pistols struck a nerve amongst disillusioned British teenagers and caused many, upon hearing 'Pretty Vacant', or 'New Rose' by The Damned, to heed the revolutionary call to arms, discard their aimless existence and embrace the nihilistic, self-expression of Punk.

Being a teenager, in any decade, is a troublesome time, especially if you're a boy. Girls, that in Infants or Junior school you'd quite cheerfully push into a patch of stinging nettles, rapidly turn into more complex creatures. Their braces, glasses and pigtails vanish by the time Senior school arrives, rapidly replaced with make-up, intoxicating perfume and a maturity that seems to belie their young years. Boys, on the other hand, embrace immaturity like it's going out of fashion - still playing football in the playground, still watching *Star Trek* re-runs on television in the summer holidays and buying *Spider-Man Comics Weekly* every Saturday morning from the local newsagent. Well, that was me, anyway.

Then hormones kick-in and that's a whole new world of confusion. Barely any kind of informative or useful teaching from school in the Biology class, plus the sheer humiliation of "The Birds and The Bees" lecture from your Dad. It all makes for a difficult time. Acne, attitude, lust along with copious sweating, resulting in the armpits of your school-shirts becoming so ossified and rock-hard they could be cracked with a pickaxe.

In the dim distant days of 1977 I was turning into the archetypal, stroppy, know-it-all teenager – angry for no good reason, rude, insolent, indolent, bone-idle, rebellious – but just when I was about to go down the path of a destructive adolescent, life had other plans.

And this is my story.

CHAPTER 1

Tubeway Days now seem quite unreal

I could almost hear the enamel on my Dad's teeth splintering and cracking as he peered over his well-thumbed copy of the crusading *Daily Mirror*. It's June 1979 and there, invading the sanctity and security of our living room on this fine Thursday night, as *Top of the Pops* reaches its weekly climax, is the UK's No.1, the best-selling single.

A-No.1.

King of the Hill.

Top of the heap.

The outfit responsible - that has sold more records than any other across the length and breadth of the country?

Tubeway Army.

And my Dad hates it.

The pounding, relentless, metallic beat of 'Are 'friends' electric?', which will steadfastly hold onto the No.1 spot for the next few weeks and divide a nation, is driving my Dad to the point of apoplexy.

"Oh, Christ, not him again!" he growls, grinding his teeth and shaking the pages of the paper as if to emphasise the point. "How come he's No.1?" he demands. "It's a load of old…" Dad struggles to find the appropriate metaphor and just stops short of calling it "shit," instead settling on "crap".

It's fair to say that Dad does not like Gary Numan or Tubeway Army at all, not in the least tiny bit. To be fair, he doesn't like any music in the charts but begrudgingly allows us to tune into each week's *Top of the Pops*, if only so that he can watch Legs & Co strutting their stuff, ideally in butt-hugging outfits. But, modern music generally? No thanks.

Although I am utterly, completely, engrossed in the performance I can sense out of the corner of my eye that Dad would much prefer to be watching something else. Despite the prospect of Legs & Co he is contemplating getting up and heading for the television to turn over and punch one of the spiteful, spring-loaded, bullet-shaped channel buttons that protrude from the faux teak fascia of our Radio Rentals TV set. Maybe something on BBC-2 or ITV? Or to maybe press the mysterious fourth button that, so I'm told, is for use in 'the future' when there might be another TV channel? But he doesn't – he just sits there glowering, incensed that following weeks of heavy radio-play the song has, somehow, reached the giddy heights of No.1 in the good old Hit Parade.

As for me, I'm lost – the song that has absolutely captivated me is pouring forth in glorious mono from the TV and I'm gone – an entrancing, soul-enriching, life-changing moment in my otherwise shapeless and dull teenage years. Gary Numan and Tubeway Army would create the key soundtrack to my blossoming wonder years – a period when music was more varied than ever before, coinciding with the point at which I cautiously started on the path that would save this shy, awkward, completely naive teenager.

I'm engrossed in the performance – Gary Numan stands virtually immobile, painfully thin, dressed in black but bathed completely in white light, lit from above and below, with the floor lights casting eerie, unnatural shadows across his face: impassive, disconnected and aloof. He has heavily made-up eyes, pale skin and jet-black hair. Other bands that I'd seen on *Top of the Pops*, for as long I could remember, had all anxiously searched out the camera as they mimed their latest three-minute pop songs – all cheery, all smiling. Chirpy and permed, they'd all wanted to get a close-up, almost as if to say, "Hello, Mum!" And it wasn't just the middle of the road, bland acts of the mid-1970s. Even the brash, insolent Punk bands that roared through the BBC-TV studios in the late 1970s, such as Sham 69 featuring the shameless Jimmy Pursey, or The Boomtown

Rats featuring the equally screen-savvy Bob Geldof, all coveted and courted the TV cameras to ensure maximum exposure.

But Numan is different. He looks like he's there under duress and would rather be a thousand miles away. No orthodox performance in the traditional *TOTP* sense, he doesn't even engage with the studio audience to any appreciable degree – just surveys the *TOTP* crowd with disinterest, disdain, almost contempt. He rarely blinks and does not register any emotion as he talks us through – it could hardly be called singing – a song rich in detail and imagery about isolation, abandoned and decrepit rooms, sinister surveillance, decay, betrayal, shadows and the unidentified 'friend'. And I've never, ever seen anything like it before.

But why him? Why a skinny, unsmiling, humourless, Bowie-clone? Why did one song have such an enduring and resonating impact upon me? For that, we need to go way, way back to the forces and events that shaped my life, not through any sense of self-aggrandizement but merely to identify who I was, how I came to be and the social structure and status of my family. More importantly, why did this song come to mean so very much to me?

I was born in 1963 and so missed out on the whole Sixties thing, man – joining the nuclear family of parents and elder brother Peter in our tiny one-bedroom flat over my Dad's shoe repair shop down Tolworth Broadway in suburban Surrey. I know that I was planned but it took several years of heaving and humping and, I believe, a miscarriage or two before I arrived on the scene. By all accounts, it wasn't an easy birth and telegrams that were sent to my Mum in the maternity ward at Kingston Hospital, re-discovered years later, were all along the lines of, "Well done – so it wasn't an elephant, then?" On my arrival at home, my brother remarked that I had "a huge purple head" which kind of set the tone of our sibling relationship for the next few decades.

The flat was spitting distance from the roaring traffic on the A3 where, in later years, I was convinced that every car and vehicle was heading away to much more exciting and interesting places. I slept in Mum and Dad's room and at night, before going to sleep, I'd listen to the traffic, wondering where the cars were going as the throaty sounds of their exhausts faded into the distance. The curtains were always open, with the lurid orange phosphorous of the street lights bathing the bedroom.

We had a small living room that had a three-bar electric fire, which served as the sole source of heat for the entire flat. A black and white television buzzed and fizzed in the corner with a set of rabbit-ear aerials on the top which were regularly paraded high and low round the room in order to get a decent picture. At the rear of the room was a huge radiogram with a walnut finish that housed our meagre collection of albums. In another corner was a floor-standing birdcage where our budgie chirruped incessantly from within.

We had a tiny kitchen which had no door as I'd locked myself in the equally tiny adjacent bathroom when I was about two years old. No amount of pleading or cajoling by Mum, Dad or Peter could persuade me to unlock the door, so Dad had to take an axe to it to get me out. As we couldn't afford a new bathroom door, he had to take the kitchen door off as a replacement.

Our spare room doubled as the dining room as well as my brother Peter's bedroom. Compact doesn't begin to describe it and it probably sounds worse than it was. It was actually a very happy environment. I can't ever remember a time when there wasn't music playing. Mum always had the radio on. My earliest memories were of her singing and dancing as I watched while crawling on the lino and evacuating my bowels into thrice-bleached Terrylene nappies. A few years later, I can remember listening to the radiogram in the living room, back home after she and I walked what seemed like miles taking my brother to school. Mum absolutely adored The Beatles and if I concentrate really hard, I can still picture her singing along to 'We Can Work It Out'.

Ah – how evocative is music? A few bars of a record – a few seconds of the intro, a soaring melody – can instantly transport you back through years or decades to a day, a place or an event, a safe place because we know exactly what is going to happen – there are no surprises. Some memories now are just a finger-tip out of reach in the recesses of my mind and all that remains is a hint, a flavour, a faded photograph of that long-lost moment. So music has always been there – a backdrop to my every day existence.

Back to my mum: the life and soul of any party whose arrival at family gatherings was anxiously anticipated because that's when the fun started. She certainly was a fun-loving woman and had a wicked sense of humour. I remember one occasion as we walked down Tolworth Broadway to the local Pay'n'Take convenience store, two nuns approached us: serene, beatific and smiling, with their long cloaks billowing behind them in the breeze. They had collection tins and stopped us to see if we wanted to make a donation. Mum obligingly reached into the pocket of her turquoise-blue mackintosh, found a couple of sixpences and dropped them into the tin.

"Bless you," said one of the nuns, her appreciation genuine and heartfelt.

"It's my pleasure," replied Mum, and then adding with a cheery wink, "Any friend of Batman is a friend of mine."

We continued to the shops, Mum giggling all the way, leaving the nuns behind us looking very confused, still smiling if a little uncertainly.

Mum was the one who was always there for us, the one we went to for love and affection, for a plaster when we'd scraped our knees, for a handkerchief when we were crying, always waving at the school gate at the end of the day to greet us, possibly even with a Mars Bar in her pocket for us if we were really lucky.

But Dad was virtually an invisible presence in my early years. He'd worked as a manual labourer since leaving school without a single qualification to his name. He was by no means ignorant or stupid; it's just that school wasn't for him so he worked with his hands in various manual-labour jobs. He'd eventually ended up working in a shoe repair shop in Surbiton, where he caught the eye of the young girl, Marian Holmes, behind the counter in the chemist shop opposite and that was that. A whirlwind romance followed and they were married soon after in 1952. My elder brother arrived in 1956 by which time they had moved out of my maternal grandmother's backroom where they'd lived for the first few years of their married lives and moved into the flat over the Tolworth branch of the shoe shop where he worked and worked and worked. The flat came as part of his remuneration for managing the shop but he was just never at home. He never took us to school, never picked us up from school, never played games with us, rarely took us out and just seemed focussed on earning as much as he could to bolster their paltry savings, which were undoubtedly drained by my arrival in 1963.

In what were still quite austere times, where the general populace didn't have much money to splurge and still had a post-war "make do and mend" mentality, Dad spent all day repairing shoes. He sometimes foolishly held in his mouth the tiny tacks he used to repair the soles with where an incautious sneeze or cough would send him gasping to Mum having swallowed the lot. By the time he ascended the stairs from the shop to the flat of an evening, always tired, always smeared black from the polish, we were just about ready for bed anyway so we didn't spend much time with him even then, leaving him to his tea and the latest episode of *The Man from UNCLE* or *The Avengers*. There was no intentional neglect on his part, as I know without question that Dad loved us unreservedly. He was just so busy, all the time, every day. Sunday drives out to Box Hill, or to the pitch and putt mini-golf course in Tolworth for instance, were rare treats indeed.

We had finally outgrown the confines of the flat and relocated on a bitterly cold winter's day just before Christmas 1968 to what appeared to be the leafy suburbia of Princes Avenue and a tidy 1930s semi-detached about half a mile away. We hadn't exactly left the flat of our own volition as Dad had had a "conflict of interests" with the shoe-shop owner. The owner had made an unscheduled visit to the shop and was appalled to find it empty, a veritable *Mary Celeste*, with no-one on-hand to either sell the leather briefcases, gloves and shoes, or take in shoes to be repaired. Perplexed, he went out to the back to the workshop and found Dad in the stockroom and discovered him *in flagranti* with the young female shop assistant. Mum, summoned from the dry-cleaners next door, went through every swear-word and profanity she knew without pause or repetition and nearly flattened him with a club-hammer. It's lucky the nuns weren't in earshot as they might have given the sixpences back. With no other choice, the owner fired Dad on the spot with a month's notice to vacate the flat.

My brother and I, looking back now, are still uncertain as to why Dad "played away from home" with the shop assistant. I suspect that he felt a bit under-appreciated, as Mum spent most, if not all, of her spare time looking after us. Dad liked his women slim, trim and tidy and Mum, when she was just 18, looked like a model. Unfortunately, after I was born, she put on quite a bit of weight, weight she'd never lose again, sadly. Maybe that's what caused Dad's eye to wander.

Who knows?

The upshot was, the family dynamic was never really quite the same after this incident. Oh, they kept us kids in the dark about what had happened and as far as we were concerned everything was fine. But, looking back, there was sometimes, very occasionally, a barely concealed, simmering contempt between the two of them which, all things considered, was not really surprising. I remember a few years later just after this incident Dad cheerfully announced that the skin on the back of your hand was virtually devoid of sensation and that if you pinched it, you couldn't feel anything. Why he should announce this was anyone's guess but he was keen to demonstrate this biological anomaly.

"Go on, have a go," Dad said assuredly, presenting the back of his hand to Peter and me. In turn, Peter squeezed as hard as he could, then I tried, puffing and breathless, all the while Dad standing legs apart, confident that we could not inflict the slightest twinge, pain or ill-effects despite our best efforts. Mum then appeared.

"Let me have a go," she said.

Dad turned to face her but in the blink of an eye, she had fastened a pair of mole-grips tightly on the back of his hand. Dad opened his mouth and screamed but no sound emerged, although stray dogs in the back-alley raised a quizzical ear and started barking. Now Mum thought that was really funny.

How Mum and Dad stayed together is a mystery but stay together they did, dealing with the immediate prospect of having to find another place to live. Moving back in with my maternal grandmother was out of the question so we faced the very real possibility of being literally kicked out onto the street. But just when the odds seemed stacked against us, The Man Upstairs looked down and smiled benignly and gave us a winning set of score-draws on the football pools, with telegram claims required, netting us a handsome £405.0s.0d. This was an absolute fortune, which gave us the opportunity to put a deposit on the house in Princes Avenue, costing a staggering £4,500.0s.0d.

Our paltry belongings barely filled the new house and without much carpet, it echoed to our footsteps. Dad had often cycled down Princes Avenue when he was younger with his ramshackle gang of mates, and thought that living there in these newly-built houses would be just paradise. The Downham family had moved out of London's East End when the bombs started falling during World War II and my paternal grandparents believed Surrey to be a safer environment. Dad now had the chance to buy a house in the road where he had once longingly gazed at what he considered to be palaces, wondering just how he and Mum were now going to pay the eye-watering mortgage that stretched ahead of them for the next 25 years.

Dad, in disgrace, was forced to take a fairly menial job at a precious-metal factory in Chessington. If he had been a virtually invisible presence while working at the shoe shop, he now vanished almost completely. He had to work 7.15am to 6.45.pm most days during the week, plus Saturday mornings, as well as working all weekend during the regular stock-takes. He must have felt like he was in purgatory.

Despite the empty, cold house, Peter and I actually enjoyed the move, oblivious to all the shenanigans that forced us to vacate the flat in the first place. We finally had our own bedrooms, which was a luxury previously unknown to us. And, my God, we even had a garden where we would later spend seemingly endless summer days kicking an old leather football about, digging holes, knocking the cooking apples out of the apple tree or just me cycling on my blue Pavemaster bicycle with white wheels and stabilizers, joyfully wheeling round the garden, mindlessly happy. On other days we'd bury our Action Man figures up to their necks in the mud-pit by the back fence. Actually, they were the cheaper knock-off versions of Action Man that we got for birthdays or Christmas but we could pretend they were the real thing. It was a fairly idyllic childhood where, lazing in the garden during the long, hot, sunny school summer holidays, drinking a glass of orange squash, maybe with a chocolate digestive, I would read the latest issue of *Cor!* or *Shiver and Shake* or one of my beloved Marvel Comics. My ambitions, such as they were at that young, care-free age, consisted of passing my cycling proficiency test and learning to swim (neither of which I achieved, come to think of it). The only thing I had to worry about on those glorious Sunday afternoons was wondering what might be for tea and when the next series of *The Six Million Dollar Man* would be on, before heading in for my weekly bath, whether I needed it or not, to sink beneath a quivering mountain of Fairy Liquid foam bubbles.

As endless as they might have seemed, Peter and I only actually had a few summers together. He had a large group of mates with whom he socialised more and more and was off down the Youth Club more often than not, wearing some damn fine, fresh-from-the-box Ben Sherman shirts and two-tone tonic strides. Being much more gregarious and outgoing than me, Peter was falling under the spell of cigarettes and whisky and wild, wild women. By the mid-1970s, he had left school and started work for militant British Rail, so he became less and less of a day-to-day presence, but no less a huge part of my young life, even if he did drive me up the wall most of the time.

With one of his first pay-packets he bought himself a beauty of a stereo system – AM and FM radio no less – with tape deck and a turntable which even played 78's. Hell, it even had an 'aux in' into which he plugged various devices – plus extra speakers, another amplifier he'd bought off a bloke down The Red Lion – along with miles of speaker wires snaking round his bedroom which became his hedonistic, Brut-scented, pleasure pad. The dangerously overloaded plug socket on the wall sagged and strained under the extra adaptors. The result was a monstrous, throbbing hybrid, which he operated at rib-rattling volume for playing his classic soul albums, one of which was his pride and joy, *Innervisions* by Stevie Wonder.

I, on the other hand, skulking in the box room, had a Hanimex portable, battery-powered tape player about the size of a breezeblock and about as heavy. This marvel of 1973's cutting edge technology had an 'in-built' microphone roughly the same size as a 1p piece, coupled with an EQ-dazzling tone control dial which went from tinny, to marginally less tinny, all operated by sculpted press-buttons similar to the ones used on consoles in the Moonbase on TV's sci-fi show, *UFO*. The whole thing was housed in Kevlar-proof plastic and rounded off with a stainless steel handle for when you wanted 'music on the go'. I would have defied anyone to move it once it had been removed from the box. I am convinced even Geoff Capes would have struggled to carry the beast for more than a couple of yards before collapsing and weeping like a school-girl.

Every Sunday night at 6.00pm, post-bath, I would place the transistor radio my brother had given me for my 10th birthday as close as I could to the 1p-sized microphone on the Hanimex brick to tape songs from the Top 20. Each edition was introduced by Tom Browne who would proudly announce that the chart was "specially compiled for the BBC by the British Market Research Bureau" (with "bureau" pronounced, in extended, mid-Atlantic vowels, as *"burrre-row"*). The backdrop to most of my home-taped compilations was usually *Innervisions* vibrating through the wall. If I ever dared enter his pleasure-seeking sanctum to ask him to turn his music down, even if I'd been driven purple with rage by the noise, he'd pick up a short-lived product of the 1970s – Aramis spray-on talc – and fire it in my direction. I'd slink back to my room, slump on the floor, dejected, defeated once more but quite, quite fragrant.

But while these tunes, which included such gems as 'Sylvia' by Focus, 'I'm Not In Love' by 10cc, 'Boston Tea Party' by The Sensational Alex Harvey Band, 'Race with the Devil' by Cozy Powell, anything by Slade and the Glam Rock canon plus, later, all the Beatles re-releases of 1976, were all very nice, and quite enjoyable, I felt no real connection to any of them. Sure, The Beatles tunes were and always will be the soundtrack to my life overall. I love The Beatles, I adore The Beatles but that's second-hand music to me. I can just about remember seeing them perform 'Hey Jude' on *The David Frost Show* but I never considered it to be my music. It was old and it was ancient history even though it was only a scant six years since they'd acrimoniously split up in 1970. But six years is a long time when you're young. I even did an essay on The Beatles for a history project at school. Then again none of the contemporary music really meant that much to me either. Slade and Glam were what other people listened to but while they released songs that I also kind of, almost co-incidentally, liked, I wasn't a fan. No pictures of a gurning Noddy Holder or posters of a leering Ga*y Gli*ter adorned my bedroom walls (lucky really). As for the other popular music, to be honest, I didn't get that much out of it – the swirling operatic epics so prevalent in the mid-70s left me absolutely stone cold.

Having made the jump in 1975 from being top of the pile at Tolworth Junior School to being the lowest of the low at Ivywood Secondary Modern for Boys and Girls, academically I had an uneventful, crisis-free two years. Classrooms then, possibly unlike now, had a definite class and caste system. At the front were the bookworms, the do-gooders, the ones who wanted to study and learn. They've all probably retired early by now after successful and highly profitable careers in the City. In the middle of the class sat those who were popular by being funny or fanciable (sometimes both). At the back, there lurked the lowest common denominators – the thugs, the brutes and, as it turned out, some jailbirds in the making. Hairy, staring, hideous beasts reeking of Rothmans – fearsome and violent, slouched on, around and sometimes underneath the decrepit old desks that lined all the classrooms. The desks were varnished each year to try and obliterate the graffiti drawn and carved into the ancient woodwork. The ink-wells, which hadn't seen a drop of ink in literally decades, were now filled instead with, by turns, pencil shavings, chewing-gum, sweet wrappers, shiny lime-green gob and the occasional contraceptive, out of the wrapper but thankfully mostly unused... mostly.

I sat just behind the do-gooders, neither too studious nor funny. In fact, I barely made any kind of impact, due primarily to the fact that my Mum died suddenly just before my 14th birthday in 1977, which was just a bit of a fucking shock, actually, now you come to mention it.

Christmas 1976 had seen my country cousins, Linda and Susan from

Plymouth, stay for what would be the last time and, on the face of it, everything seemed fine. But between Christmas and New Year, Mum and Dad had argued a lot, with one memorable shouting match occurring up in their bedroom while I sat alone downstairs with my cassette-player turned up as far as it would go, listening to an old compilation tape featuring 'Golden Years' by David Bowie and 'I Believe in Father Christmas' by Greg Lake, desperately trying to drown out their raised voices.

The decorations came down, the unopened Watney's Party Sevens were consigned to the back of the cupboard under the stairs and I remarked to Mum that it was "back to boring old normal." Mum replied that life was never normal and we didn't know what the new year of 1977 would bring. If only we knew.

First off, I had a late present from Santa – the on-set of puberty. Seemingly overnight, my pituitary gland went into overdrive and like Bill Bixby on TV transforming into the beast that dwells within us all, The Incredible Hulk, I changed from innocent teen to angst-ridden monster. I just seemed to get angrier and angrier. My voice had broken the summer before but now acne reared its unwelcome, festering head, commencing with a huge boil on my nose that looked like it had been designed by H.R. Giger.

I remember in early 1977 returning home from an overnight stay with Mum and Dad as we'd been away for a wedding. On a truly horrendous day, with the rain pouring down, we arrived back at Princes Avenue where I hopped out of the car and headed into the house, wilfully leaving Mum and Dad to carry all of the luggage from the car to the house. Mum was struggling to carry her vanity case but lost hold of my cassette box of precious tapes, which went clattering into the puddles on the drive.

"You stupid woman!" I bellowed, my voice still yo-yoing between that awkward pre- and post-pubescent range, apoplectic with rage that all my lovingly recorded Top 20 tapes were ruined. And in that moment, as Mum tried to pick them up, the rain still pouring down, the look on her face was not one of anger but one of loss. Perhaps she could see that her 'little soldier' was not so little anymore? I fully expected to get a good-hiding from Dad, but the incident went unpunished, Mum just so desperately sad.

And typically for most boys at that age, the rebelliousness started. I seemed to have a repertoire of smart-arse answers, disparagingly delivered. I declined to give a sensible response to any question I was asked, rather lacing my replies with oh-so-funny cynicism and weary sarcasm. Despite being told repeatedly to the contrary, I *did* think it was big and I *did* think it was very clever indeed. My school-work immediately began to suffer as, with the hormones raging inside me, I just didn't care. Not a bit. Mum tried to keep me in line but seemed to be fighting a losing battle. A mate came round one school day morning so we could amble up to Ivywood together and I left the house not exactly wearing a complete uniform. Mum caught sight of me from her bedroom, opened up the window and shouted at me to go and get dressed properly but I was already half way down the road, ignoring her protestations.

"Does your Mum always shout like that?" my mate asked.

Scornful and cocksure, I replied, "She bloody well does these days."

And then everything changed. As spring loomed, Mum had started to feel unwell, but it was nothing sinister, just 'the change' as she called it. But she felt progressively worse and none of the doctors she saw throughout that spring, nor any of the medication they prescribed, seemed to have any lasting effect. Dad was clearly worried and they seemed to have finally put behind them Dad's indiscretion back in the shoe shop. Indeed, on Mum's better days, they were actively looking forward to their Silver Wedding Anniversary and had started to make tentative plans. But Mum began to feel even worse, so she was finally taken into Kingston Hospital on Monday 11th April 1977 for some tests. One of these tests involved an exploratory operation, which was scheduled for Friday 15th April. While Dad went up to visit her each night of the week when she was in hospital, neither Peter nor I fancied going with him. I mean, hospitals – horrible places, no? I had a fear of men in white coats – I didn't even like going to the barber's. Besides, Peter had plans most nights and even though it was the Easter holidays, I had homework…probably… So, we were, gosh – well, I don't know – just kind of busy, OK? We had a vague idea to maybe go and see her after the operation. After all, she wasn't going anywhere, right? Friday morning came, Mum was taken into surgery, the exploratory op started but a hitherto undetected blood-clot, which had been silently travelling round her system, hit her heart and killed her stone-dead on the operating table.

Dead at 42.

To my eternal shame, when Dad came home from the hospital in tears that Friday lunchtime, my first thought when he told me, through great heaving, guttural sobs that "poor old Mum just died," was, "Well, who's going to look after us now?"

To say the next few days and weeks passed in a blur would be an understatement, none of us able to fully comprehend why this could have happened. And how could this have been allowed to happen in the first place? Wasn't there a kind, loving, benevolent, bearded God in the sky who looked after all His flock and who made sure that children didn't lose their parents like this and husbands didn't lose their wives? I prayed for several nights after she died, literally curled up on my knees by my bed prostrate on the floor, hands clasped until my knuckles were white, eyes tightly shut, praying to God to 'please make this not have happened' but each day saw the same diminished household, haunted by all Mum's things just as she'd left them when she went into hospital. While Dad and Peter consoled themselves and had friends, neighbours and relatives to support them, I had no one. These days there are child bereavement counsellors who would have been all over me like a rash but obviously back in 1977 no such support network existed. It was, however, gratifying to receive lots of support from the teachers at school....no, wait...they were completely insensitive bastards. My form teacher, an insufferable prick who wore an ill-fitting toupee, threatened to have me removed from his class because I was "miserable." My few friends, only aged 13 or 14 themselves, were hardly in a position to offer any wise or sagely advice either. How could they? I tried to mention it once by telling a mate of mine, Andrew Burton, on the first day back at school that 'something bad had happened during the Easter holidays' but he cut me off before we could discuss the unbearable truth of the matter with a terse, panicky, "I know."

Dad, in emotional turmoil, became both Mother and Father overnight, a man who had barely made any kind of impact on my life suddenly had to become the cook, the 'housewife', the cleaner, the sole-provider. Although we no longer needed plasters for our scraped knees or handkerchiefs when we were crying, we still needed love and affection but that didn't come easy.

The funeral itself I only recall from mental snapshots of the day, like old faded, colour-bleached Polaroid photos – sat in the car following the funeral car containing the coffin adorned with flowers and seeing Dad's reflection in the limousine's window, seeing him desperately trying not to cry; the family and friends in the chapel all sad beyond belief; the crippling knot of nausea in my stomach as the eulogy was read; looking helplessly at Dad and Peter when the coffin travelled slowly behind the curtains as no one had actually told me that Mum was going to be cremated. I had expected a graveside service and a gravestone, like how every death on TV seemed to be portrayed. I wasn't ready, I hadn't composed myself to say goodbye. But the coffin disappeared, the curtains slipped silently shut and the mournful piped music began. We walked, shell-shocked, out into the bright sunshine, the spring flowers blooming in the gardens around the crematorium, with the lush green lawns like snooker baize.

After the funeral, Mum's death was almost never discussed, at least

not with me and it was literally years before I found out what had
actually killed her. The upshot was, in the absence of any kind of
support, I kind of retreated into myself, not really interacting with
anyone, just completely immersed in the frustration of my own
inarticulate depression, spending more and more time alone in my
room. The arrogance stopped, the cocksure answers stopped, the
burgeoning rebelliousness stopped. Everything stopped.

CHAPTER 2

Punk passes me by, while Bill Grundy has a momentary lapse of reason

The growling, gobbing beast that was Punk-rock started to roam the Union Jack-bedecked streets of Jubilee Britain in 1977 but even then, it passed me by. I was always just at the wrong age – way too young for the 60s, too young for Glam and Bowie, and unlike my future best mate Dave Okomah (a mere year older than me but positively brimming with tales of his new wave misadventures) *just* too young for Johnny Rotten and his anarchic ilk. Besides, if the papers were to be believed, a Punk band was coming to *YOUR* town where they were likely to burn down the church, raid the off-licence, nut a Chelsea Pensioner, then mug your grandma. They were animals and, by God, they weren't going to get away with it. And unlike the several thousand Police fans who now claim they were part of the nine-strong audience at one of the earliest Police gigs in the USA, I actually saw the infamous edition of the tea-time *Today* programme in December 1976 where Bill Grundy, who may have subsequently regretted having one for the road at lunchtime in the Thames Television bar, invited the equally lubricated Sex Pistols plus bondage-clad entourage to say something shocking. Which they did: quite loudly and frequently, with absolutely no sign of fear, regret or intimidation. Profanities saturated the airwaves, and sweet suburbia was shocked to its core, with our household being no exception. As I sat watching these barbarians in our painfully middle-class home – as evidenced by the regency-stripe wallpaper in the hall where a plastic chandelier cast its sickly yellow light on a hostess trolley complete with an ice-bucket shaped like a pineapple and a little-used soda-syphon – I squirmed in embarrassment as Grundy, in the dying seconds of the show and, as it turned out, his TV career, vainly groped for a response to being called a "dirty fucker".

'God Save The Queen' by The Sex Pistols was released on my 14th birthday, released with impeccable and calculated timing to cast a shadow over the otherwise joyous occasion of the Queen's Silver Jubilee. Everywhere, there were souvenirs, flags, toys, gifts, pennants and posters, all released to cash in on the nationwide holiday, all plastered with Union Jacks, coats of arms and crowns and almost all cheap tat, imported from China.

You could understand why the more angst-ridden or vulnerable teenagers of 1977 felt abandoned and betrayed. Unemployment was rising, there were strikes, the three-day working weeks and power cuts were still a bitter recent memory and yet some believed, with perhaps some justification, that money that might help their future was instead being wasted on such a frivolous celebration. It has been said that The Queen thinks that England smells of fresh paint. I could see why. During the Jubilee celebrations, where The Queen travelled the length and breadth of the country, I'd seen roads blocked off, with armies of men in beige overalls removing every last tiny bit of litter from the grass verges while their colleagues in white overalls hastily repainted the white lines on the road, before the Rolls Royce carrying Her Majesty sailed past, her gloved and bejewelled hand waving from the rear window.

I had no opinion either way. The Royal Family did a worthwhile job, I supposed, but a lot of cash seemed to be spent on painting a veneer over the cracks of a very disjointed and disconnected Great Britain.

The powers that be in the music industry, the purveyors of good taste and common decency, conspired to keep The Sex Pistols from the coveted No.1 spot on the weekend of the Jubilee so were 'selective' with their chart data and which shops to approach for sales statistics. Despite the fact that almost everyone my age was buying 'God Save The Queen', it was Rod Stewart's 'I Don't Want to Talk about It' that ostensibly claimed the top spot, much to the disgust of my peers. I didn't care much for Rod Stewart's song to be honest but it didn't make me want to rush out and buy 'God Save The Queen' either. In fact, I didn't want to rush out and do *anything*. I just felt so numb, so morose, so broken that I could barely muster any energy or enthusiasm to do much at all.

On the day of the Jubilee itself, part of Princes Avenue had been cordoned off for a street party and Dad suggested I go, just to get out of the house. Reluctantly, I wandered the quarter of a mile or so down to the party and witnessed lots of very young children plus parents and grandparents all enjoying the event. There was no one there of my age, just lots of squealing little children eating jelly and ice-cream, beneath yards of Union Jack bunting that crisscrossed the street. When I ambled up to the organiser, she eyed me up and down suspiciously and asked for my name. Checking a list on a clipboard, she found my name and gave me my ticket for the prize raffle. I glanced down at the ticket and nearly choked – the ticket was a torn-off slip from the letter that had been posted to all the houses in Princes Avenue months ago and my name had been written by Mum in her neat, instantly recognisable handwriting, signed off with her elegant signature, 'M.E. Downham'. I screwed up the ticket and put it in my pocket, totally unable to cope with the unexpected reminder of Mum. Indeed, in the half hour or so I stayed there, I wandered from one table to another, almost like I was immersed in a huge bubble. Sounds seemed muffled, images seemed indistinct and opaque and I was incapable of talking to anyone. It was like everything was in slow motion and it felt like everyone was staring at me.

This had been happening more and more of late, especially in public places or when meeting strangers. It was like a switch was flicked somewhere deep in my brain and if I felt I was being stared at or had unwittingly become the centre of attention, this bubble would form, a kind of protective self-defence. I would just clam up, silent and unable to communicate.

Completely out of place, I left a short while later and hurried home, passing a house where, through the open windows of the upstairs bedroom, some rebel was playing The Pistols' 'God Save The Queen' at full blast, just as huge drops of rain started to fall.

The Sex Pistols genuinely seemed to be a threat but I can't say that I felt the urge to join my comrades in the streets, with a torn blazer and razor blade earring, to tread on the corpses of the still twitching rock dinosaurs. Thousands of others obviously did, later perfecting their Sid Vicious sneers in photo booths up and down the country and adorning their bondage gear with anarchy badges and safety pins, while I remained safe in some kind of music and fashion time warp.

And yet strangely the year wasn't a total music revolution. At the end of 1977, Paul McCartney and his band of merry minstrels, Wings, released 'Mull of Kintyre', a bagpipes-driven whimsical paean to McCartney's Scottish retreat. Despite it being completely at odds with the seismic changes that were occurring in popular music, it went on to sell two million copies. You'd imagine just red-faced whisky-soaked Scottish ex-pats or elderly aunts and uncles were buying it, but no. I remember sitting in class and overhearing a conversation between two of the Neanderthals at the back, both staring into the middle-distance, both of them probably craving their next John Player Special at break-time, which they cunningly concealed down the centre of a packet of Polos. The painfully slow conversation went along the lines of:

Thug One: 'Ere...have you...have you heard that...er...that...er... new Wings song?

[Long pause]

Thug Two: Yer...

[Long pause]

Thug One: S'good, innit?

[*Interminably* longer pause]

Thug Two: Yer...

These were two teenagers who should have embraced the ethos of Punk, teenagers with possibly no future, no prospects and little hope of leaving school with anything other than a trail of failed examinations, a 20-a-day cigarette habit and, possibly, VD. But no, their song of choice was a three-chord ballad over Punk's finest one-chord howling revolutionary call to arms. So another genre-changing revolution slipped by not only me, as I continued to listen to my Top 20 tapes off the radio, but also it seemed some of my peers.

CHAPTER 3

A pivotal journey to the thriving Mecca of Downtown Kingston

At school, there was a guy who every other guy wanted to be. He was the 'David Watts' of Ivywood and went by the name of Jack Mason. During the early years at secondary school, I'd lumped him in with all the other hooligans who, grunting, dragged their knuckles along the floors of the halls of learning. As we poor innocents shuffled between classes along the narrow corridors of the Albury building, like the workers trudging to work in *Metropolis*, these hooligans administered dead-legs on a painfully regular basis, causing us to stumble against other hooligans, thereby inviting their violent wrath in the process, too. Everyone was a target though and these sadistic, imbecilic thugs took obscene pleasure in inflicting random acts of quite unfeasible violence on the younger, smaller and fey school-boys who squeaked like gerbils as they crumpled crying to the floor.

But as far as Jack was concerned, I was wrong to have originally branded him a hooligan – Jack was clever and so didn't get streamed with all the other jailbirds-in-the-making that ended up in the lower-*lower*-thirds. Here were the monosyllabic, chain-smoking thugs who were often spared taking lessons to actually whitewash over the graffiti on the walls of learning.

Jack was in my class – he was cool, was one of the first people I saw with an earring and always seemed to have a girl hanging off him. He was funny, he was a rebel and he didn't beat the shit out of me. In fact, we got on alright, me and Jack, even if I did silently vow to maim him when he least expected it as a result of a rumour that he'd played 'hide the sausage' with a girl who was one of my many desires, a girl who probably didn't even know I existed.

In the spring of 1979, faced with the prospect of O-Levels, we were often allowed study days at home where we could pore over our gradually disintegrating wallpaper-covered textbooks straight out of the 1950s and endeavour to cram as much into our post-pubescent brains as possible. The aim here was to obtain bits of paper that stated we were clever and which meant we wouldn't spend our lives whitewashing walls. Me? I preferred to go shopping.

On one such day, having dragged myself out of my pit to stare aimlessly at pages and pages of physics text for a couple of hours, I all-too easily gave up and decided to go out. Dressed in hand-me downs and absolutely conventional C&A clothes, I scraped around for the few pence that would get me down to the roaring Mecca of Kingston town centre. On the top deck of a 281 bus we passed Ivywood School and the school bus-stop. Here, for years, there was graffiti carved into a wall inviting the curious to "Fart Frequently" which proved that the English Language wasn't lost on all the pupils at Ivywood as 'frequently' was quite a tough one to spell. And, come to think of it, it's not a bad philosophy to have in life. On that spring morning there was no-one alighting or disembarking at the school bus stop but I still ducked down out of sight in case some eagle-eyed teacher spotted me. From 400 yards away, on a speeding bus? Through the steel, glass and brick work of the school? Who did I think these teachers were?

Slumped among the dog-ends in the back seat, I'd missed seeing Jack power down Butler's Road and just catch my bus at the next stop. This was a few weeks after a memorable lunchtime incident at school. On that occasion I'd been studying the list of names on the gym notice board to see if I'd been selected to play badminton that week in the three-period games lesson on Friday afternoon, rather than rugby or football at the school playing fields a few miles away.

This was probably during one of the last full weeks of *proper* school before the schedule of home-study and exams began. If I was down to play badminton, and thus be spared the brutality of the football field, I might have been able to engineer a game with Linda Henson, a girl I relentlessly, hopelessly, fantasised about.

As I studied the list of names, one of the notorious, mono-browed thugs named Eddie Midmore, who was usually surrounded by sycophants and who had the invincible shield of larger, hairier brothers at home, barged into me, jarring me sideways. My lunch box was knocked out of my hands, spreading the sandwiches Dad had made for me, as he did most days, all over the floor. I'd muttered something under my breath but Eddie just laughed, a deep, hacking, rasping laugh, the inevitable consequence of his 20-a-day smoking habit. His hangers-on, his henchmen, all laughed as well. It's ironic that their blatant defiance of the official school uniform was instead replaced by a uniform of their own – collars turned up, ties knotted so thick that the knot itself was as big as a fist, top button undone, shirt out, blazer sleeves rolled up, shoulders hunched plus vicious, black Dr. Marten boots. Some of the henchmen had been OK, non-threatening, polite kids in the first couple of years at Ivywood; kids who back then were studious, probably bought *Look-In* each week ("The Junior TV Times"), kids who probably helped their mothers around the house and who kept their bedrooms impeccably tidy and no doubt anxiously awaited the latest episode of *Dr.Who* on a Saturday evening. But faced with the daily torment of bullying, many elected to seek safety in numbers as part of the retinue of the real bullies such as Eddie and, Christ, how I hated him.

After depriving me of my lunch, which was now being trodden into the tarmac, Eddie then made some passing, snide comment to Jack, who was also checking the gym notice board, probably hoping he'd been selected for football at the playing field, which meant he could easily bunk off. Jack, while no saint himself, hadn't laughed when my lunch had been knocked flying. Since the fourth year, he had sported a skinhead haircut replacing his former blonde mop-top in anticipation of a much-rumoured brawl with the thugs from Southfield School in Chessington, Ivywood's sworn enemies. He wanted to look the part and certainly looked menacing enough these days so, responding to Eddie's snide comment, told him to "fuck off". Eddie, momentarily taken aback that someone had the audacity, the sheer gall, to not be intimated by his menacing authority and, worse, had given him some lip back, took a vicious swipe at Jack and caught him a blinder under his nose, bringing forth a nosebleed of biblical proportions. Jack wiped his nose, saw just how much blood was gushing out from both nostrils and looked squarely at Eddie.

It wasn't really clear what exactly happened next. Maybe it was adrenalin? Maybe it was bloodlust? Maybe it was the fact that, after five years of tolerating this fucking idiot and his years of tyranny, he'd had enough?

Jack, having fallen against the wall of the gym when Eddie's fist had smashed him in the face, regained his posture and threw off his blazer. Eddie sneered and, in a show of bravado, held his fists up. They circled each other for a minute or so and from nowhere, a crowd of a hundred kids appeared, drawn mindlessly to the affray by the hastily telegraphed message, "Fight! Fight!! Fight!!!" However, Eddie's sycophants saw something in Jack's eyes that sensibly warned them to get out of the way, leaving just Jack and Eddie in the centre of the huge baying crowd. Eddie, devoid of all protection, had just enough time to realise this wasn't going to end well.

In a second, Jack laid into him, a blur of well-aimed swinging punches, propelling both of them into the assembled crowd who all stumbled and fell as Eddie tried to defend himself. But it was all in vain. Eddie, though bigger than Jack, was no match for Jack's almost berserker rage and it was only the timely arrival of the Deputy Headmaster and the PE teacher that prevented Jack from inflicting some major injury. Jack had to be literally hauled off Eddie who had nevertheless sustained a swollen, blackening eye, a split lip and a pretty impressive nosebleed, too. The teachers bellowed and kicked at the crowd to disperse who duly obliged and ran helter-skelter for cover. The adversaries were then dragged away separately to have their wounds tended to. Eddie, in an effort to save a very red, bruised and tear-stained face, tried to shout at Jack, "You're fucking dead! You wait!! Just fucking wait!! I'll get my brothers onto you!!" but it just came out as a snot-filled croak. The remaining observers just laughed at him. I know I did. If I had been a couple of feet closer, I would have kicked him as hard as I could as he lay squirming on the ground. How I wished I'd had the balls to stand up to him during the five years of endless bullying.

That incident had seen Jack hailed as an urban hero at Ivywood as everyone, even most of the teachers, were monumentally sick of Eddie. Jack had worn his bruises and cuts as badges of honour but they'd faded now as he ascended the stairs of the bus as it continued on its journey. Unusually, he was on his own, but catching sight of me, as he climbed up to the otherwise empty top-deck, he came and occupied the seat in front of me. Getting his breath back from the 100m sprint, he looked like he'd been up all night shagging and, damn it, probably had.

"How you doing?" he asked.

"Yeah, not bad thanks. How are all your war wounds?"

He laughed.

"Yeah, they're getting better! That fuckin' idiot."

"Didn't it, like, really hurt?"

"Nah, not at the time, only later. He nearly took one of my fuckin' teeth out, though!" he said, opening his mouth wide and showing me a loose molar.

"Well…well…good for you, Jack. He had it coming," I said, a little bit embarrassed, both appalled at the ferocity and brutality of the fight but also envious that Jack had finally stood up to Eddie and shown him in his true colours – a coward, as all bullies are.

"I fuckin' *hate* him! We got suspended for a week, so I ain't seen

much of him since. Listen, though, if you see any of his fuckin'
brothers hanging around outside school, you let me know, yeah?"

"Yeah, course I will, Jack," I said, and we exchanged pleasantries
as the bus lurched through Surbiton towards Kingston.

As we talked I marvelled at his jet-black, leather biker's jacket. He
was cool, clever, up all night shagging, had an earring and a leather
jacket. Did he have no limits? Apparently not; he was also quite a
good artist. On the back of the jacket, he had stencilled in bright
white paint the names and logos of his Punk and New Wave heroes –
The Skids, Siouxsie and The Banshees...plus a group called Tubeway
Army. The first two I knew, especially The Skids who had performed
an energetic version of their song, 'Into The Valley' (the first Punk
single I ever bought) on a recent edition of *TOTP*. But Tubeway Army?
I'd never heard of them so I asked him who they were. Rising from a
momentary lull in the conversation, he was suddenly animated with
unbridled enthusiasm.

"Tubeway Army? Ah, they're fuckin' great!" he declared. "Haven't
you heard their stuff? Their lead singer is Gary Numan and he...is...
fucking...*BRILLIANT*!!! He never ever smiles. Ever! He's amazing!"

He went on and on about the group and the singer and
recommended I get their latest album, *Replicas*. While I went
shopping a lot, I never seemed to have any money and, even if I did, I
was more a singles buyer rather than albums. Nevertheless, I agreed
to accompany Jack on his mission that day to see if he could get
Tubeway Army's 'Down in The Park' on 7-inch single from a Fagin-
like record dealer in Kingston market. A mate of Jack's, similarly
enthralled by Tubeway Army, had told him it was out on limited-
edition blue vinyl but we had no luck. Back then there were few local
outlets for non-chart music, with Kingston's high-street purveyors
of pop limited to WHSmiths and Woolworth's and a tiny branch of
HMV. We tried them all as well but to no avail.

We mooched around all afternoon and, entering the dark and
moody independent record shop, Beggars Banquet, down Eden

Street, Jack finally and triumphantly showed me Tubeway Army's *Replicas* LP, released on Beggars Banquet's own record label. It had a stark, almost bland cover; there appeared to be a bleached-blonde, pale-skinned android on it, dressed completely in black, standing beneath a light bulb that seemed to bathe the vacant room in an unpleasant almost waxy yellow glow. The android appeared to be staring mutely out of the window across a dark and menacing street to 'The Park', where an eerie crescent moon hung in the sky. If you looked carefully, you noticed that he didn't match his reflection in the window.

"Well, that's certainly unusual," I said, casually. "That's Gary Numan, then?"

"You have GOT to get this!" Jack went on insistently, jabbing the sleeve of the LP at me. "It's brilliant!! It really is!"

I flipped the LP over and saw the photo on the back – an extreme close-up of a heavily made-up eye but, shockingly, the pupil was flat and vertical, not round. It was just as eerie as the front cover. And the song titles were perplexing: 'Me! I Disconnect From You', 'Praying to the Aliens', 'Down in The Park', 'I Nearly Married a Human', along with something called 'Are 'friends' electric?'. The whole package appealed to me – the imagery, the vaguely sinister song titles, the robotic persona, the weird eye... and what was 'The Park', *where* was 'The Park'? Even then it was clear that this was all rooted in science-fiction which, with exposure to all of my brother's DC Comics at a tender age, had started my own comics-habit in 1972, which has lasted to this very day. This, combined with sharing my Mum's somewhat incongruous love of science-fiction films, meant that something was stirring in my currently direction-less mind. Mum, by the way, once took me to see a re-run of *Beneath The Planet of The Apes* in the Summer of 1975 at Kingston Odeon and little did I realise that a couple of dozen miles away, my future best mate, Dave Okomah, was with his Mum, watching the same film, on possibly the very same day, similarly enthralled by this oft-maligned sequel.

I wish I could say I bought the *Replicas* LP there and then and had a life-changing 45 minutes at home, listening to the unearthly and alien music, but I was skint and reluctantly gave the LP back to Jack. But my curiosity was certainly pricked and absolutely piqued and pretty soon there would be no getting away from him. Over the next few weeks, I started to hear the name Tubeway Army and Gary Numan more and more and then, with very little fanfare that I recall, Beggars Banquet, Tubeway Army's record label, lifted a second track off the album, 'Are 'friends' electric?' as the new single.

CHAPTER 4

You know I hate to ask... but are 'friends' electric?

I first heard the track on one of the Radio 1 Sunday night chart run-downs, which I think had now been extended to cover the Top 40. It was announced as a new-entry and once Tubeway Army had been mentioned, I rolled off my bed and crawled across my bedroom floor and turned up the radio, thinking, "Ah, I know these." Remember, at this time I hadn't even heard any of Numan's music – but on it came and with no big intro, no count-in, no great build-up to the song, it finally came crashing into my insular world. The drums, bass and synthesisers starting together on the same note, on the same beat, commencing a five-minute, 25-second aural assault on my impressionable psyche:-

The unyielding, relentless, unpretentious drums – plain, steady, no ostentatious fills or solos – driving the song through from start to finish.

The bass, augmenting the drums – efficient, practical, clinical.

The synthesizers picking out a plaintive, yearning sequence of notes, no swirling self-indulgent grandiose chord runs.

And then the voice – the voice, the voice – melancholy and monotonous, metallic and disparate, desperate and yet dispassionate, spoke directly to me, and I was lost:

"It's cold outside...and the paint's peeling off of my walls...."

The song absolutely floored me even though the words made no immediate sense – I had no idea who the 'friends' were, I didn't know what "deals with SU's" meant or their relevance but the whole essence of the song, the mood, the sound and the rhythm, instantly appealed to me. And anyone who sang, "...and it hurts and I'm lonely...," must have unwittingly known what I was feeling, at that precise moment and, good God, it seemed as if they were reading my confused, churning, teenage mind. The song reached deep inside me and touched me in a way no song has done before or since.

Even two years after losing my Mum I was still deeply troubled by her sudden, cruel, inexplicable, unexpected death. I'd endured two years of inarticulate depression, unable to discuss my loss with anyone, singled out as being a loner at school and bullied mercilessly for "not fitting in". If you weren't one of the cool clique, or in one of the gangs of thugs who, as we've established, invariably had older and equally violent brothers at home (thereby making them generally invincible in the school yard) then it was imperative to try and stay as invisible as possible. It was vital not to stand out at school and be "different" as you just invited daily scorn, ridicule, intimidation and victimisation, whether for being too fat, too thin, too tall, too short, too clever, too stupid, too gay, too 'specky', too ginger-haired or for being too "weird". And God help you if you wore a turban.

I kind of fell into the "weird" category and suffered regularly for it because I didn't fit the macho, football-loving, fuck your parents, fuck authority, cigarette-smoking, rebellious stereotypes that so many of my contemporaries became once puberty set in. I would have effortlessly followed that path myself but Mum's death had stopped me in my tracks. It made me stop and question, with wisdom beyond my teenage years, the whole rebellious streak.

Why? Why rebel?

What was the point?

Why would I want to wilfully upset my Dad?

Didn't he have enough to deal with?

But in the words of a strange, unearthly, electronic ballad, somehow, someone was talking to me – remotely – and that, slowly, gave me some comfort, some reassurance and helped me make sense of my troubled teenage years. I didn't consciously realise this at the time –

how could I? – but I knew, absolutely knew, I'd never heard anything like it before. It even seemed to be two separate songs somehow welded together and the searing, soaring synth seemed almost out of key. Nevertheless, this, for the first time, was MY music and the multi-layered self-indulgent 1970s prog rock operatic anthems that annoyed the crap out of me seemed a very long way away indeed.

There was nothing in the charts that matched it or could suggest that it was part of a new genre of electronic music. Witness some of the 'chart-bound sounds' of June 1979 – 'Silly Games' by Jeanette Kay, 'Ring My Bell' by Anita Ward and bloody 'Bright Eyes' by Art Garfunkel. As we've established, 'Are 'friends' electric?' swept to No.1 within a few weeks and you either loved it or hated it. But amongst my peers – my generation, man – nearly everyone pretty much, at the very least, thought it was OK. You couldn't really ignore it. I couldn't wait to hear it again. That in itself presented a problem. If you hadn't been out and bought the single, you taped it off the radio, risking having the questionable wit and the debatable wisdom of the likes of DJ Mike Read talking over the intro or outro. Or you could endeavour to track it down on TV – unreliable at best as, apart from TOTP, there really weren't that many outlets for music on TV. The immediacy of access to music today would have seemed like some science-fiction future fantasy back in 1979. Tubeway Army's first appearance was memorable – unearthly and alien – but each subsequent appearance saw Numan's confidence increase with the performances more staged and more elaborate, although still a million miles from the more traditional TOTP performances.

By now, I had enough money to splurge on disposables such as records and music papers, having secured a part-time job sweeping the floors at Woolworth's in the evenings, thus ensuring, with no time or real inclination for revision, that I would quite spectacularly fail nearly all my O-Levels. When I finally bought 'Are 'friends' electric?' a week or so later from MJM Records down Tolworth Broadway I was dismayed to find that:

a) My copy came in a plain white paper sleeve.

b) The quality of the vinyl was, as was seemingly the case with all the Beggars Banquet records I ever bought, atrocious.

Nevertheless, I played the record over and over again. Finally, I was faced with an ultimatum from my Dad along the lines of ... "If you play that bloody record one more time, the next time you see it, it will be in pieces in the bin." I believed him, too. Once, years before, my brother Peter had arrived home from his weekend Youth Club with a SuperBall – transparent, roughly the size of a small Satsuma and with a coloured rainbow-swirl of plastic snaking round the interior. When thrown against a hard surface it turned into a lethal and potentially eye-removing projectile. Bored out of our tiny minds that Sunday afternoon, we tested it out to its fullest, taking it in turns for what seemed like hours to lob the ball at the living room wall and then, squealing in part fear, part excitement as it ricocheted at lightning speed back and forwards, thumping on other walls, furniture and the goldfish bowl, we hurled ourselves noisily out if its way. It was amazing that we found such enjoyment in this escapade. I fully suspect that Peter was aiming to maim me in some fashion, although he would have been satisfied with inflicting significant bruising, I'm sure. Alas, he never got the chance – as much as we enjoyed the deadly dodge-ball, Dad, next door trying to read *The News of The World*, could only hear the thumping and screaming.

Thump, thump, thump – scream.

Thump, thump, thump – scream.

Thump, thump, thump – scream, over and over and over again.

I recall that I heard the sound, distantly, of a newspaper being screwed up. Then, with speed belying his age, Dad appeared in the living room, wordlessly but with a face the colour of a bruised plum. In a blur of cardigan and Marks & Spencer's slippers, he scooped up the ball in one fluid, almost acrobatic move, literally kicked open the locked French windows and threw it with all the power of a seasoned county cricketer into the blue suburban sky. Before it was a dot on the horizon, possibly reaching escape velocity, and as wordlessly as he had appeared, he returned to the front room, firmly closing the door behind him. Elapsed time? About eight seconds. Time before Peter or I dared talk or even move? About an hour. So I kept my playing of 'Are 'friends' electric?' to those occasions when Dad was at work, which now, as the sole income provider, was usually six and sometimes seven days a week.

As much as I loved – and, believe me, I *loved* – the record, what I didn't know was that that there were numerous bands in the UK who wielded the same instruments as Gary Numan and Tubeway Army. They were huge instruments: valve-driven synthesizers, patched together with endless cables and connectors with user-manuals the size of phonebooks, producing sounds that pulsed and resonated with robotic efficiency. The new sounds were being made by bands with exciting names like The Human League, Ultravox! and Orchestral Manoeuvres in the Dark. All having worshipped at the altars of Kraftwerk and Berlin-era Bowie, they were gathered in their respective towns. Against a backdrop of urban decay, despondency and increasing unemployment, the likes of John Foxx and Phil Oakey were writing songs for their bands which had no orthodox set-up – invariably no drummers, no guitars – just synths and tape machines. They performed to trench coat-wearing audiences, audiences perhaps disenchanted with the 'Anarchy in the UK' Punk ethos. After all, there had been no posthumous chart-entries following the demise of The Sex Pistols and no great outpouring of grief after the hapless and entirely hopeless Sid Vicious overdosed in America, pumped full of Grade-A drugs so potent they that would have instantly rendered a cow stone dead. This was an audience searching for their own voice who found it in the music created by bands who had plied their trade for a number of years, at pubs, clubs and universities, hauling the wardrobe-sized synths to and from pub and student union gigs with an eye on securing record deals and chart success. Plenty of bands had frequently released records that hadn't exactly bothered the Top 40. But then some little-known guy from Middlesex, who had enjoyed only limited exposure on the live circuit, and even then with a faux Punk band, came along seemingly out of nowhere and beat them to it. No wonder, then, that Numan's peers were not best pleased with his initial, limelight-stealing success.

But who exactly was he? Looking at his childhood photographs, like John Lennon's or John Lydon's before him, there was nothing to suggest in those innocent family snaps that he was destined for musical stardom, as a high-profile, highly visible, world-famous musician, loved and reviled in equal measure. Indeed, Numan's childhood was idyllic in as much as he came from a hard-working, ethical, close-knit and protective family. His Mum and Dad worked all hours, with often several jobs between them to ensure that he and, later, his adopted brother, while not spoiled to any measurable excess, wanted for nothing, as long as it was within their limited and frequently hard-earned means. Indeed, there is nothing in those early photographs – ears sticking out considerably – to suggest that this boy, Gary Webb, was destined for a career of anything other an orthodox 9.00 to 5.00 office job. Studious and focussed all the way through Junior school, he was very much the star pupil until the step up to Senior school, and the on-set of the dreaded puberty. During those early teens, the lure of music, Bowie, girls and their heart-flattering attention was strong. As he later said in an interview, he was always the idiot at the back who said something outrageous or provocative to become the focus of attention in the classroom. He slipped further and further down the academic ladder until he was ignominiously expelled.

Drifting along with no qualifications to his name but possessed of the absolute unshakeable belief that he was going to be famous, Numan, proud owner of a Les Paul electric guitar - albeit a cheap copy - joined various bands and fell further under the spell of Bowie and, later, Punk music. He even auditioned for The Jam! It's true!

See page 26 of Numan's autobiography, *Praying to the Aliens*! These disparate influences guided him away from the cabaret pub circuit and focussed his desire to be a rock star. Joining a group called The Lasers as their guitarist, the band rehearsed and gigged with a catalogue of angry songs. They weren't exactly protest songs, but aggressive, three-minute numbers that, while satisfying the glue-sniffing Punks in the audience, didn't satisfy Numan. His own song-writing was increasingly influenced by the science-fiction greats, like Philip K. Dick and J. G. Ballard. Later, at Numan's suggestion, they underwent a name-change, with Tubeway Army being the favourite choice. The band continued to churn out clichéd Punk tunes, with Numan progressively taking more of the vocals and centre-stage.

While the line-up of Tubeway Army changed over the following months of 1978, the core members of Numan (then performing under the stage name, 'Valerian') and his key-supporter in the band, bassist Paul Gardiner, remained constant. Taking over the musical direction, they touted demo tapes around the main record companies, generally instigated by Gardiner as Numan was always too shy to make the initial contact. Alas, they were turned down by every single one of them. They finally approached the fledgling label, Beggars Banquet, who took a chance and released their first single, 'That's Too Bad'. Buoyed by reasonable sales, Beggars committed to another single and, later, an album. Deciding that Valerian wasn't a name he was comfortable with, the boy Webb set about choosing a new stage name, famously leafing through a copy of the Yellow Pages in Beggars Banquet's reception and finding a plumber by the name of 'Neumann'. Losing an 'e' and an 'n', Gary Numan was born. He later commented that he liked the dual meaning (New man/Numan) and liked the fact that it emulated, to a degree, the quirky spelling of one of his early music heroes, Marc Bolan (Marc with a 'c', not Mark with a 'k').

So, equipped with a new name, a recording contract, some booked studio time and new songs to record, he set about preparing his first album, with himself on synths, guitar and vocals, Paul Gardiner on bass and his uncle, Jess Lidyard, drafted in on drums. Slowly the nation awoke to a new dawn of electronic music. Budding musicians were realising that the mood and menace that the press of a few bass notes on a PolyMoog could convey far outweighed the effort and practice required for fumbling fingers to fret an E minor on a guitar. I wonder if Numan really knew, if he could have really anticipated, what was going to happen next?

CHAPTER 5

We don't need no education

By the end of June 1979, my mandatory school days came to an end. As I've said, working after school in Woolworth's, with little inclination for revising meant that I failed most of my O-Levels. I just about scraped through with three – Maths, Art and English Language – but failed all the rest, where I even faced the shame of having some of them awarded the dreaded "U" mark (unclassified), they were so poor. To say Dad was disappointed would be an understatement. It's not that I was stupid or ignorant – no whitewashing of school walls for me – it's just that there didn't seem to be any encouragement, either at school or at home. Apart from classes taken by a few select teachers, learning at Ivywood amounted to endless copying of text from blackboards into exercise books and seemingly very little else. The old, greying, chalk dust-covered purveyors of learning would have been more at home in the 1940s or 1950s. Their teaching methods were so antiquated. At home, Dad was always working to keep us fed and housed, while Peter, at 23, was quite rightly enjoying himself, having just come out of a long engagement to his childhood sweetheart. It's not that there was any neglect on their part – it's just that they didn't seem to have the time to sit down with me to see what I was doing and how I was faring at the time my compulsory school days were coming to an end.

My last full day at school, before the schedule of CSE and GCSE examinations, consisted of saying goodbyes to peers and teachers alike, getting the bibles presented to us at our last school assembly signed by all and sundry and gawking in disbelief as Sharon Hayes elected to get parts of her perfectly rounded body signed instead. During the day I managed to take a few photographs on a new 110

Instamatic that I'd received from my brother for my birthday. At lunchtime an illicit bottle of Pomagne appeared and having glugged quite a few mouthfuls I spent the final hours in a quietly happy daze, intent on seeking out Linda Henson, my classmate for the past five years and the girl of my dreams. The alcohol reddened my face, already flushed from the new joys of shaving. But, despite this, I was going to tell her, finally, that I'd loved her from the moment I'd set eyes on her. I searched everywhere for her, finally opening a door to a remote cloakroom to find two other members of my year engaged in some pretty heavy petting. They momentarily untangled their tongues and told me in no uncertain terms to "fuck off". As for Linda, she was nowhere to be found. One of her friends finally told me she'd already gone. Dejected, I left and walked down Ewell Road on my own and, having said some very final goodbyes, promising to keep in touch with a select few people, arrived home. I got my house key out of my pocket, still with the piece of red ribbon knotted through it, which my Mum had attached years ago so I didn't lose it and which I couldn't bring myself to remove. I let myself into the typically empty house, having been a latch-key kid for years. I dropped my school bag on the floor, went into the back room, turned the TV on, watched *Magpie* and kind of vaguely thought, "What am I going to do now?"

I had no plans at all – I'd never even thought of what I was going to do next – it had never even crossed my mind. There were some schoolmates with jobs already lined up and a few would even be starting work within a few short months, even weeks, after the schedule of exams. But, in my blissful ignorance, I thought I'd sit around for a bit and see what happened. I was certainly not going to follow the careers advice that I'd had in the last term at school. A formal interview had been arranged with an external assessor where we were going to have a full, frank, in-depth discussion about what I could constructively do in the great, wide world outside of school. I was asked what I liked doing, what I was good at (English, Maths and Art) and after a full, frank, in-depth discussion of less than a minute's duration, the assessor, dragging his finger along a huge drawer of A5 index cards, triumphantly plucked one out and announced, "Here's the ideal job for you!" I read the card in disbelief. It described a vacancy that involved helping deliver carpets for Bentalls department store in Kingston. Ill-equipped to argue the matter, I reluctantly agreed on the spot to join as an apprentice but decided as soon as I left the room that delivering carpets was not what I wanted to do with my life and just didn't turn up for the July start date. Shortly thereafter, letters arrived from Bentalls asking where I was. These I promptly threw in the bin and they gradually petered out, the message finally getting through that I was not going to be joining the work force at Bentalls and carving out a career in the inspirational industry of carpet delivery. Facing a limitless summer holiday, I decided to spend my time doing things that I wanted to do.

In the small ads pages of the music papers I would buy and voraciously read each week, I kept seeing among such ads for "Pistols/Vacant/EMI", reference to "Tubeway Army/Blue Vinyl LP Limited Edition". The asking price for this limited-edition LP amounted to several weeks' wages for sweeping up the detritus that the Tolworth denizens had stomped into the wooden, creaking floors of Woolies, where I still had a part-time job. I decided to try and get a copy. Early in my possibly permanent summer holiday, with my exams now behind me, I again caught the 281 to Kingston, bought a Golden Rover ticket from Kingston Bus Garage and caught a chain of buses that eventually, via a convoluted and lengthy journey, deposited me at Oxford Street. Having desperately saved a few pounds I headed for a little second-hand record shop that I knew from a previous trip up to London taken with my brother in 1978. While the shop dealt primarily with 60s music, I thought it might be worth a shot as they also had all sorts of weird and wonderful records in vast, coffin-length boxes or temptingly displayed, out of reach, on the walls behind the counter. Summoning up the courage to descend the stairs into the subterranean vinyl time warp, I waited patiently. Then, from the back pocket of my slightly flared C&A jeans, I produced a crumpled ad I'd clipped from *Sounds*. Showing the ad to the owner of the shop, I asked, in a voice that despite dropping a few semi-tones virtually overnight during the long, hot summer of 1976, still had a tendency during times of stress to slip back into its stammering pre-pubescent high pitch, whether he had a copy of Tubeway Army's blue vinyl album. From the look on his face, I might as well have been a trainee from the London County Council's new Scrotum Review Board, asking him to drop his trousers so that I could examine his balls.

"Tubeway Army?" he sneered from behind his large, coloured-framed glasses which predated those worn by Trevor Horn from Buggles by a good eighteen months.

"Tubeway Army?" he went on dragging out "army" across several syllables and with a look on his fat, smug face that suggested he might have a swollen, suppurating boil rubbing somewhere intimate.

He held the ad between the very tips of his fingers as if I'd produced the item not from my jeans but from the crack of my white Marks & Spencer's underpants.

"No…we don't carry *that* sort of stuff in here," he said and literally tossed the ad back to me.

He looked across to another customer who was clad from head to toe in greased denim, then jerked his head in my direction with eyebrows raised as if to say, "Did you hear that? Did you hear what this moron wanted?" The guy in greased denim sullenly and wordlessly agreed, shook his pony-tailed head with an audible and physical sigh and went back to examining a copy of the *Led Zeppelin IV* LP.

I left the shop red-faced and humiliated but took great delight in discovering a few years later that the shop appeared to have been torched. Nevertheless, swallowing my disappointment and quite public embarrassment, I headed up to HMV, which was then based at their original store just past Oxford Circus. I checked under both 'T' and 'N' in the 'New Wave' section but could only find Gary Numan's previous offering, *Replicas*. I decided to check the singles to see if they had 'Down in The Park' on blue vinyl instead but there was nothing. I even asked a shop assistant for help, deciding that they couldn't be any less helpful or condescending than the earlier shop owner. And for once, I was right. A guy who wasn't that much older than me listened to my quivering enquiry with genuine interest and disappeared into the stock room to check. I waited for his return and a few minutes later he came back struggling under the weight of a well-thumbed record catalogue roughly the size of a wallpaper sample book.

"Well, good news and bad," he said, studiously examining the catalogue. "The blue vinyl *Tubeway Army* LP sold out months ago and I can't see that 'Down in The Park' was ever released on blue vinyl." (He's right – it wasn't). He went on: "We've got it on ordinary black vinyl. It was released on 12-inch though with a picture sleeve – we've got that in stock. D'you want that instead?"

We went to a counter and he eventually produced the two singles – I was immediately taken by the 7-inch version as the cover replicated the *Replicas* LP sleeve while the cover of the 12-inch version looked boring. My brother had a few 12-inch soul singles which I think were imports from the States and which generally featured extended versions – I should know, I heard them often enough vibrating through the bedroom wall. I asked if this was the case here. The guy studied the sleeve and the record catalogue.

"Uh, dunno," he said finally, "looks like it's the same version on both."

"I'll take the 7-inch version then," I said, mumbling a genuine thank-you and anticipating just how pleased my Dad would be with another Gary Numan record in the house.

I handed over my hard earned cash, little realising that it would be another 20 years before I finally got hold of the 12-inch version in mint condition, paying a princely sum in the process.

Arriving home, the house as empty as ever, I headed for the living room and Dad's hi-fidelity stereo. I carefully removed the single from its sleeve, dusted it down with a pale-yellow anti-static cloth that seemed to attract every dust mote in the room and carefully placed the needle on the vinyl. Greeted with the rainfall-like hiss of the Beggars Banquet vinyl, the music crashed in and I was again transported to another world.

The song itself was as stark, cryptic and alien as 'Are 'friends' electric?', although the tempo was slower and much more menacing. Laden with echo, it was evident to me even then that this was very much the Tubeway Army style – sparse, efficient but utterly compelling. The words again meant no sense to me, with the evocative lyric telling a tale of a park in some dystopian future where atrocities were inflicted on humans by heartless killing machines and where the rich and the powerful watched from the safety of a club as the humans were hunted down. There was no direct 'message' this time around but it was a song that I played over and over again. Numan's vocal was as dry and un-emotive as before and he sounded disconnected, like he was casually narrating a story to his audience as a remote observer. He sounded aloof – the "Oh, look…" line delivered dispassionately, with no shock at the atrocities or condemnation of the rape and murder; he even sounded confused – was it a car crash? Was it a war? Or perhaps something else? The musicianship was as clinical as ever, although the standout instrument was the deep, resonating bass synth, which permeated the song with menace and oppression. The song shuddered to a climax, the bass synth fading out over a simple repeated 8-note riff, to me suggestive of the sun rising over an apocalyptic landscape of the dead and the dying.

I was totally hooked.

CHAPTER 6

'Numania' and the 'Are 'friends' electric?' picture disc

With my exams out of the way, all I had ahead of me was… nothing. No obligations, no school uniform, no rules, no timetables, no studying, no traipsing back and forth along the Ewell Road between home and the Ivywood halls of learning.

Nothing.

Peter and Dad would head off to work early in the morning, Dad to his position as precious metal stock-controller at Engalhard's in Chessington, and Peter off to Croydon to do…well, I never figured out what he actually did but it seemed to involve draining the local pubs of beer each lunch time. They'd inevitably rush out of the house – Dad always ready on time, Peter trailing behind him to cadge a lift to Tolworth Station – with a hasty "Goodbye!" as the door slammed shut behind them. I'd then think about getting up myself. But having lived by the rules epitomised in an old Terry Scott novelty song from the 1960s which was played every Saturday morning on BBC Radio 1's Junior Choice – "Every night when we're wide awake, they make us go to bed…and every morning when we're fast asleep, they make us get up!" – I'd inevitably slip back into my slumber and have epic, wild, almost hallucinogenic dreams in 3-D, 70mm, super-surround sound.

I wasn't the only one in this blissful period of post-school/pre-work. A mate of mine, Chris Freeman, who, along with Andrew Burton, was one of my very few real friends from school, was also contemplating what he was going to do. But, like me, he was happy to see what happened over the next few months. Chris had a couple of older brothers, one of whom was in the police, so he was thinking he might follow suit. But that was a decision for much later on. In the meantime, he and I would hangout round his house most days. He had a huge, mouth-watering collection of Marvel Comics including a near complete run of *The Uncanny X-Men*, which I would longingly leaf through, while he'd play music on his stereo. While we both loved comics and both had an unhealthy fascination with Cheryl Ladd from *Charlie's Angels*, our musical tastes couldn't have been more different. He was a Status Quo fanatic with a sideline adoration of Queen, so the cold, clinical, synthesised sounds of Gary Numan and Tubeway Army were a complete anathema to him and his rock fixation. Each to their own, of course, but, like my Dad, he *hated* Gary Numan. Not just a, "Oh, I don't like that song much," but a real, "I cannot *STAND* Gary Numan!!!" and I, of course, couldn't see why. This was brand new music – strange, thoughtful, stark, thought-provoking music. Even some of my beloved Beatles songs seemed so very old and out of date in comparison.

This was the future for me but not everyone was going to join me. Indeed, the music press almost immediately started to slate Numan, presumably due to his obvious comparison to Bowie. Well, *obvious* to most people, but not me. Last time I really recalled being really aware of Bromley Dave was his duet with Bing Crosby on a "Crimble mit der Bingle" TV special a few years before. Hardly cutting-edge stuff, surely but then, as with many things, I'd completely missed the Berlin-trilogy, the epic 'Heroes' single and Bowie arguably at the height of his creative powers.

Chris Freeman was also the proud possessor of a genuine Les Paul electric guitar which he'd got for his 16th birthday. He'd had a tatty old guitar for years and had learnt is craft and was now a good, if metal-fixated, guitarist. This Les Paul, though, was a just a wondrous bit of kit which he seemed to play effortlessly. I'd eagerly take hold of the beast when I could but just didn't have his natural, innate ability. Even when he patiently guided me through a Play Electric

Guitar in a Day book which I'd impulsively bought in Kingston, it was clear that even the basics were beyond me. But the thought of playing in a band appealed to me, even if I didn't know what role I'd play (probably lead electric tambourine).

So, the summer of 1979 continued, spending hours day-dreaming, listening to music and doing what I wanted. I continued saving my money from sweeping the floor at Woolies each evening to fund regular trips up to London, usually with Chris, to spend my hard-earned wages. He would cycle round to my house in the morning, we'd run down to the bus-stop at the end of Princes Avenue and leap aboard a 281 bus as it pulled away and journey down to Surbiton Station. Here we'd catch a train up to Waterloo where the excitement and anticipation of going up to London was palpable. The old slam door trains, the blur of suburbia speeding by, travelling past a huge advertising hoarding on the side of one ancient warehouse just outside Vauxhall where, for years, there was a gigantic advertisement for Sandeman Port. Opposite that hoarding there was a row of now long-demolished soot-black tenement buildings where the graffiti on one roof once proudly proclaimed that 'Toad Lives Here'. After the final juddering journey into Waterloo, we'd then descend into the Underground on ancient, dirty escalators.

I loved the Underground. It was dark, it was crowded and I was completely anonymous among the commuters and tourists, buffeted by the strange, tepid, diesel-tainted winds that blew along the platforms, heralding the arrival of the next tube train where, in some carriages, commuters were still allowed to smoke.

After a short subterranean journey on the Northern Line, we'd emerge into Tottenham Court Road opposite The Dominion Theatre. Our first port of call was always the Virgin Megastore a few yards along Oxford Street, a huge, cavernous shop that had row after row of records in tightly packed racks. You could buy almost anything released in the UK, along with obscure, shrink-wrapped foreign imports to stretch the wallet. This was the mother ship of record stores – my local store, MJM Records, could have easily fitted into it a hundred times over. It was vast, with stock across several floors and where picture disc LPs, priced way beyond my meagre weekly wage, adorned the walls like works of art. The four solo albums by the members of Kiss were displayed on one wall, *A Single Man* by Elton John was on another, *Abbey Road* and *Sgt. Pepper* were on another. Elsewhere, the elfin and 100% erogenous zone that was the young, barefoot temptress Kate Bush pouted from the *Kick Inside* ultra-limited edition picture disc, tantalizingly out of reach, both literally and financially. Seven-inch singles and the new 12-inch singles could be found in one department and racks of posters of your Punk and New Wave heroes could be found in another. We would spend hours in there, flicking through rack after rack of albums and singles, lost in that brief moment in your life when you have nothing else to worry about, other than the here and now.

Clasping our lurid orange Virgin carrier bags, we'd then head further down Oxford Street, dodging the ever-present human billboard, the terrifyingly eccentric Stanley Green, who urged passers-by, in his low, monotone voice, to eat less protein and to lead less lustful lives. We never bought any of his pamphlets as I quite enjoyed being lustful – I just didn't have an outlet for it! The 'Less Protein' sign and assorted pamphlets are currently on display in The Museum of London. Free entry and well worth a visit!

Leaving Green in his flat hat and overalls and brandishing his eight-foot tall 'Less Protein' billboard we'd then more often than not hear the "tish, bong-bong, tish, bong-bong" of Indian percussion instruments, heralding the arrival of the orange-clad, shaven-headed devotees of The Radha Krishna Temple snaking down the street, chanting the Hare Krishna Mantra. All in a state of blissful fulfilment, one of them would have a canvas bag of their LPs and encourage the Oxford Street shoppers to buy a copy (usually us, after foolishly making eye contact):

Devotee: "Hey, there! Hey, there, man!"

Me:(suspiciously) "What?"

Devotee: "I see you like 'ell-pees'! For a small donation, you can buy our *Radha Krishna Temple* album!"

Me: (trying to side-step past) "No!"

Devotee: "It will change your life!"

Me: (desperately) "No!"

Devotee: "It's on the Apple label!"

Me: (running away) *"NO!"*

Devotee: (in the distance) "But it's produced by George Harrison!"

Escaping their clutches, we'd head to The Oxford Walk, a collective of shops and stores under one roof. The site is currently occupied by the HMV flagship store but back then it had about 50 small retail units across three floors selling all manner of goods, with each store looking like an old shop with fake upper storey windows and faux cobbled-streets and lampposts. On the first floor, just by the top of the escalators, there was a shop that made T-Shirts using headache-inducing chemicals, possibly toxic, as part of the printing process. They also sold badges, thousands of them – Punk badges, New Wave, The Beatles, Heavy Metal, small mirrored badges, some with reflective material that glinted and swirled in the light, along with the iconic penny-farthing badges from the recently repeated but still almost incomprehensible *Prisoner* TV series starring the enigmatic Patrick McGoohan. I bought the penny-farthing badge with '6' on, but elected not to buy '2' or '1' and couldn't imagine for the life of me why anyone would want one with '69' on? I also purchased a Tubeway Army badge, which emulated the London Underground logo. In the basement, strangely enough, was another Virgin store, much smaller than the Megastore but still selling mouth-watering items, with Japanese 7-inch singles seeming to be a speciality. It was here, later, that I'd drool over imported Gary Numan singles after his fame spread worldwide, when his star shone… brightly, fiercely, memorably but all too briefly.

Days like these usually continued with a trip to Dark They Were and Golden Eyed, a science-fiction book and comic shop named after a short story by sci-fi great, Ray Bradbury. It was located in Berwick Street in the depths of Soho where, pre-censorship and government clampdown, we would pass seedy sex shops with window displays full of gynaecologically pornographic magazines and cine-films, along with all manner of sex toys, vibrators and packets of something called 'Spanish Fly'. Indeed, in some doorways, prostitutes lurked wearing garish make-up and overcoats, which would sometimes blow open to reveal stockings and suspenders. We would hurry on to the sanctity of the comic shop, perplexed and embarrassed and yet somehow strangely curious at this flagrant and blatant display. Dark They Were and Golden Eyed, on the other hand, was a magical place. On the ground floor were shelves groaning under the weight of books by the science-fiction greats, books with glorious painted covers of starlit skies where exotic spaceships took off into the twilight of Dali-esque landscapes amid towering spires of alien cities. Descending the stairs into the belly of the beast, the basement revealed boxes of musty comics along with, a rarity, the latest imports from America. Marvel and DC Comics in those days had a three-month lead date on their publications, so a July 1979 dated comic would actually be on sale in the US in April 1979. We in the UK had to wait until the actual cover date before they were distributed to our local newsagents, if they were distributed at all. So, if we hadn't spent all our money in the Virgin Megastore, we'd carefully choose which of these precious imports to buy, usually *The Uncanny X-Men* for me, in a desperate attempt to start an *X-Men* collection to rival Chris's, while Chris himself was building a pretty good collection of *Iron Man* comics.

Sometimes we'd visit a small, dingy record shop in the heart of Soho that Chris wanted to check out, as they stocked obscure American import albums. The shop, seemingly lit by only a couple of 40 watt bulbs, was staffed by two elderly rock music enthusiasts who had clearly lead quite the rock'n'roll life. Every time I see Ozzy Osbourne on TV, I am reminded of these two guys, slumped in denim and shades behind a counter strewn with well-thumbed music papers, both smoking ridiculously large roll-ups which, through second-hand fumes, made us quite light-headed before we finally emerged back onto the street, giddily blinking in the sunlight.

Laden down with more bags, we'd finally end up in McDonald's, then located on the corner of Dean Street and Shaftesbury Avenue, for a very late lunch of Big Mac with fries and a chocolate shake of such thickness and wallpaper-paste consistency, that it would bring on a throbbing headache, purple spots before the eyes and maybe even a mild seizure when trying to suck it up through the straw.

The days passed, my passion for music increased and my status as a Numan devotee was getting more serious. Aside form the regular jaunts up to London, I'd devour the weekly music papers, ever hopeful that there might be a favourable review or critique of Tubeway Army. Two things caught my eye one week – one was the headline 'Tubeway Army Split' which reported that Gary Numan was going solo. I don't remember being that concerned about it as it reassuringly went on to elaborate that Gary Numan was indeed going solo and that his new single was about to be released. I couldn't wait.

The other item was an ad in the back pages of the *NME*, where someone was specifically advertising 'Tubeway Army AFE picture disc. Limited Edition. Offers.' It was released on picture disc? I had no idea! The images of those beautiful picture discs at the Virgin Megastore meant that the more I thought about it, the more I coveted it. My favourite song, 'Are 'friends' electric?', the song that had touched me on so many levels and which was never far from the record-player, was released on a picture disc? I *had* to get it. But from where? No way was I going to get it via an ad in the paper as there was no question of me asking Dad to write out a cheque on my behalf. I had to think. Certain that none of the stores up in London would have a copy, I thought I'd try the record dealer in Kingston Market. When Jack and I had trawled round Kingston earlier that year for the non-existent 'Down in The Park' on blue vinyl, I remembered that the dealer had boxes of singles on his stall, a few more expensive ones pinned to a wall and had occasionally disappeared under a trestle table, emerging, with eyes cast left and right, to surreptitiously pass an album or single in a brown-paper bag to the more discerning record-collector. It couldn't hurt to give it another go, could it?

That Saturday afternoon I caught the ever-reliable 281 bus down to Kingston and made my way to the record stall in the market. I certainly felt bolder than of late but still anxiously walked up and down eyeing the dealer and his customers before electing to make my move. He really was a Fagin-like character, usually clad in a sheepskin coat, wearing tinted glasses and sporting a not entirely successful perm. He had weather-beaten skin prematurely aged by chain-smoking roll-ups or John Player Specials clenched between a set of Terry-Thomas teeth. The cigarettes were often passed to him by his regular customers who would engage him in endless conversations about his music knowledge and the availability of obscure Bob Dylan records. Seizing my chance as he stopped for a breather, I entered the stall, idly leafed through some recent releases then, quite boldly for me, asked whether he had this holy grail, the 'Are 'friends' electric?' 7-inch picture disc? He eyed me up and down, lit another cigarette – paused – and finally said that he did indeed have it, and that it was a first edition to boot.

"First edition?… "What?"… Excuse me?"

He elaborated further between rattling coughs. "There were 20,000 copies initially pressed on picture disc and I know for a fact," with 'fact' emphasised by a gust of nicotine fumes and the sickly sweet smell of whiskey, "that Beggars Banquet re-pressed it several times. Three times, at least."

"Really?" I said, not really in any position to doubt these words of seeming wisdom and insider knowledge. The dealer sucked deeply on his cigarette before continuing.

"Yeah, that's why some copies don't have the inlay card 'cause they're second or third editions. But this," he said, plucking the disc from his secreted stash under the stall, "is an original."

And there it was – the 7-inch picture disc, with a blonde-haired Numan looking more robotic, more alien, more un-earthly than ever, with eyes that appeared to be glowing, beneath that same crescent moon from the *Replicas* LP cover. He slipped it out of the PVC sleeve and showed the reverse, which was the eye from the back of the *Replicas* LP, complete with the flat, vertical pupil. I was dumbstruck…it was a thing of beauty.

"Hard to come by, these," said the dealer sagely, weighing the disc in his right hand, keeping it just out of my reach, nonchalantly flicking ash from the cigarette cupped in his left hand.

Then came my inevitable question: "How much?"

Without a moment's hesitation, the dealer shot back, "Fifteen quid."

Parts of my body – including trachea, esophagus not to mention sphincter – went into spasm.

"How much?!!!!!!!" I spluttered, somehow managing to go from a barritone bottom E to a falsetto top E in just one breath. Fifteen quid amounted to a small fortune – LPs cost about a fiver, and I still wasn't at that stage of being into buying albums. He was expecting me to pay three times the cost of an LP for a single! I was lost for words.

"We-eelll, if you don't want it," the dealer said, nonchalantly sliding it back into its PVC sleeve.

"No, no, no, no…I didn't say that," I added quickly, panicking, conscious of the fact that some of his regular customers were congregating round the stall, all looking in my direction. Not having the street-smarts or nous to say, "Fifteen quid? Are you having a laugh? I'll give you ten, final offer!" I stammered and stuttered and said, "I'll take it."

"A very wise decision, young man," the dealer said, smiling as he quickly bagged up the disc in about two seconds flat, gleefully accepting the fifteen quid in pound notes and 50 pence pieces that I produced from my wallet and pockets.

I eagerly took the bag, keen to get away from the stall, guilty that I'd spent so much on it, equally conscious of the fact that Dad would be furious if he ever found out how much I'd spent on a record, but also tingling with excitement that I had the precious, limited edition picture disc in my hands.

Had I been ripped off?

Was it a first printing after all?

Was it a second edition?

Did the dealer have dozens of them secreted away under his stall?

Or was he at that moment, as I made my hasty exit, calling Beggars Banquet from the nearest phonebox, saying, "Dave here…down to me last couple of 'friends' picture discs…can you rattle off another couple of dozen for us with the inlay card? Yeah? Sweet! Cheers, nice one!"

I didn't care. All I knew was that I had it and it was mine, although my joy was somewhat tempered by the prospect of a long fucking walk home as I no longer had enough money for the bus fare.

CHAPTER 7

I feel safest of all...

Money was starting to become a problem, especially after spending my limited savings on ludicrously priced picture discs, buying music papers each week, making regular trips up to London and buying the occasional Marvel import. I didn't earn that much from sweeping up the detritus at Woolworth's which, to be honest, was becoming just a bit too much like bloody hard work. Pocket money had stopped, quite without any warning from Dad, following the eventual arrival of my woeful examination results. The envelope arrived and even though I hoped for some kind of miracle, the contents confirmed what I had feared, in that I had failed most of them. I had just scraped by with English, Maths and Art but the rest? Chemistry, History, Physics? Utter failure. As I've said, Dad was dreadfully disappointed. A man of few words, he looked at the official confirmation from school and silently assessed the results and the implications. He knew I wasn't stupid, I knew I wasn't stupid, it just seemed that I hadn't had the right support, on so many levels and for so many reasons.

"What you going to do now, son?" he eventually said, less of a question, more of a criticism and an accusation.

I really didn't have an answer.

To tell the truth, I hadn't really bothered actually looking for a job but here I was shame-faced into admitting that I had no plans, no aspirations and faced the realisation that a magic pixie wasn't going to come fluttering along, wave a wand, and offer me a job.

My brother Peter was clever – very clever – but I really felt I'd let Dad down and he really didn't need the added aggravation of worrying about me and just what the hell I was going to do with my life.

One option was to go back to school and join the 6th Form at

Ivywood and see if I couldn't re-take some of the exams to try and get some better results.

"Maybe you'd better do that then," Dad wearily, but firmly, said.

He sounded so down and, working all hours, looked very, very tired. Maybe he was disappointed with himself too, realising that he hadn't exactly provided the support or encouragement I needed. It was difficult to tell with Dad, never one to wear a heart-shaped patch on the sleeve of his M&S cardigan.

My pocket money being stopped was, I think, a combined punishment and a life-lesson. Had I been any younger, I may well have got a good-hiding but as I now towered over both Dad and Peter, that was never going to happen, even with Dad's increasingly rare but nonetheless infamous, red-mist tempers of old.

Consequently, I attended a 6th Form Open Day on a gloriously sunny day before the September term started and committed myself to further learning, studying for the re-takes scheduled for spring 1980 where, hopefully, I would get better marks. I wasn't that enamoured with the idea of going back to school after what I thought had been a very final farewell but Dad wasn't prepared to allow me to slouch around the house indefinitely. So my day-dreaming days and regular weekday trips up to London seemed to be coming to an end. It wasn't an ideal situation but I had no other option. I was pretty fed-up about it to tell the truth, as I genuinely, if naively, believed that my school days were over and the thought of going back to Ivywood filled me with no small amount of dread. I had no money to speak of, no real prospects and Dad was obviously, evidently, visibly disappointed with me. It seemed I didn't have an awful lot to look forward to.

The following week, 'Cars' was released.

I'd seen the ads in the music press for the new single by the newly solo Gary Numan, with the name Tubeway Army now consigned to music history. I'd been perplexed by the ads because my new hero seemed to be covering his face with a pyramid. What the hell was that all about? Nevertheless, I bought it on the day of release from MJM Records in Tolworth, interrogating the assistant behind the counter with several, eager, impatient questions.

Me: "Does it have a picture sleeve?"

MJM Girl: "Yes."

Me: "Is it out on picture disc?"

MJM Girl: "No."

Me: "Is there a coloured vinyl version?"

MJM Girl: "No!"

Me: "Is there a 12-inch version?"

MJM Girl: "NO!!"

Actually, there was a 12-inch release but that was an import so, as far as the UK release was concerned, 7-inch, black vinyl, picture sleeve and that was your lot. I raced home. As ever, I had the house all to myself and went to my room and over to my wire record rack where, amongst all of Mum's old Beatles records, plus the few singles that I'd bought over the years ('Lola' by The Kinks, 'Sugar Sugar' by The Archies, 'How Does It Feel?' by Slade), I retrieved my 'Are 'friends' electric?' picture disc and my 'Down in The Park' single then retired to the front room to play this brand new song.

It's strange but, as I'm writing this, I have thousands and thousands of songs lined up on my PC and iTunes, literally several days' worth of songs available at the press of a button. But back in the long-lost days of 1979, if you wanted several songs played in a row, you either taped your singles and albums onto a cassette or stacked up your singles on a record-player and watched as they all span like a potter's wheel with, if you'd had more than five stacked up, some interesting warped tremolo effects by the time the last single crashed down to be played. I lifted the lid on Dad's hi-fidelity stereo, slipped the single from its sleeve and placed it on the turntable. There was the inevitable rainfall hiss as the needle touched down on the Beggars Banquet vinyl and here was the new single by Gary Numan.

Safe to say it was short on lyrics, meaningful or otherwise, but good God above, the sound? It was awesome! There are very few records that render you breathless on first hearing them – I was in the rare position of having two singles in quick succession that did just that. From the phased, robotic opening, the whole atmosphere of this new record was much richer, much thicker than 'Are 'friends' electric?' Less echo, more resonating bass synths, bass guitar no less clinical and this time the drums seemed a lot more percussive, more up front, more "rocky". The thing that did it for me was the plaintive hook – it was mesmerising. The multi-tracked final minutes of the song with three distinct synth riffs was haunting, evocative, lamenting and completed by the overriding sadness of the song right up to the final notes at the eventual fade out. While far more of a production than the sparse previous singles, the essence of this new song still centred on remoteness and isolation and that appealed to me immensely.

I played it over and over again, loudly, playing along on imaginary drums or synthesizers. If a neighbour had chanced by our house and peered through the net curtains, they may well have thought I was having a fit. Frequently I would study the picture sleeve to observe Numan, as pale as ever with heavily made-up eyes, dressed in what appeared to be quite a sober, conservative double-breasted suit (I'm sure my Dad had something similar in his wardrobe). And his hair, jet-black on all previous TV appearances on *Top of the Pops*, was now a mousy brown, not unlike mine. It was perplexing to say the least. But I didn't buy the single to listen to the cover though, right? If the song itself knocked me out, then the video was unlike anything I'd seen before.

I can't recall where I first saw it but I don't think it was on *Top of the Pops*. When he performed the song in the studio as the highest new entry that week, the band, Tubeway Army in all but name, were to the forefront of the band set-up, with Numan curiously relegated to the rear. Later performances saw him front and centre but I don't remember ever seeing the video on *TOTP*. Having said that, there weren't too many other outlets for music videos then, and none that I recall on ITV (and that ever mysterious fourth channel for use 'in the future' was still some years off). So where exactly did I see it? I don't know. But in this day and age, at the press of literally a couple of buttons, I can access it instantly on YouTube. It was innovative then, it's rightly rated as a modern classic now. The phased opening saw Numan, now black-haired again, stalking in slow motion into shot – cold, aloof, unblinking. Skin bleached white by the neon lights, painfully thin, he enters a fluorescent-framed pyramid, where he morphs from wearing his familiar black suit, black shirt with red and blue tie, into a red leather jumpsuit…it was astonishing. The video was replete with split screens, spinning images and new technical special effects. The band's appearance was mean and moody on an array of synths…and, good God, what was that weird creature on drums? As an accompaniment to the song, the video was astonishing. I couldn't wait to see it again but there was no telling when you might see it next, so you had to absorb every nuance, every effect, every pose and commit it to memory.

I loved it as did his fans, unfazed by the fact that Tubeway Army was no more and, within a couple of weeks, 'Cars' had effortlessly sailed to No.1. Dad, unsurprisingly, was less than impressed although my Quo-loving mate, Chris, thought it a lot better than 'Are 'friends' electric?'

Chris had been a bit elusive of late and it transpired that he had started jamming with some of his former class-mates at a rehearsal studio above an Indian takeaway restaurant in Surbiton. I was in a different class to Chris at Ivywood so I didn't really socialise with his other mates who were similarly-minded in terms of music: loud, heavy and Zep-based. Andrew Burton attended a few sessions and told me years later that at one exceptionally loud jam he nearly passed out when, mid-session, he stooped in front of one of the speakers just as one of the guitarists was in mid-flow, eyes tight shut, playing an ear-drum-bursting white noise solo. I may not have socialised with these other guys but I was still annoyed that I hadn't been invited along. I mean, I could have sung a tune if nothing else, couldn't I? Maybe my fascination with all things Numan meant I was automatically excluded from these head-banging sessions? Perhaps it was for the best, as I loathed heavy-metal with a passion. It would have been nice to have been bloody-well asked, though!

CHAPTER 8

Back to Ivywood, getting a job at Fine Fare, and the suspicions of PC Thorogood

September 1979 arrived and I dutifully returned to Ivywood School. I witnessed the new first year arrivals – young, eager, some lost within huge, ill-fitting uniforms, most with shiny new briefcases, all facing five long years of secondary education. How I pitied them. Had I really been that small when I started back in 1974, clutching my own new leather briefcase which contained a fountain pen, spare cartridges, a mathematics set, a pencil case, a biscuit and, at Mum's insistence, some toilet paper ("Just in case…")? But, strangely, there was also a small pang of regret, with the realisation that I had thrown away five years of my life with very little to show for it, other than a wardrobe of school uniforms that, bought new at the beginning of each autumn term, no longer fitted me by spring as, once I hit puberty, I seemed to grow taller by the week.

Leaving the newbies and their excited, nervous chatter as well as a few tears, I met at the assembly point for the new 6th formers, which was in the Common Room in the Lower Stables block by the main Albury Building. I suspect that Ivywood had once been a vast private school or even a private house and all the old outbuildings had been converted into usable classrooms, the stables being no exception. I arrived with some of my former classmates who were either attempting retakes like me or were looking to increase their haul of O-Levels and A-Levels. I was delighted that none of the thugs who had made my life a misery over the past few years were present. Some of the thugs in question were destined for lengthy unemployment, others headed for building-sites, paint-covered overalls, sweeping roads or emptying dustbins. A couple of others, I later learned, had a spell banged-up at Her Majesty's pleasure following a hapless attempt at a bank robbery, while another was found dead of a drugs overdose on a fetid houseboat moored on the Thames in Kingston. But those assembling with me in the common room, with its lurid orange walls adorned with notice boards, Dali prints, huge Bowie poster, ageing second-hand sofas, plus an ancient record player in one corner, were OK. In fact, I got on well with most of them, although none were what I would call really close friends.

By way of an introductory roll call, my new colleagues included:

Jack, the Numan-loving 'David Watts' who had returned looking cooler than ever. During that morning, he asked if I'd got the new Gary Numan single, which, of course, I had.

"Fuckin' brilliant, innit?" he enthused. "Listen to it on headphones!!" His vicious skinhead haircut was thankfully growing out.

Terry Easton: He'd been in our class for a couple of years but I hadn't really got to know Terry that well. In fact, it looked like we were destined to be sworn enemies when, a few months before the end of the Fifth Year, he'd crept up behind me as we descended from the top floor of the three-storey Valiant school block. All he'd done was thump me on the shoulder, not even that hard, but I'd swung round, instinctively punching him in the stomach, knocking the wind out of him, and watching in horror as he fell down a flight of stairs. I was amazed that he hadn't tried to kill me after that little incident.

'Budgie': Terry's sidekick and not the sharpest knife in the drawer.

Andrew Burton: I'd known Andrew since the age of four when we'd started at Tolworth Infants School together on the very first day of term. One of the cleverest people I knew. He wasn't coming back for re-takes, that was for sure, but to amass more exams before going to Uni.

Linda Henson: Oh, be still my beating heart! Lovelier than ever, she had continued to bloom during the summer holiday, blossom, and effortlessly exhibit female pulchritude and luminosity in abundance.

Kyle Lynch: A guy who had been in most of my classes throughout the previous five years. He was a bit of a joker, originally from the Midlands and we all towered over him, even the girls.

Kim Taylor: Another old class-mate; we'd also known each other since Infants school, taking our educational journey together to Ivywood School. Gosh, she was lovely, turning into a young, beautiful woman while we boys still raced round gibbering and farting like the minions in *Despicable Me*.

Anne Mithra: I could never work out exactly what her ethnic background was. From her previous staid, snobbish persona she had emerged from the summer chrysalis as a part Punk, part New Wave proto-Goth, dressed entirely in black, with a leather jacket, jet black hair, blemish-free smooth olive skin and an attitude. God, she was menacing, and hot at the same time!

Shriti Dhavda: Another girl from 'overseas'...India? Dubai? I had no clue...not one. But I did know that she was gorgeous, a mane of natural black hair atop a body that was developing in all the right areas. She was quite stunning.

Suzanne Laine: One of the Laine twin sisters. She was clever and lithe, with long blonde hair and a tendency to wear tight, buttock-clinging blue denim jeans.

But back to that first day in September 1979: We listened with varying degrees of interest to the introductory talk, hosted by a huge bear of a teacher called John 'Uncle Vock' Vockings. The essence of the talk welcomed us back to the hallowed halls of learning but the clear implication was that it was entirely up to us whether we actually attended or not. As far as Ivywood was concerned, they'd completed their obligations by teaching us for the mandatory five years – anything else was none of their real concern. I got the distinct impression it was a case of: attend, don't attend, it's up to you. I didn't mind – there was no regimented structure now, no registers in the morning, no strict time keeping, no more detentions, no more punishments, no more PE or sports and, how wonderful, no more school uniforms. As much as I'd been dreading coming back, this actually seemed like it might turn out to be OK.

So, for the time being, things settled into a not unpleasant weekly schedule of attending classes, actually being talked to by the teachers as adults, doing a bit of revision and, when not attending class, heading into Kingston or going home! Marvellous! Dad was reasonably happy that I wasn't lounging around the house all day, and I was reasonably happy that he was reasonably happy. What I was reasonably unhappy about was the job at Woolworth's where I had decided that I had suffered quite enough from sweeping their floors. There's only so much enthusiasm you can muster for clearing up the crap left behind by the shoppers of Tolworth. Sometimes I wondered what they had actually trodden in. It was disgusting. So I, with little regard for what I'd do for money now that my pocket-money had stopped, handed in my notice. On my last evening there, I was tasked with sweeping the floors of the upstairs stockroom which I think was a punishment by the Napoleon-like store manager (short, odious, delusions of grandeur…). As the stockroom was completely empty of other staff, I took the opportunity to peruse the shelves and, remembering a tip from my brother who had worked there years before – "If you're going to nick something, make sure it'll fit down your pants 'cause they can't search you down there!" – I pilfered a couple of bits and pieces: a miniature travel manicure set, a bottle of awful aftershave, along with a copy of Bowie's *Lodger* album on cassette, just for the sheer bloody hell of it. And when I got home, I threw them straight in the bin – a short-lived thrill at best. I kept the Bowie cassette though but sought out a bottle of TCP from the medicine cabinet, as the pointed, sharp edges of the cassette box had done quite a number on my testicles.

I was actually enjoying myself back at Ivywood – the work wasn't too taxing, everything was pretty laid-back and I looked forward immensely to spending time in the Common Room, especially if Linda was there. God, I yearned for her but wouldn't have had a clue what I'd have done if she'd turned round and made a play for me, not that that would ever have happened in a million years, even a billion years. She was lovely though and every time she walked into the room, my stomach went into spasms of unrequited love.

On one wall of the Common Room was a dartboard and I discovered I wasn't that bad a darts player. Over time I could even manage a three-dart 101 finish and was overjoyed whenever Linda played... or Suzanne, or Shriti. Anne never played – when asked she would just sneer at how pathetic and plebeian we were. And yes, I had to look 'plebeian' up in the dictionary. If we weren't playing darts, we would sit around playing poker where Jack always managed to win. I wondered how he managed to get so many aces, five or six at least.

The radio was always on and music papers and magazines were strewn about the place – I loved reading the latest news in what I acknowledge was an era not really comparable to the rock'n'roll revolution of the 1950s or the psychedelic 1960s but it was my time, my music and my generation.

There was an eclectic mix in the charts – the dying echo of the original Punk movement with the likes of The Stranglers and The Skids; the New Wave acts like The Police and Elvis Costello; the burgeoning 2-Tone ska revivalists like Madness and The Specials; the Mod movement championed by The Jam and Secret Affair; the rock acts that still endured like Quo and Rainbow. We still had disco and soul for those so inclined but at the forefront of the new synth revolution was my hero, Gary Numan. He was the topic of several fevered Common Room debates, along the lines of:

"Have you seen the video for 'Cars' yet? Fuckin' great."

"That bit with the pyramid is brilliant!"

"I liked the bit where the band were just hitting the synths at the end…just bang, bang, bang."

"Yer, one of 'em's the bass player."

"I thought it was the guitarist?"

"Nah, he don't have no guitars no more – just synthesisers."

"Then who was playing guitar on *Top of the Pops* when he did 'Are 'friends electric?' (That was me asking).

"Dunno."

"An' who was on drums? Weird ain't he?"

"Yer, he looks like an albino golliwog!"

"Them suits they were wearing looked pretty good."

"I want one of them red and blue ties!"

"They sell 'em down Kings Road."

"I want a red leather jumpsuit, like what he was wearing!"

"Numan's got his left ear pierced…does that mean he's a poof?" (That was Terry – another Numan fan it transpired).

"Nah, it's the right ear if you're queer, innit?"

"Innit his right ear he's got pierced?"

"I've got my right ear pierced and I'm not a fuckin' *poof*." (That was Jack).

"Are you sure?" (Terry again - this resulted in a savage beanbag-chair fight instigated by Jack at the very suggestion he might be gay).

"Of course, everything he's done, David Bowie has done before, far better."

That last voice of dissent came from Anne who was an ardent Bowie fan and highlighted every part of Numan's act and persona, confidently telling us where and when Bowie had done it first. That didn't stop her from going to see Numan live when he undertook his first UK tour that autumn.

The tour was in support of his new album *The Pleasure Principle* which, following the international success of 'Cars', also went straight to No.1. Jack, of course, had tickets as well and went on the same night as Anne to the Hammersmith Odeon, Friday 28th September 1979.

"You not going then?" he asked me one idle day between lessons. I tried to act cool, or as cool as I could (which was the polar, not to mention stellar opposite, of cool).

"Nah, I'm skint," which was true – most days I didn't even have any money for lunch. Besides, how could I actually get to Hammersmith Odeon? Public transport? I think not – I could manage getting to Waterloo and my familiar wanderings round Soho and the West End but Hammersmith? Not a clue. Dad would never have taken me, nor would I have even asked him, considering he sometimes got lost in Tolworth. And where did you actually get the tickets? Would I have had to have gone and queued up for one like at the cinema? Or could I have sent off a postal order? God, I was naive.

"I got the album the other day…it's fuckin' brilliant. You got it yet?"

"No, but I'm hoping to…when I get some cash. I need a job first though."

Jack thought for a second. "Why don't you come and work at Fine Fare in Tolworth? Me and Terry Easton work there – it's a fuckin' great laugh!"

Fine Fare was a huge supermarket at the foot of Tolworth Tower, built in the early 1960s. For a while, it was the largest supermarket in Europe. Once replete with a bar that served coffees, doughnuts and tall, chilled milkshakes, you could look out onto the art deco forecourt where a huge, multi-layered concrete structure featured a wild, cascading waterfall surrounded by fountains at its base. That was until the local hoodlums found that if you threw in several bottles of Fairy Liquid with their lids off, the churning water would whip up a thick blanket of foam that swamped the forecourt and parts of Tolworth Broadway. So the water supply was subsequently and permanently turned off, the waterfall never to flow again. My brother still maintains (not very convincingly, it has to be said) that he was not one of the hoodlums that put the Fairy Liquid bottles in the fountain, although the suspicions of PC Thorogood at Surbiton Police Station were well documented. As for working at Fine Fare? I said I'd give them a ring.

The following Monday, Jack came thundering into the Common Room, animated to the extreme about the Gary Numan concert. He had the tour programme and was brandishing a rolled-up poster he'd bought outside the venue, which he immediately put on the wall, partially covering the poster of Bowie on stage from his 'Sound and Vision' era.

"Ah, mate you should have been there. It was fuckin' amazing!!! It was packed – completely sold out!! I was up in the balcony and could see everything!! He had these huge panels that lit up in time with the music…he done 'Are 'friends' electric?' at the end and it was great. And 'Cars'!! And some of his old Punk songs!!!"

Damn!!!

Anne strolled in soon afterwards, as aloof and as cool as ever, stashing her cigarettes and lighter in her bag.

"What did you think of the concert?" I asked excitedly.

Barely stifling a yawn, she eyed-up the poster on the wall.

"It was", she said slowly, barely able to hide her sheer contempt, "a load of old crap".

She and Jack then had a huge row about the show. Me? I just wish I'd been there, for this was the beginning of "Numania". That was the phrase Martin Mills, the managing director of Beggars Banquet, used years later, when the swarming crowds outside the theatre after the first night of the tour prevented Numan and the band leaving. He knew then he had something pretty special on his hands. The UK tour was sold out, the fans were becoming more fervent than ever and in the unlikely event that you hadn't heard of Gary Numan before now, there really was no escaping him from this point on for the next couple of years. He appeared not only in the music press but also in the nationwide British press, on TV, on *TOTP*, everywhere. It's a cynical thing, the music press though – Numan regularly appeared on their front pages as arguably one of the biggest starts in the UK at that time, so a prominent photo on the cover would guarantee an increase in sales, right? I'm sure it did but, as I've mentioned before, save for a few lone voices championing his rising star, most of the press were blithely indifferent and even contemptuous of Numan, who they saw as nothing more than a Bowie clone. It made little difference to me – in the words of Jack, I thought he was fucking brilliant, and, positive press or not, I began collecting the articles about him, not sad enough to cut and paste them into a scrapbook (because that would have been, like, *totally* sad, no?) but instead keeping them loose in a foolscap folder which I had labelled, with rub-on Letraset letters, 'The Numan File'. And if there was a really good cover, I'd pin it on my bedroom wall where, before long, I had quite a gallery.

We've well established by now that my Dad hated him, but my brother was equally disdainful of Numan and my infatuation with the man and his machine music. Now I can see one of the possible reasons. He felt threatened. Maybe he realised that his time of having his finger on the pulse of popular music, being at the forefront of the latest styles and crazes, where he owned at least 50% of the Top 20 singles, was over? He was 23 and when you've reached that age, the popular music of the day, the chart-bound sounds, the music of youth, is just that – a young man's game. His beloved disco, soul and funk singles and albums were completely out of synch with what was happening – really happening – in the music scene of 1979, so maybe that was why he derided me so often, usually in front of his equally contemptuous peers. Maybe it was something else? Beyond the usual sibling rivalry in any brotherly relationship, maybe he was still angry that, when he moved out in 1978 to briefly set up home with his long-standing fiancée, I had transferred all my books and comics and other possessions into his still Brut-scented pleasure palace but had refused point-blank to return to the box room when he moved back in eight months later after his relationship spectacularly failed? Maybe he was still angry that he had felt compelled to move out in the first place, as he had unwittingly slipped into the role of chief cook and bottle-washer after Mum had died and Dad kind of relinquished the role? Whatever the reason, he took great pleasure in belittling my Numan fascination.

One fine day, as the autumn sun bathed the Art block at the back of the school, I joined some of my fellow 6th Formers, including Kyle Lynch, to attend a discussion group that was being held in one of the empty upstairs rooms.

He and I climbed the stairs, the sunshine blazing through the windows revealing smudged finger-tip graffiti, such as 'Spurs Rool', 'I Luv Suzanne Hall', 'Chelsea FC', 'Suzanne Hall is a slut', 'ML luvs DV', '69', plus a pair of spiky-haired, melon-sized balls beneath a biologically disproportioned ejaculating cock. Kyle caught sight of my attire.

"What the fuck are you wearing?" he asked, eyes rolling in disbelief.

"Eh?"

"I said…what the fuck…are you wearing?"

"Er, it's what I was wearing yesterday," I replied, uncomfortable at the criticism being levelled at me.

I looked down at my sartorial inelegance: an ill-fitting t-shirt, flared C&A jeans that flapped voluminously round my ankles (because I thought I had big feet and that the flares would hide them), all rounded off by a pair of beige C&A trainers that had a gaping hole, revealing a pair of ginger-coloured towelling socks. If it had been raining I would have been wearing my beige parka, not even a green one where I might have been mistaken – at a great distance – for a Mod! I hadn't had my hair cut in, like, forever and shaving brought no pleasure, only a rash. Consequently, I had an unruly mop of brown hair when all my contemporaries had theirs cut short, along with a patchy, moustache-less beard that Brian Blessed would have mocked – MOCKED! – it was so pathetic.

"No-one wears fucking flares anymore!" Kyle went on exasperated and I had to admit, I was still stuck in the fashion time warp.

"For Christ's sake get some different ones! You look ridiculous!"

I didn't have much fashion sense, it had to be said. That was another thing my Dad could never understand about me. Dad was always well turned out, never without a tie - even in the sultry summer months - and prided himself on his appearance, hair always in place, never unshaven, topped off by a dab of Old Spice. Even back in the austere post-war years when rationing was still in place it was not uncommon for Dad, only then just in his late teens, to spend an entire week's wages on a new sharp suit and a shiny pair of shoes that he would polish until you could see infinity in them. Me? Not a clue. I hated clothes shopping and in the past Mum had usually bought things for me. Apart from my C&A flares, I now just wore Peter's hand-me-downs, but given that I was now at least a foot taller than him his old trousers and my socks were separated by a good two-to-three inches of pale, white, hairless calf. As for shoes, I owned two pairs – the trainers that were gradually falling apart and my last pair of school shoes with the heels worn down. And that was it. I was embarrassed about the situation and resolved to buy some new clothes. That would necessitate me getting another job. So, before picking up the phone to ring Fine Fare, I asked Terry for more information about working there.

"Ah, it's a complete doss," he said. "We just muck about in the warehouse. It's easy!"

And he didn't look too shabby in his blue drainpipe jeans and sweatshirt so it must have been paying well. I had little choice really. I finally gave Fine Fare a ring and was called in for a chat where the deputy store manager, Maureen, interviewed me. I was offered a job on the spot. I'd work on the tills Thursday and Friday night from 5.00pm until 8.00pm, then all day Saturday from 9.00am until 5.00pm. It was as simple as that.

I started the job virtually straight away and turned up at Fine

Fare on my first Thursday in early October 1979 for my induction. I
was given a brown overall with a name badge attached, which read
'MR MR DOWNHAM'. As my middle name is Richard everyone I
encountered thought it must be a mistake. Peter often said that about
me anyway come to think of it, (he didn't really but that was just too
good a joke to pass up).

I was introduced to a girl named Clare and was gob-smacked at
how stunning she was. She could only have been a year or 18 months
older than me at most but she came across as so mature, so worldly-
wise that I felt completely immature and inadequate. She was slim,
blonde with slightly curly hair, and had the most hypnotic blue-grey
eyes. Having a figure to die for was no bad thing and I struggled to
avert my gaze when she sat me down at one of the long line of tills at
the front of the shop to teach me how to operate them and generally
show me the ropes. Over the next couple of hours, we went through
several dummy baskets of shopping, and she showed me how to
enter the price, select the department (black button for general,
green button for veg, red button for meat), a very manual process.
It will come as no surprise that I kept getting it wrong – remember,
this was decades before scanning items with bar-codes; all the
produce was labelled in store and if it was frozen goods, the price
had generally fallen off anyway. During that training session, Clare
and I exchanged idle chitchat and I think it was probably the longest
conversation I'd had with a girl since establishing the exact rules for
'It', 'Chase', 'Chain-He' and 'Feet Off Ground' with Kim Taylor in the
playground at Tolworth Infants School. Terry and Jack wandered
past a couple of times, similarly decked out in their brown overalls
and gave me either a thumbs up or grief.

"You know these two, then?" asked Clare.

"Er, yeah, we go to school together."

God, that made us sound like children! I should have said "college"
or something but, no, the first thing that popped into my head was
"school". Not for the first time, I flushed with embarrassment.

"Be gentle with him!" Terry called as he ambled back to the warehouse.

"Oh, get lost!" Clare replied, but it was all in good humour.

I started my job properly the following night and was introduced to more of my new work-mates on my first all day shift on Saturday. Not only were there Terry, Jack and Clare, there was also:

Jillian: Her ethnic origin eluded me, too, but she had a mop of jet-black hair like Anne, and Terry always seemed to be hanging around with her.

Steve: A smug, bighead who sported a smudge of a moustache that, given another 15 years and a liberal daily sprinkling of Baby Bio, might just have grown enough to be visible from a distance. Genuinely believed he was God's gift to women.

Katie Smith: Short, bubbly and another object of Terry's affections.

Katie Webb: Petite, short blonde hair, very pretty, a lovely smile... and a boyfriend. I liked her a lot though!

Josie: Tall, blonde and still with, somewhat incongruously by 1980, a Farrah Fawcett hairstyle.

Roger Howman: Or, as he was summoned by the managers so frequently for his numerous unwitting misdemeanours, generally suffixed by, "Office, please."

Gary: Slightly younger than me, he doted on an utterly cheerless, po-faced girl who also worked on the tills.

Gill: In her mid-30s, blonde, buxom and good humoured.

Ian: A cool as Jack (maybe fractionally cooler!) who played bass in a New Wave band called The Docs and always had a pocketful of plectrums.

Kevin: Worked on the meat counter, older than then the rest of us, possibly late 20s, and with a strong West Country accent. Looked a bit like Barney Rubble (possibly with the same IQ). He always had plasters and bandages around at least two of his fingers, so Kevin and razor-sharp meat cleavers were clearly not a good mix.

Zoë: She was Jack's current girlfriend, a year younger than Jack and was just gorgeous.

Dad was pleased, as I expected him to be, that I was actively "doing something" – anything that didn't involve me slouching around the house where, it has to be said, I didn't exactly contribute much in the way of general housework. The Fine Fare job was no bad thing in his eyes. Idleness was not a failing of Dad's as he worked very hard indeed, sometimes too hard. Peter and I often thought that, of late, he looked very grey and drawn.

My self-imposed (self-inflicted?) solitary life was slowly coming to an end, and incidences of the protective bubble were becoming less and less frequent. I could no longer hide behind my shyness and social ineptitude in my new job as I would be dealing directly with the public, while at school, I had to discuss my course work with the tutors and couldn't conceal myself in the middle of the class amongst my 30+ classmates as I'd done during the previous couple of years. Someone had once said that I was a bit of a loner but I always thought of myself as more self-sufficient. I didn't rely on the company of others and didn't engage in social activities such as sport. This was another thing that must have disappointed Dad – he had been quite a sportsman back in the day, winning local tennis, squash and table-tennis championships. Peter was no slouch either, being part of a winning rugby team at Tiffin's Grammar School, where he also held county records in athletics and cross-country. My sporting prowess at Ivywood was under-whelming at best – as far as athletics went, if it was a 100m sprint, you couldn't touch me; over 200m I'd struggle; if it was the sheer sadism of the punishing 5000m I'd be at the back vomiting, trailing along in last place with the kid with asthma, who had sticking plaster over one lens of his glasses, and a strangely fey but grossly overweight lump who'd wander off into the bushes chasing butterflies. Then I'd head wheezing back to the changing room and the humiliation of the showers, where we more sensitive kids were allowed to wear swimming trunks, while the more confident, hirsute boys would bound naked into the swirls of steam and piping-hot water, some displaying meat and two veg that were even bigger than my Dad's. But even those boys, who fearlessly waved their genitalia at a knot-hole in the wall where, it was rumoured, the girls could spy on us from their changing rooms, kept an eye out for a certain teacher, hoping he wasn't prowling around the showers. He was not someone to get caught in the changing rooms with and even the bravest boys used to flee with their hair still damp and shoelaces undone to escape his attentions. So, no, sport was not my bag, baby. All I could do was write stories, I was not too bad at maths, could draw a bit and could tell you, without hesitation, who the fill-in artist on *The Uncanny X-Men* #106 was. It was Bob Brown with a framing sequence by regular X-Men artist Dave Cockrum if you are at all curious!

The routine of part-time school – a bit of studying at home, spending as much time as I could in the Common Room and working Thursday night, Friday night and all day Saturday – suited me fine. During this period I started to get on really well with Terry and we began to hang out together more. He was a sporting dynamo and loved Chelsea, which caused no end of arguments with the Spurs-loving Jack. Terry was also a massive Gary Numan fan but, like me, hadn't had the money to go and see him at Hammersmith like Jack and Anne had done. Oh how I really wish I'd gone. Amongst Numan's fans, it was a pretty special tour, which had continued into October 1979, with *The Pleasure Principle* album effortlessly topping the UK charts. Perhaps somewhat incongruously, Numan was also gaining significant exposure and chart success across Europe and the rest of the world, with 'Cars' and *The Pleasure Principle* making a momentous and possibly unexpected dent in the US singles and album charts, much to Beggars Banquet's delight no doubt. Consider though that this level of instant, 'overnight' stardom had occurred within less than six months.

How do you cope with that kind of fame when, barely a year

before, Tubeway Army had been playing in pubs and clubs, riding on the coat-tails of the Punk movement, already dismissed as a Generation X rip-off, performing their 90 mph, three-minute Punk songs in pubs where the audience were less inclined to listen to the music and more inclined instead to extrude as much phlegm and snot as possible and gob it at the band?

How do you go from wistfully driving past Hammersmith Odeon in your battle-damaged, beleaguered Morris Minor Estate thinking, "One day I'll get there," then, seemingly in the blink of an eye, arriving at the same venue in the tour bus with full entourage, watching roadies manoeuvring huge cases of equipment with 'Numan' stencilled on them, pressing through the throngs of fans anxiously waiting for you?

How do you go from practicing guitar in front of a mirror in your bedroom, to performing to thousands of people, night after night, and proving to yourself, your fans and your fiercest critics that you actually know how to do this and that you deserve to be in that spotlight as much as anyone?

How do you go from gob-flecked performances in a club, to waiting in the wings at Hammersmith Odeon – with Orchestral Manoeuvres in The Dark's Kay's catalogue synth and reel-to-reel tape machine hastily removed from the stage, with the dying notes of 'Airlane' resonating around the theatre and the opening notes of 'Me! I Disconnect From You' driving the audience into a frenzy – and then stride out on stage to the universal roar of delirious delight from 3,500 plus fans? Keeping a few hundred glue-sniffing Punks reasonably entertained in a pub is one thing, starring and professionally performing at the Hammersmith Odeon, now that is something else.

How do you prepare for that level of very public exposure, with the fear, both figuratively and literally, of falling flat on your face and leaving yourself vulnerable to the barbs and criticisms of the media?

How do you deal with The Musicians' Union who, allegedly, tried to get you banned from performing on TV because, by using synthesizers, you were "taking work away from real musicians"?

There were two major problems with that argument:

The first? Numan used synthesizers, true, but had proper drums, a proper bass guitar and, certainly on *Replicas*, a real guitar. Synths augmented the sound.

Secondly, electronic synthesizers had been in use for years! Witness, for example, performances on *TOTP* by Space and 'Magic Fly, 'Oxygene' by Jean Michel Jarre, 'I Feel Love' by Donna Summer, and going back to the early 1970s, 'Popcorn' by Hot Butter and even 'Son of My Father' by Chicory Tip!

So that argument was utter bollocks then, clearly!

Numan has said that he didn't expect to get so famous so quickly – he thought that the release of 'Are 'friends' electric?' might make him popular and generate a small cult following upon which he could slowly build his career in music. But this? This was huge. He summed it up best when he likened this whole phase of his career to standing on a station platform, with the 'train to success' hurtling along the tracks towards him at a phenomenal, eye-watering speed and, as it roared past, *just* grabbing onto the last carriage by his finger-tips and trying to hang on. You go from being an unknown, unemployed wannabe, to being in every paper, on every TV screen, with your name plastered on billboards and theatre hoardings. Suddenly his image was everywhere, even emulated in the iconic Lee Cooper jeans advertisement on TV, where Numan sang 'Don't Be A Dummy'. The advert featured neon-eyed, bleached-blonde Punks, not too dissimilar from Numan's image used on the cover of *Replicas*.

He was relentlessly pursued by the media for opinions on everything from music, image and influences, to demanding to know his stance on the current state of British politics and, while you're at it, cheers, Gaz, can you clue us in on the meaning of life?

It can't have been easy, not helped by the fact that few of his contemporaries had a single kind word to say about him. And speaking of contemporaries, it's interesting to note that OMD often neglect to mention that it was Numan who sought them out and personally chose them to be the support act on *The Touring Principle* tour, that it was he who gave them nationwide exposure and enabled them to pursue their own successful career. I read an interview with them recently where they talked about their early days and they boldly stated that it was getting a record deal that got them out of the clubs and on their way to fame and fortune. And Numan? Not mentioned once, the miserable, ungrateful buggers.

But while Numan was getting some considerable exposure and column inches in the music papers, the journalists started to become far more vitriolic and spiteful with attacks becoming much more personal. The metal-favouring *Sounds* hated him, the New Wave bible *NME* barely tolerated him and the disco-loving *Record Mirror* loathed him. Maybe part of his appeal to me was he was the underdog? Certainly another part of the appeal was that my Dad couldn't stand him. I would never do anything to upset my Dad and I had absolutely no out-and-out rebellious streak but this was just a small way of sticking two tiny Action Man–scale fingers up at Dad and authority in general.

CHAPTER 9

Finally, a make-over!

I was finally earning a reasonable wage at Fine Fare, bolstered by a bit of occasional overtime so I figured it was about time I bought some new clothes, as I had always intended to do. Venturing down to Kingston one Saturday morning on a rare day off from my usual stint at Fine Fare, I set about improving my wardrobe. As embarrassed and nervous as I'd been about asking the dealer for the 'Are 'friends' electric?' picture disc, I went into some of the boutiques along Eden Street, including the Top Man shop, opened in 1978 with an in-store appearance by porn star and model, Fiona Richmond. I searched the racks and finally purchased some new sweatshirts and some new, black, straight-leg jeans. I even bought a black, button-down collar shirt along with a black tie – I toyed with the idea of going to the shops down the Kings Road to see if I could get a Numan blue and red tie but decided against it.

At home, I anxiously tried on the black jeans, black shirt and black tie and thought I actually looked OK. Dad however, on his way to the bathroom with a canary in a cage for his customary mid-afternoon crap, saw me and looked dismayed.

"You going to a funeral or something, son?" he said and left me to gaze somewhat deflated at my reflection in the bedroom mirror.

I could have thumped him. And that was one of the problems with Dad – I don't think he really meant to upset or belittle but, blimey, he could be a bit thoughtless sometimes. Years later, he'd regularly remark to Peter how well one of Peter's old schoolmates was doing, who now lived in a sprawling mansion worth an absolute mint down in Weybridge and who possibly owned most of Surrey and was now greedily eyeing up Kent.

There were a few other examples - once I came home from school and saw that Dad's car was up on blocks in the driveway, a steady stream of oil dripping from underneath. Rather than staining the brickwork of the drive, the oil was being soaked up by a large piece of cloth; not by one of the Brentford Nylons bed-sheets that we'd bought years earlier but which we'd consigned to the back of the airing-cupboard as we were all fed-up with the static electric shocks that would arc around our fillings in the night; nor by the barely-used, candy-striped hideously uncomfortable flannelette sheets that were similarly consigned to the airing-cupboard. No, the first object he laid his hands on was my burr-burr – my furry comfort blanket that I'd had as a baby which had Mrs Rabbit pictured with Peter Rabbit on. I don't know where he'd found it as I certainly hadn't seen it literally in decades. Nevertheless, I glanced at the once blue fur that was now being drenched black and nearly cried.

"What did you use that for?" I asked, exasperated.

"Well, you weren't using it any more, were you?" Dad replied, wiping his hands on an old handkerchief.

"Yeah, but...but...it was my burr-burr?"

Dad was unconcerned.

"Ah, well," he shrugged.

I looked again at the now ruined memento from my infancy.

"It's done the job though, eh?" he said, cheerfully oblivious to my obvious upset then turned tail to go indoors to make a cup of tea.

On another occasion I had cause to venture into the garden shed, anxious that one day I wouldn't emerge having been devoured by the FUCKING great big spiders that lurked in there (and, no, they were never more afraid of me than I was of them). Keeping my visit as short as possible, I happened to see a recently opened pot of emulsion. Resting by the side of the pot, covered in paint and bent at a perfect 45 degree angle, was the screwdriver that I had painstakingly made in Metalwork at school, with months of fine tooling, filing, firing and suffering nightmares the night before using the monstrous lathe where, so popular school myth had it, a boy had had his fingers ripped out of their sockets.

"Dad? You bent the screwdriver I made for you?" I said, once again exasperated at his casual thoughtlessness.

"Did I?" he replied absent-mindedly.

"Yes! Look!" I said, holding up the paint-covered item.

"Oh, yeah…was that the one you made for me?"

"Yes!! Yes, it was!!"

"Yes, well, I didn't want to ruin one from the set I got for Christmas."

"But…I *made* this for you!"

He shrugged apologetically.

"I'm sorry, son…but maybe next time make it a bit stronger."

Regardless of Dad's criticism of my new clothes, I started to smarten myself up a bit, wearing some of my new sweat shirts to the 6th Form and relegated my C&A flares to the back of the wardrobe and started to wear my new black jeans. I also began to shave more regularly, despite the accompanying shaving-rash, and even decided to get a long overdue haircut. Ambling along to Dad's trusted barber shop – they glimpsed me a fraction of a second too late before they could turn the 'open' sign to 'closed'– I plopped myself down in the barber's chair where they faced quite a challenge to cut my shaggy mop of hair. But the barber, who was aged somewhere between 70 and 150, persevered and I left the shop with a new look, not too short you understand – kind of Beatles 1965 – but leaving the wheezing red-faced barber slumped in a chair with his colleagues wafting a jar of Brylcreem under his nose in an effort to resuscitate him.

The autumn term continued at Ivywood, now very much settled into the routine of attending my elected lessons, dossing about in the Common Room and working at Fine Fare. The weather was getting decidedly cooler as the leaves on the trees in the gardens to the rear of the main Albury school building turned brown. Autumn was, and remains, my favourite time of year, still with the occasional warm day but the mornings getting cooler, the sunlight more watery and the nights starting to slowly creep in. On one such day, I had finished my last lesson of the day, which had overrun, and ambled back to the

Common Room to drop off some textbooks and also to see if anyone was around. Strangely it was empty, save for one person – Suzanne Laine. She was curled up on the sofa, shoes off, wearing a light brown polo neck jumper, tight blue jeans and reading a book. I wasn't sure if she'd seen me and I hesitated for a second, debating whether to go in or to make a discreet exit.

"Hi, Martin," she said and nearly frightened the life out of me. "What are you doing?"

"Errrrrrrrrrrrrrrr," I said, "Errrrrrrrrrrrrrrrrrr….", rooted to the spot.

She looked at me quizzically, momentarily closing her book.

"Errrrrrrrrrrrrrrr," I continued, "I've…er…got to drop off a book."

"Oh," she said and smiled just the sweetest, innocent smile.

"Are you staying long?" I blurted out and wondered for a second who had spoken, before realising it was me.

"About an hour," Suzanne replied, "I just thought I'd catch up on some revision."

"Oh," I said.

There was a long pause.

"Are you just going to stand there?" she asked.

"Er…no, no, I, er, I'll just drop off this book."

I thought for a second.

"Anyway, I've got to hang around as I've forgotten my door-key ha-ha-ha-ha-ha so I can't get into my house as no one will be home before six so I may as well hang around here if that's OK with you but if it isn't I'll head off but I'll have to wait on the doorstep."

I was startled with my on the spot, barefaced lie that had come tumbling out. My door key at that moment was almost being bent out of shape concealed in my clenched hand.

"No, no…that's fine," she said reassuringly and I went and sat at one of the tables near the sofa.

We sat and talked for a while, about nothing in particular, but I cherished just being in the same room as such a beautiful girl, who laughed often and freely at what tended to be my self-deprecating humour. The shadows in the Common Room lengthened as only a few lights were on, while the lights in the rest of the school blinked out one by one as the remaining teachers and pupils went home. It was soon 6.00pm and the clatter of the cleaners outside meant that we'd have to leave before the rooms had, at best, a cursory tidy up and then be locked up for the night. I walked out with Suzanne to the school gates and said goodnight. I watched her walk off towards to her house, hoping that she might turn round and wave, but she didn't. So I headed for the bus-stop to get the 281 bus home, pausing to watch a spectacular sunset over Surbiton Station from the railway bridge, the sky ahead dazzling red, white and gold while the sky behind me was a deep, deep blue.

I entered the house, Dad and Peter having been home since about 5.00pm, and headed to my room where I rummaged around for the Five-Year Diary that Mum had bought me for Christmas 1974. Determined to fill it in regularly, I never seemed to get past April of each year. I made some brief notes about what had just happened – what Suzanne was wearing, lying about my key, the sunset – although I'm not sure why I felt compelled to write it down. It wasn't as if I'd asked her out, or we'd kissed or lost my virginity, but I just didn't want to lose the magic of that fleeting, sweet, innocent moment.

As it turned out, it was virtually the only sweet, innocent moment that we had and didn't, alas, herald the start of a long, passionate relationship. But it did start the beginning of a completely platonic friendship that lasted for the duration of our time in the 6th Form before we eventually, inevitably lost touch. But considering my complete lack of experience with girls, my crippling embarrassment, and my general social ineptitude, a sweet, innocent friendship was no bad thing.

CHAPTER 10

A Betamax video-recorder and The Beatles

Dad was happy with the way things were going as far as I was concerned – back at school, earning some money, not slumped in my room reading comics or listening to "that bloody Gary Numan" – so just before November tipped into December 1979, he decided that we should all have a bit of a treat. He'd seen that the BBC over the Christmas period were going to show all The Beatles films and, knowing that I liked the band (*they* were OK as far as he was concerned, it was just that monotonous, repetitious "ner-ner-*NER*, ner-ner-*NER*" of Numan's music that got on his tit) he announced to Peter and me that he was going to invest in some new household technology and was thinking about getting a video-recorder. We were stunned. The last bit of cutting-edge technology that our house had seen was one of the first colour televisions in Princes Avenue, which we rented from Radio Rentals back in 1971. Back then we had awaited its arrival, barely able to sleep the night before, and watched in silent, breathless awe as the engineer installed it in our back room. An electrical smell emanated from the grille at the back as the tube warmed up, to show us our favourite programmes in glorious colour. I remember my Mum was disappointed when we saw *Star Trek* in colour for the first time as she always thought Mr. Spock was green! My Nan meanwhile, who Dad brought round every Saturday lunchtime after he finished work, couldn't wait for *World of Sport* on ITV and the prospect of seeing Jackie Pallo and Mick McManus in full sweaty colour as they grappled in the wrestling ring. Dad and Peter would then turn over to BBC-1 and *Grandstand*, commanding absolute silence for the football results and the pools news, on the off-chance of another win. But now, without any warning, Dad decided he wanted a video recorder.

"Are you sure?" we asked. "Aren't they, like, really expensive?"

"We'll have a look and see what's what," he said.

We three visited the local branch of Curry's down Tolworth Broadway and, upon entering the store, were hit by the distinctive electrical smell and a barely audible white noise from all the TVs with their sound turned right down. Among all the TVs, music centres, cassette decks, fridges, kitchen appliances and radios, there was a small selection of video-recorders. The shop assistant slid over to our side as we stared blankly at each machine.

"How can I help you?" he asked, every inch an East End barrow boy but with a tie and a name badge.

"We're thinking of getting a video recorder," Dad said somewhat vaguely, "what can you recommend?" The assistant's beady eyes sparkled at these words.

"We-he-hell, sir," spake the man, "I'm sure we'll be able to oblige. Did you have any particular model in mind?"

We didn't – I think Peter had looked in the paper to see how much they generally were but that was about the extent of our market research.

"Well, there are two types to choose from – Betamax or VHS."

"What's the difference?" Dad bluntly asked.

"They're two different formats. You have," said the assistant, presenting two blank tapes, "the VHS tape and these smaller, more compact Betamax tapes."

Dad asked the obvious question, "So you can't play VHS on Betamax then, no?"

The assistant revelled in our general ignorance.

"Oh, no, no, no, no, no, sir, they're quite incompatible."

He looked about the store and his voice lowered to just above a whisper.

"But if you want MY opinion, sir..." (We gathered closer into this conspiratorial huddle), "...the Betamax is a far, far superior format – it's a better picture, better quality and, honestly? I don't think VHS will last."

Dad loved being called "Sir" and, rarely for him, prepared to throw caution to the wind. He by-passed the VHS models and turned his attention to a Sanyo VTC-9300 Betamax machine. It was huge...the shelf it was on was buckling under the weight and, if it fell out of a tree, it'd kill you.

"Beautiful model, that one, sir," said the assistant as if selling a new car, running his finger across the matte-black finish. Dad was like a rabbit caught in the lights of an oncoming car, mesmerised by the green neon display and shiny piano-like keys protruding from the front.

"You can record one channel and watch another one at the same time," the assistant went on, "and," he added with a flourish, "it has a remote control!"

Sanity prevailed, but only for a fleeting moment.

"Are you sure we won't be stuck with the wrong format?" Dad asked, distantly, but his mind was already made up.

"Sir, I would never *willingly* give you wrong advice," the assistant said, smarming and charming Dad as he went. And then Dad sealed the deal with the immortal words – "Is it available on HP?"

I thought the assistant was going to collapse in orgasmic delight.

"Why, yes, of course it is, sir" he replied, already thinking he might shut the shop early.

We signed the hire purchase agreement, thereby committing the three of us to spending, over the next five years, the same amount of cash it would have cost to buy a new Mini. I think it weighed about the same, come to think of it.

And so the Downhams entered the modern-age with the delivery of the Betamax, and we all know what happened after that. Betamax was a superior format but the battle for supremacy over the VHS format was short-lived, lasting about three years, seemingly only ending when the porn-industry sided with the latter, with the likes of the *Electric Blue* soft-porn series ultimately only available on VHS. But, briefly, we had a piece of kit that other households didn't have, able to record TV programmes – unbelievable! – and enjoy the 'luxury' of the remote control which consisted of a long cable plugged into the back of the Betamax which paused or un-paused playback. This video-recorder beast squatted under our TV for the next few years until we eventually caved in and bought a VHS. But, for now, the Betamax did exactly as it said on the tin and recorded TV programmes and we could play them back with, what seemed to us then, perfect clarity. We'd sit and set the timer to record a programme in, say, five minutes time, then watch in wonder as, 30 seconds before the start of the programme, the video sprang into life to the sound of clunking belt drives and gears from within. Then we'd sit back and witness the machine actually recording a TV programme. Astonishing! Dad said that I could record The Beatles films over Christmas on one of the three blank tapes we'd got with the machine. We had to be careful though as a new tape cost £14.75 (I've still got a receipt somewhere!) but it was worth it. Being able to watch – when I wanted to – the rarely seen *Magical Mystery Tour* or *Let it Be*, in what we then thought was stunning audio and visual clarity, was just amazing.

CHAPTER 11

'Complex' on 12-inch and Dame Dave throws a hissy-fit

My friendship with Terry grew. We were fast becoming best friends, and we talked endlessly about music - not just Gary Numan, but other synth bands too. In the 6th Form one lunchtime, I read in one of the numerous music papers strewn about the Common Room which, to be frank, was starting to resemble a squat, that Beggars Banquet were lifting a second single from *The Pleasure Principle*, a song entitled 'Complex'. Naturally, I had to have it. I also saw with great delight that there was going to be a 12-inch 'limited edition' – fatal words for me, those! I noted the release date that was set for the following week and I was determined to get it.

Came the day, on an afternoon when I didn't have any lessons, I left Ivywood attired in my black jeans and black shirt and caught the 281 bus down to Kingston to seek out the object of my desire, tingling with anticipation but also genuinely worried that, as it was a limited edition, I might not actually be able to get it. I mean, what if the record shop had sold out? What then?

Terry, who didn't have any lessons either, came with me. Unlike on my visit with Jack, I lead the way round Kingston, sidestepping the likes of Woolworth's and WHSmiths and heading to a proper record shop. We hit pay-dirt first time when we went into the tiny HMV store on Clarence Street. It was a one-unit shop which, back in 1977, had brazenly displayed the poster for the Sex Pistols' *Never Mind The Bollocks* album in the window before they were ordered to take it down, replaced instead by a censored, sanitised 'Never Mind The Sex Pistols' version. Tiny it may have been but here, on this cold autumn afternoon, it was packed full of all the latest releases, posters and badges adorning the walls. I lead Terry to the 12-inch singles rack and, holding my breath, leafed through the new releases.

And there it was – 'Complex' on 12-inch black vinyl. I plucked it from the rack – I may have even emitted a little whinny of delight – and gazed at the cover. It was purple, with a shaded picture of an indistinct, almost invisible, Numan, except for the eyes – always the eyes – which were a bright, luminous white. I flipped the single over and examined the back – it was a picture taken from the recent tour with the band in full flow, Numan centre stage, in front of the dazzling light panels that Jack had raved about. Damn, I wish I'd been to the concert.

Two tracks were on the B-Side – 'Bombers' and 'Me! I Disconnect from You'. God, it was another thing of beauty! Terry examined the single with me but was clearly unimpressed.

"Hmm," he said, "what's the point of getting a single on 12-inch?"

Oh, I was quite smug! "Well, sometimes you get extended versions, other times you get extra tracks on the B-Side. Here," I said selecting the 7-inch version of the single, "you only get 'Bombers' on the 7-inch version. On the 12-inch you get another track. Got to be worth it, no?"

Terry remained unimpressed and elected to get the 7-inch version.

"Well, I'm getting this," I said and moments later we emerged into the street, the afternoon already getting dark.

"What are we doing now?" I asked.

Terry looked up and down the street, drawing his coat collar up as it was getting cold.

"Dunno," he said, "I might pop down to Beggars to see what they've got in. If not, I might go to the pub."

Really? A pub?

I didn't really consider going to pubs to be a viable option for me, not that alcohol had ever been banned or frowned upon at home. Indeed, Christmases in the mid-1970s at Princes Avenue had seen the hostess trolley in the hall laden down with bottles of Cinzano, Martini and Bols Advocaat, along with tiny bottles of Babycham and huge tins of Watney's Party Seven beer. I would join my country cousins, who journeyed up from Plymouth for each Christmas between 1973 and 1976, and have little snifters of them all, while 'I Wish It Could Be Xmas Everyday' by Wizzard provided the musical backdrop to family parties in the front room – everyone engulfed in the smoke from my Uncle Reg's Hamlet cigars.

When Peter had moved out in 1978 to briefly set up home in Horsham, his mates had helpfully assisted the move by throwing some of his possessions out of the back of the removal van during the journey from Tolworth. This was to impress two girls who were in an open-top sports car behind us who initially laughed but whom I doubt appreciated the mass, hairy-arsed mooning that followed. Peter's mates insisted we stop off at a pub en route. They refused point-blank to buy me a soft drink, so, after a few pints of Stella Artois lager, I spent the rest of the day deliriously out of my skull, with 'Ça Plane Pour Moi' by Plastic Bertrand echoing round my head after Peter's mates thought it would be hilarious to play it repeatedly on the pub jukebox until the landlord threw us out.

So, booze and me were not exactly strangers but we were hardly bosom buddies either.

"I'm off home then," I said, deciding I'd probably join Terry in the pub another day.

Anxious to play my latest addition to my Numan collection before Dad got home, I headed round to the bus station.

"See you tomorrow," I called back as Terry disappeared amongst the throng of shoppers.

"Yeah, cheers, Mart", he called back.

And that was a moment, right there.

Everyone, but everyone, called me "Martin" (except for Peter who called me "Tit-head" from time to time). I'd always been slightly envious of other kids at school who had names easily abbreviated or had cool nicknames. Terry was "Tel", Andrew was "Andy" etc. I didn't think you could really do much with "Martin" and despised "Marty" but "Mart"? Do you know what? I was OK with that.

I caught a 281 bus home, anxiously holding the HMV bag, stealing glances at the precious contents. Dad was still at work so I decamped to the front room and Dad's stereo and placed the single on the turntable. Examining the sleeve, I listened to the new Gary Numan single. Immediately apparent was the change of tempo – it was much slower and as light on lyrics as 'Cars' had been but the atmosphere still very much emphasising feelings of loneliness and isolation. So how could I not like it, right? And I *did* like the song, but on first hearing, I didn't *love* it. It's the widely held belief among the Numan fan-base that he should have released 'Metal' instead and I agreed with them. It was a bold move, though, releasing what the comic-loving broadcaster and writer, Paul Gambaccini, declared was the first electronic ballad. However, flipping the disc over to the B-side, I absolutely adored the two live tracks. 'Me! I Disconnect From You' was just a tour de force from the outset, the Numan backing band a complete machine, delivering a performance that made me wish even more that I'd got my wits about me and gone to the concert. And 'Bombers' was just incredible. I had no idea at this stage that it was a reworking of an earlier Punk song by Tubeway Army and it would be a while before I heard the original, faster, angrier version. I played the two live tracks more than the A-Side but, with regular playing, came to love all three. However, after hurtling into the charts, it stalled at No. 6, which was disappointing to say the least.

What was also disappointing was that I didn't get to see the video for the single. Well, that's not true – I *almost* got to see it. One of the drawbacks of working at Fine Fare on a Thursday night was that I missed *Top of the Pops*. As I've said, blank Betamax tapes cost a fortune so you couldn't casually record things that idly took your fancy, or set up series links like you can now on your Sky or Virgin box.

One evening in late November, with 'Complex' having entered the Top 10, I'd headed off to work at 5.00pm, on what was a truly horrible night – dark, wet and blowing a gale. With Christmas looming, and as Fine Fare was the largest supermarket for miles, it was horrendously busy, with queues of 15 customers on every till. I didn't even get a tea break, so by the time I'd finished I was knackered, not to mention hungry. I got my coat and headed out into the night where the weather was getting worse. I trudged home, squelching all the way as the rain came down in torrents.

The glow of the lights at our house in Princes Avenue was very welcoming as I arrived home, hair plastered down my face, steaming slightly, absolutely drenched. I could smell that something had been cooking – something chippy! – and went into the back room. Peter was reclining with feet up on the sofa watching TV, a can of Stella in hand with a John Player Special wedged between two fingers. An empty plate on the floor by the sofa betrayed the last smears of tomato sauce that had, I suspect, judging by the enticing odours, probably recently drizzled some chips but possibly also a couple of Bird's Eye beef burgers as well. All had evidently been mopped up by a slice of bread and butter.

"Alright?" I asked, wondering if anything had been cooked for me. There hadn't.

"Yep," Peter said, making himself comfier on the sofa, taking a long drag on his cigarette.

"Where's Dad?"

"Upstairs."

There was a pause as Peter took a swig from his Stella and drew on his cigarette, both clutched in the same hand.

"Oh, your mate was on *Top of the Pops* tonight," he said absently.

"Who?"

"Your mate – old fuck-face."

"Gary Numan?" I said, as I continued to steam in the warmth of the house.

Another drag, another swig.

"Yeah, him."

"Was he in the studio?" I asked, anxious for more details.

"No, it was a video."

Another pause, another drag, another swig.

"It was a good video, though."

"Really?" I asked eagerly.

"Yeah, it was all purple and animated and his eyes were all weird."

Bugger!

Another drag, another swig.

"Best video I've ever seen, actually."

"Really?"

"Yeah."

I looked at the Betamax squatting under the TV.

"Did you record it for me?" I asked hopefully.

Peter took a long drag on his JPS, and drained his can of Stella.

A long, guttural belch preceded his reply.

"Did I fuck."

So it was literally years before I saw the video for 'Complex' as 'in and out' best describes its chart action when it plummeted out of the Top 10 the following week. But I was nevertheless delighted with the addition of the 12-inch limited edition single to my burgeoning Numan collection of records (still no albums though!). Terry was pretty impressed with the single when we inevitably discussed it in the Common Room, although he didn't seem overly bothered that the song had failed to hit the coveted No.1 spot.

Beggars Banquet cashed in on the unqualified, unimaginable, inconceivable domestic and international success of Numan during 1979 by re-releasing the first two Tubeway Army singles, 'Bombers' and 'That's Too Bad' as a double 7-inch pack, and also re-promoted the eponymous first *Tubeway Army* album sporting a new black and white line drawing of Numan's face on the cover, a drawing that would become his trademark, enduring to this day. I cut out the ads Beggars Banquet had placed in the music press heralding this re-promotion and added them to my 'Numan File' of press cuttings.

Back in the 6th Form, spirits were high as Christmas was nearly upon us and parties were being planned with great excitement and anticipation. Alas, my invites to these must have been lost in the post as I was excluded from every single one. But I was satisfied with my close friends and, like I say, Terry and I were getting on really well. He was always a good laugh at Ivywood and certainly made things entertaining at Fine Fare. One evening, as I went up to the canteen for my tea break, I saw him and Kevin from the meat counter playing football with bread rolls in the warehouse which, after being kicked from one end of the warehouse to the other, ended up back in the breadbin for unsuspecting customers to purchase, hopefully oblivious to the fact that the bits of black grit on each roll weren't sesame seeds.

After term finished, I prepared for Christmas as best I could. Christmas these days was hard to get through. The memories of Christmases-past, with the house full of friends, family, laughter, booze, cigar smoke and music, all centred round the kitchen where Mum cooked the Christmas dinner, were all still painfully fresh. This year it would just be the three of us – me, Dad and Peter. Peter was still young (-ish), free and single and didn't seem to have any lingering regrets about the collapse earlier in the year of his long-term relationship. He still wasn't happy about being stuck in the box room but I still refused to move out of his old bedroom. He was nevertheless living a hedonistic lifestyle and had even managed to go on a Club 18-30s holiday in the summer so he was happy enough. He had, however, made mention of a girl called Susan he was introduced to at his office party.

On Christmas Day itself, we were invited over to my Uncle John and Auntie Rita's house in Chigwell for lunch and Dad drove as he rarely drank. Before we left, I carefully set up the Betamax to record the penultimate film in the 'Beatles at Christmas' season on BBC-2, which was *A Hard Day's Night*. And, yes, it did record properly and, no, I didn't record The Queen's Speech on BBC-1 by mistake.

Climbing aboard Dad's gold Series II Rover 3500, me in the back, Peter riding shotgun, Dad's seatbelt knotted and unfastened as always (Dad always believed – genuinely – that if he crashed, the steering wheel would protect him from harm), we headed off on what was a cold, miserable day, driving past homes with curtains open revealing warm, glowing, festive households with Mums, Dads, children and grandparents, all smiling and happy and embracing the Yuletide spirit. We drove past house after house, gold foil decorations to the fore, windows steaming up as Christmas dinners cooked, relatives wearing coats and scarves arriving at the doors, carrying bags and parcels and bottles, smiling and happy as they entered on a day that, even though barely lunchtime, already seemed to be getting dark.

Happy families, all.

How I envied them. I felt denied a loving, maternal presence in the family and resented it even more. I didn't have any grandparents – my paternal grandfather had died in December 1962, just before I was born. This was at the beginning of the notorious 'Big Freeze' when Britain froze under layers of snow until March 1963. The undertakers were worried that they wouldn't actually be able to bury him as the ground was frozen as hard as concrete. My maternal grandfather died in 1964 when I was still a toddler, my paternal grandmother, who we rarely saw, died in 1972 and my maternal grandmother died in 1978 after a series of debilitating strokes, completely unable to comprehend that her youngest daughter had died. No parent should ever outlive their children.

Mum was gone and her absence was still achingly felt, certainly by me. With Peter, I think he drowned his sorrows and years later admitted that when she had died, he vowed he would never, ever be as sad again as he was in 1977. And Dad? Up until now, he never talked about Mum's death, never opened up about how he was feeling, not to me anyway. But there was one exception, in 1978, on the first anniversary of Mum's death. I was helping him decorate the back room and was stripping some of the wallpaper. All the furniture was up-ended and dustsheets were everywhere. Dad was on the other side of the room, kneeling down, stripping paper when he stopped and paused.

"Well, it's a year today since Mum died," he finally, sadly, said.

"I know, Dad," I replied (how could I *not* know?). Then he burst in to tears, crying into his hankie with great heaving sobs. My eyes filled up and I was choked.

"Please don't cry, Dad?" I said tearfully and gave him an awkward hug, as he was slumped on the floor while I remained standing, uncertain as to whether I should sit down with him.

"I know, son, I know, I know, I know. I'm sorry," he said, wiping his tear-reddened eyes. He eventually composed himself.

After a few minutes, we carried on with the decorating with an uneasy silence between us. How I wish I could have offered some words of comfort to him but as an inexperienced, troubled 15-year old, I just couldn't articulate anything remotely helpful. Dad must have been in agony – we didn't even have any photographs of Mum on display in the house; the pain must have been too much for him. How he must have struggled. My poor Daddy.

Let me tell you a bit about my Dad, Jim Downham. Dad was the eldest of four brothers – Dad, John, Reg and Roy – and was born in Bermondsey in 1928. He always said he was a true blue Cockney, born within the sound of Bow Bells, and his early years were tough to say the least. Not only was he born into a very, very poor family, living in a rat-infested tenement not far from the Thames where the family, as Dad remarked years later, "didn't even have a pot to piss in," but also his start in life couldn't have been more difficult. He was born with a large brown birthmark that stretched across his right cheek, down his neck and into his ear. It was like a huge mole. When he was a baby, his parents kept a woollen balaclava on him to try and conceal the mark for fear of upsetting their neighbours. Dad told me that he remembered, aged only four or five, being paraded before rows of doctors in huge, polished wood, high-ceilinged consultancy rooms, all trying to determine what had caused the disfigurement and what exactly could be done. Dad's face was photographed at length and he was eventually referred to a surgeon, Harold Gilles, who was a pioneering specialist in the new discipline of plastic surgery. He performed a new procedure on Dad whereby he grafted the skin from Dad's shoulder onto his cheek to cover most of the birthmark, a process that required Dad to be physically linked to his shoulder, with his head and neck at an uncomfortable not mention painful angle for months while the skin graft took place. The process was a complete success and the plan was to perform further plastic surgery on Dad's ear to remove the growth but the outbreak of the war put paid to that notion. Gilles, along with Archibald McIndoe, went on to perform near miraculous plastic surgery on soldiers horribly disfigured in World War II, soldiers who would have otherwise faced a lifetime of ridicule, scorn, revulsion and isolation. Dad eventually had the process completed in 1976 but for all his life, he hated having his photograph taken, despite the fact that unless you got really close, Dad's face looked perfectly normal. I contacted the administrators of the Gilles and McIndoe archives years later to see if the photographs might still exist of Dad as a little boy but they couldn't find any trace. Nevertheless, I'm proud that Dad was himself a guinea pig for the process that would change the lives of soldiers in the famous Guinea Pig Club.

Back to Christmas Day 1979: We drove to Chigwell, traversing several streets more than once and this was before we even left the environs of Surrey. Dad, for all his sensibilities, capabilities, knowledge and wisdom, had absolutely no sense of direction. We sometimes called him "Captain Compass". Peter had the radio on and produced a cassette from his pocket.

"Here, have a listen to this!" he proudly announced, slipping the cassette into the car stereo.

It was 'Rapper's Delight' by The Sugarhill Gang and we all laughed at the lyrics, for this was the extended version with one of the singers making reference to satisfying Lois Lane with his super-sperm. This cheered us up a bit, so by the time we eventually got to Uncle John's we were all in a better mood. We didn't see John and Rita that often but like the numerous families I'd seen on the journey over, we were welcomed into their house. Their maisonette was lavishly decorated and from the kitchen came the smell of a full Christmas dinner cooking with all the trimmings. On a table was a Fortnum & Mason's hamper, so it was evident we were going to be well fed.

That evening, after consuming our body-weight in food, with several bottles of Black Tower and Blue Nun consumed, Peter and I retired to the kitchen. Dad, even though he'd only had a couple of glasses of wine at most, sat with his brother John in the living room, joyfully reminiscing about the old days, laughing about their childhood, marvelling at how the four young brothers could have possibly have played hide and seek in the double-bed they all shared. Meanwhile, Peter and I picked off bits of cold turkey and cold stuffing from the huge bird that Rita had cooked and polished off some cold roasts as well. Maybe it was the fact that Peter had downed several glasses of wine with dinner and a few pints in the pub we popped into with Dad and Uncle John before dinner: Maybe it was the fact that I'd had a couple of glasses of wine as well, but we sat at the kitchen table and chatted about things, nothing too specific, nothing too life changing, but just talked.

Peter has come across as quite the villain of the piece in my story so far and, make no mistake, he was an absolute swine sometimes. He once tried to poison me and once, quite successfully, set fire to me. A word to the wise, if anyone says, "I bet you can't break a match-stick in half," *don't* rise to the challenge, the results are painful (not to mention hot). However, throughout our sibling rivalry, he demonstrated quite random acts of kindness. He'd suffered just as Dad had when Mum died and whilst I withdrew into a private and often impenetrable world of my own, he supported me as best he could during his own period of mourning and obvious despair. Other, more tangible, gestures included the time he bought a huge mirror from a shop in Croydon that had The Beatles etched into the glass. It was massive, at least four feet by three feet, but he ferried it home from Croydon on the train, just for me. Another time, he arrived home from work and dropped a big brown paper bag on the floor next to me as I was doing my homework. Inside was the entire stock of DC Comics that had shipped that week which he'd bought from a newsagent outside Croydon Station. There was also one memorable summer Sunday morning when he decided, without warning, that we were going to go on a comic spree and drove me from the newsagent at the very far end of Tolworth Broadway, to every newsagent down to Surbiton where Peter bought me every comic I wanted, speeding between shops before they all closed at 1.00pm on the dot.

Pretty much from this point on, as I matured a bit and our waistlines became more synchronous, we started – slowly – to develop a much better relationship. He was no longer the third parent he'd appeared to be when I'd been growing up, and no longer the surrogate parent.

The memorable year that had been 1979 ended with me, my mate Chris and Dad watching the *Will Kenny Everett Make It Into 1980 Video Show?* on Thames TV. This was an hour-long, star-studded affair which began at 11.00pm. Among the truly hilarious sketches were some pretty rare musical performances, culminating in a chilling acoustic version of 'Space Oddity' by David Bowie. It later transpired that Gary Numan was supposed to have been on the show too but Dame Dave, holding court in the studio green room with Bob Geldof plus other assorted celebrities *de jour*, saw his 'clone/rival/young pretender/arch-nemesis', stamped his foot 'pon the Thames TV carpet and said that Numan must be removed from the premises, 'ere he would cancel his performance, summon his limousine and personal man-servant to fetch him to Soho where he would imbibe the leaf of the opium plant with Mick Jagger and Lou Reed. When I saw Bowie's rendition of 'Space Oddity', I thought how much like Gary Numan he looked!

Came the bells at midnight, and after The Greedies (aka Thin Lizzy plus Jones and Cook from The Sex Pistols) performed their spirited rendition of 'We Wish You a Merry Christmas/Happy New Year' to see out the programme as well as the year, Dad drove Chris home. I went too, stunned by the crystal clear frosty night and a perfect full moon complete with 'moon-bow' that encircled it. Back in my room, before I retired to bed, I wondered what 1980 would hold for me?

What indeed.

CHAPTER 12

'I Die:You Die' on *The Kenny Everett Video Show*

In sweet suburbia, the 1980s began inauspiciously enough with the depressing task of taking down the decorations and preparing for the bleak nothingness of January. Cold, dark, with little to look forward to, I hate New Year – always have, always will.

But what of our hero? The man himself decamped to America in early 1980 as a prelude to a full US tour later in the year. A few promo appearances were arranged, notably on the ground-breaking TV show *Saturday Night Live* where a nervous-looking Numan performed 'Cars' (with a second camera trained on that weird creature on drums, the inimitable Cedric Sharpley) in addition to 'Praying to The Aliens'. I didn't see this performance until recently, but as far as exposure in the US goes, it was a pretty lucrative gig. *Saturday Night Live* was an iconic TV programme and securing a slot on that was akin to The Beatles appearing on *The Ed Sullivan Show* in 1964. 'Cars' and *The Pleasure Principle* were still high in the singles and album charts Stateside and, who knew, would go on to have a massive influence on a diverse array of artists, citing the melancholic themes of the album as modern classics while the drum and bass of 'Films' were later sampled by hip–hop artists. Weird, eh? Bowie-clone starts band, gigs a bit, pisses off peers by having a worldwide smash hit No.1 single and becomes cited as critical influence on a wide spectrum of music, all within a few months. Tricky to stay sane in a situation like that, I would imagine. Fortunately, Numan had his family around him to keep his feet on the ground and wasn't swayed by a retinue of 'Yes Men' to act on his slightest whim.

The video that Numan had prepared for the Kenny Everett New Year's Eve show premiered in the first episode of season three of the regular series broadcast in February 1980. I knew from the TV listings that he was going to be on and even though I watched the programme religiously, I made sure that I taped the episode. And I'm so glad that I did. Everett introduced the performance with the line, "Gary Numan...is he human? Yes, he probably is. But for little old ladies and persons of a nervous disposition, let me tell you that this bit only lasts for two minutes." Dad remained behind the newspaper, brother Peter was slumped on the sofa and I sat mesmerised by the new song, which accompanied a spectacular video. The song was 'I Die:You Die'.

As floored as I'd been when I'd first seen 'Are 'friends' electric?' on *Top of the Pops*, I was as equally breath-taken by this performance. It was incredible. In two short minutes it showed a man possibly approaching the very peak of his creative powers – a much more animated performance – angry, bitter, sneering, belligerent – coupled with video effects such as the then ground-breaking split-screen images; a bleached-out face that highlighted his eyes – always his eyes – showed that this was no android standing immobile and aloof. This was a ROCK STAR who, derided by the music press but adored by his loyal followers, was sending a clear and concise message to the critics, the mockers, and the naysayers. And that message was, "Fuck You."

Even Peter, without a hint of sarcasm, said the video was pretty good. I watched it over and over again, as captivated as ever. In the 6th Form the following day, it was one of the many topics of conversation.

Jack, unsurprisingly, was bowled over by it, Anne hadn't even bothered to watch as she thought Everett about as funny as death, and Terry was cursing because he'd missed it. I invited him round to watch it on the Betamax Beast.

The following week, on Episode Two, Everett introduced another musical segment, announcing a performance by "Gary *OLD*man" (oh, you witty punster, Everett).

"Oh, Christ, not him again," Dad moaned.

But there came no Gary Numan song, just Everett dressed up in a leather jumpsuit, face bleached white, eyes heavily made up, robotically dancing and singing a song about Margaret Thatcher. I had to agree with Anne that, on this occasion, he was about as funny as death.

Back at school, I was anticipating the exam retakes and felt sure that I'd do better this time. Well, I probably would. I couldn't do any worse (could I?). The schedule of exams was announced but, alas, when I should have been revising, I was arsing about in the common room, playing darts, reading music papers and listening to the radio, especially on Tuesday lunchtimes when the new Top 40 was revealed. When 'Going Underground' by The Jam went straight in at No.1, the roar of approval from Andrew Burton could have been heard in New Malden.

I was really enjoying myself in the 6th Form, where Terry organised a mixed-doubles darts tournament. Somehow I'd asked Linda Henson to be my partner and against all odds, she'd said yes. Linda really was a special girl – I'd known her since my very first day at Ivywood and she was just so sweet. With lovely eyes, a beautiful smile, she had a touch of the Jenny Agutters about her. This was no bad thing, especially when the beautiful actress's film *Walkabout* was shown late one night on BBC-1 back in 1978 and we young boys, onanists all, discussed in detail Jenny Agutter's famous nude scenes.

I fancied Linda like crazy and had, over the years, dialled the first few digits of her home phone number dozens and dozens of times to ask her out on a date, dragging my finger through what seemed like wet cement dialling the sixth digit, never having the courage to dial that final all-important seventh digit. I'd then hang up, frustrated and angry. She'd gone from being an awkward, slender young 11-

year old and had become a beautiful young woman. How come then, I still looked and behaved like a child in comparison?

It was a couple of days before the tournament and I'd been practicing at home, not wanting to let my partner down. Indeed, I was perfecting my five-dart, sometimes three-dart, finish in the common room early one morning when Linda arrived.

"Hi," I said excitedly.

"Hi, Martin. How are you?"

"I'm alright thanks," I replied but could see that her normal, sunny, smiling face had clouds of concern blowing across it.

"Listen, I've only come in to pick up a few things and head off."

I didn't understand what she was saying.

"Oh?"

"Yes. And I've got to return a few text books, too."

"Oh?"

Somewhere, high above, a huge penny trembled.

"I know. Kind of nervous but hey."

"Oh?"

The penny wobbled some more.

"It's been good fun though."

"Oh?"

Look out, below! That penny is going to fall!!!

The expression on my face must have betrayed my complete and utter clueless bewilderment.

"I'm leaving. I've got a job."

The penny dropped, crashing to the floor.

"Oh," I said dejectedly.

"I'm finishing today so, er," she hesitated, "I won't be around for the darts thing…"

"Oh, right, right. Well, don't worry," I said but I was so upset.

"Not disappointed are you?" she said, all smiles.

"Me? Nah. No, really, I'm fine," I lied. She turned tail and headed off.

"That's alright then."

It was her turn to lie.

"I'll see you later then?"

"Yes. Good. Later, then," I said, but she was already heading out of the door. 'Goodbye Stranger' by Supertramp was playing on the radio.

And that was the last I saw of her. I was literally heartbroken and she left just as I was starting to get on with her. I wonder, did she have the slightest inkling of how I felt about her? She became a sort of icon of my time at Ivywood, becoming the subject of a song I wrote years later entitled 'Albury Days' (Me? Write a song?).

Terry became a regular visitor to my house where we'd play records and watch stuff I'd carefully taped on the Betamax, including the 'I Die:You Die' performance which he was very impressed with. We also fiddled about with my guitar. My mate Andrew Burton, realising that his future did not lie within Chris's heavy-metal band, now named Vlad The Impaler, had sold me his Yamaha SG copy for £30.00, which included a practice amp, but I still had absolutely no idea how to play. Dad was less than delighted when I brought it home.

"Does it have headphones?" he asked, mournfully.

Yes, Dad, yes it has a headphones socket.

I had a *Beatles Complete* songbook which had pictures of chords. So I fumbled my way through some of the basic shapes...E, G, D, C but couldn't play an F to save my life. The first song I learnt to play was 'Eleanor Rigby' because just by moving a few fingers, I could play a vaguely recognizable version. Terry loved the guitar but was no more competent than me. But we'd hit strings and notes at random, playing with the basic effects on the amp and creating a cacophony of sound, not that tuneful but certainly creative nonetheless.

I dutifully sat the examinations and hoped for the best but I knew, deep down, I'd blown it again. I didn't know with absolute certainty of course, until a further envelope arrived a month or two later with the bad news. When you sit an exam that has a two-hour time-limit and you're twiddling your thumbs after 45 minutes because you've run out of things to write, you pretty much know you're not going to be paraded in front of the school as an outstanding, A++ student, destined for Oxford or Cambridge.

Life in the 6th Form kind of fizzled out after that. I'd fulfilled my obligation to sit the retakes, as had several of my schoolmates, so, with little need to attend classes anymore, we all kind of drifted off. I went to the common room a few times after the exams but with fewer of my peers there, with no darts leagues, no massive bean-bag chair fights, no gathering round the radio for the latest releases and chart news, there didn't seem to be much point. Unlike the last day in the 5th Form, there was no big farewell, no celebration of all that had gone before, no tearful goodbyes, no signing of bibles or Sharon Hayes' heaving cleavage or bare bum. Nothing. It just...finished: a huge anti-climax, but definitely finished and for good this time.

My life returned to lounging about the house all day, sleeping as long as I could, doing some drawing, trying to learn more guitar chords, attempting to master that near-impossible F chord (and as for E flat, forget it). On Thursday, Friday and Saturday I'd do my stint at Fine Fare. That was something I actually looked forward to as, even though it could get hellishly busy, it could be quite fun. On Saturday evenings we even started heading over to the Charrington Bowl based by the Tolworth roundabout next door to The Toby Jug pub for a few games of Ten-Pin bowling. The regular crowd would be me, Terry, Jack, Zoë, Katie Smith, Roger, plus anyone else who fancied joining us. Terry was by now well into his Numan phase, as he started wearing a black tie, black shirt and black jacket while I wore my black jeans and black shirt. I still wanted the red and blue tie though! My complete lack of sporting prowess continued at the bowling alley as, inevitably, I'd come last, even managing once to hurl myself down a lane when I got my thumb stuck in a bowling ball. This was yet another example of my complete lack of skill in anything remotely sport-related but it was fun and Zoë was just a little cutie and I liked talking to her as I made her laugh. We'd follow-up the bowling with a few games on these new-fangled Space Invaders machines. Make no mistake, Space Invaders was huge – a cultural phenomenon – where people would crowd round these fridge-freezer sized machines and watch in envy as the more-skilled players wiped out the marauding pixel aliens to attain the coveted high score. I would take my turn and would be greeted with the "Game Over" screen almost immediately, which raised riotous but good-natured laughter from my colleagues. So, do you know what? Life wasn't too bad.

CHAPTER 13

The Touring Principle, *Telekon* and The Toby Jug

Inevitably, we started to stray over to the adjacent Toby Jug pub for an illicit pint or two. The Toby was a landmark in Tolworth and had hosted a veritable Who's Who of bands in its time, not least of whom was David Bowie. His legendary Ziggy Stardust tour actually started at The Toby (It's true! Go and check for yourself…I'll wait). Other rock luminaries included Free, Jethro Tull, Fleetwood Mac, Squeeze, Traffic, Status Quo to name but a few. My brother could also vouch for the fact that sometimes they had strippers of a Saturday lunchtime with one notable buxom exotic dancer who would particularly seek out bespectacled men in the audience, sit naked astride their lap, pluck off the patron's wire-framed glasses, pop out the lenses and stretch the frame across her boobs with a nipple poking through each eye hole. These shenanigans occurred during his infamous 50-pint weekends where him and his mates would have 10 pints each Friday lunchtime, 10 Friday night, 10 Saturday lunchtime, 10 Saturday night and 10 Sunday lunchtime. But, amongst my small gathering at The Toby, there were no strippers or rock gods, just a few pints of fizzy lager, a few packets of crisps, lots of laughing and regular visits to the jukebox.

Spring of 1980 started Phase III of Numan's career. Phase I was starting a band and Phase II was the international success of 'Are 'friends' electric?'. The worrying Phase IV and "The Increasingly Poor Decisions of Gary Numan" were yet to come. This, though, was the wildly exciting Phase III, which brought a new wealth of Numan products that stretched my budget somewhat, but, oh, what products they were!

The first item to empty my savings account was a video featuring a show recorded at the Hammersmith Odeon from Numan's 1979 tour entitled *The Touring Principle*. It was available on VHS and Betamax and beat Blondie's *Eat to The Beat* video release by a week, thereby making it the first commercially released music video cassette in the UK. Take THAT, Debbie Harry! It cost an absolute fortune but I had to have it, right? I bought it from HMV up in London on one of my reinstated weekday visits. With no 6th Form anymore, I could fill my days pretty much as I pleased, although I was conscious of the fact that Dad was keeping an eye on me.

Laden down with HMV, Virgin and Dark They Were and Golden Eyed carrier-bags, I anxiously examined the video-cassette on the train home where the sleeve notes declared that it was "a video journey to rock's electronic future" (quite prophetic when you think about it) and I could not – could NOT – wait to watch it. I arrived home, peeled off the cellophane wrapper and placed the cassette into the Betamax Beast – always a bit concerned by the grinding of gears and the sound of scrunching tape – and waited anxiously. The Warner Brothers logo appeared on the screen and then, for my viewing pleasure over and over again, were extracts from the tour, topped off by the promotional video for 'Cars'. The first live track I immediately recognised from the live B-Sides of 'Complex', as 'Me! I Disconnect From You' which roused the audience to fever pitch. There followed tracks from *Replicas, The Pleasure Principle* and the eponymous first *Tubeway Army* album, including a stunning version of 'M.E'.

The performance, which also included a blinding version of 'Down in the Park', was enhanced by more of what were then considered ground-breaking video effects – strobe effects augmented the stage lighting and slowed down, coloured images of Numan crossed the screen. It was a thing to behold. If there were still any disbelievers who labelled Numan a pretentious, talentless pretender, all they had to do was look at his performance in the opening number, 'Me! I Disconnect From You'.

With no trace of fear, no sign of nerves, no evidence of stage fright, he exudes confidence bordering on arrogance like he's been playing to packed venues for years, and he delivers the song with passion and utter, utter conviction.

The performance is all the more surprising when you recall Numan's earlier painful shyness. Even on stage with Tubeway Army at early Punk gigs, he wasn't exactly comfortable or confident. Listen to the *Live at The Roxy 77* bootleg – while the band are perhaps unexpectedly tight, Numan is clearly not at ease, almost wearily advising the crowd at the beginning of their set, "This won't take long...then we'll be gone." You have to wonder what happened between these gigs (actually from 1978 and not even at The Roxy!) and the masterful, confident performance captured on film at The Hammersmith Odeon. It is quite a transformation.

The stage set was pretty spectacular, too – Numan was, naturally, at the front of the stage while the backing band were in four illuminated stacked boxes to the rear: Chris Payne on synth top left, on synth top right was the sublimely talented Billy Currie, whose presence was felt all over *The Pleasure Principle*, Paul Gardiner on bass bottom left, while the quirkily named Rrussell Bell was bottom right, on synth plus guitar for the heavier tracks. Ced Sharpley was quite a sight on drums at the back of the stage but, apart from Numan, I was most captivated by Rrussell when he played guitar. He was quite flamboyant and added a harder edge to some of the older songs, especially when they performed 'We Are So Fragile'. Silhouetted against the neon lights of the stage set, he looked a bit like me (a little bit, anyway). I decided that I'd have another look at that *Play Electric Guitar in a Day* book!

I bought this concert again on DVD recently and had two options – either watch the original presentation, or watch without the effects.

I find that I *can't* watch it without the effects, as antiquated as they now seem in this multi-media, multi-format, multi-platform 21st Century.

A second must-have item released in May 1980, in time for my 17th birthday and with Numan fresh from his tour of the USA, mainland Europe, Australia and New Zealand, was his brand new single, 'We Are Glass', a prelude to his fourth album in three years, *Telekon*.

Let's take a moment here – *his fourth album in three years.* Phenomenal, no? Who these days can match that for recorded output? OK, so the likes of The Beatles in their early days were churning out two albums a year and had gone from 'She Loves You' to 'Tomorrow Never Knows' in a similar time frame but, even so, four albums in three years was no mean feat.

And what of this new single? My initial thought was one of disappointment as I'd been hoping that the angry, pounding song 'I Die:You Die' premiered on the Everett show would be the next release.

Nevertheless, I bought the single from the Fagin-like dealer in Kingston Market, surrounded as ever by his entourage of hangers-on, keeping an eye out for passing Plod while dispensing bootleg singles and albums from beneath his stall. There were no nerves this time, no hesitation, no embarrassment and I boldly entered the inner sanctum of the stall, eargerly leafing through the new releases. In the 'N' section, I found the new single and examined the cover. In those days, the cover was such an integral part of a record, whether a single or and album. In this case, the sleeve was black with red stripes down the side and the bottom, with a ghostly image of Numan in the centre of the sleeve. It looked good but it still wasn't 'I Die:You Die'. I then chanced upon the re-release of 'That's Too Bad' coupled with 'Bombers', Tubeway Army's first two long-deleted Punk singles, now released as a double-pack to cash-in on the chart success of 'Are 'friends' electric?'. A mean, moody peroxide Numan gazed from the cover along with the (then) members of Tubeway Army, all attitude and eyeliner.

I knew there were no special editions, coloured vinyl or 12-inch versions of 'We Are Glass' so returned home with the latest additions to my Numan collection. It was a bit of a paradox playing these singles, two from the outset of Numan's career and one from the up to the minute, here-and-now of 1980. This was a time when the charts were starting to see more and more synth bands and artists making their mark. In Basildon, the neophyte Depeche Mode were seeing just what a synthesiser and a good tune could do, while The Human League, their place in history as synth pioneers forever trumped by Tubeway Army, were dabbling with self-penned numbers, releasing experimental singles (including a throbbing electro version of G**y G****er's 'Rock & Roll Part 1'). Meanwhile Orchestral Manoeuvres in The Dark were showcasing their new songs, the newly solo John Foxx was about to unleash the epic menace of 'Underpass' and the recently revitalised Ultravox (sans exclamation mark and John Foxx but adding jobbing front man Midge Ure and poaching back former member Billy Currie from Numan's backing band) were in the studio plotting their return.

And there's another one right there – Midge Ure. Here's a man who had a modicum of success in the mid-1970s as part of the hardly world-dominating Slik, then hitched up with ex-Sex Pistols bass player Glen Matlock to form the arse-achingly awful but blissfully short-lived Rich Kids and had, until recently, been a substitute lead guitarist in Thin Lizzy. So here, tempted by the potential of synths, appetite whetted by Visage, he was approached by a newly flush Billy Currie to reform Ultravox. Fame and fortune beckoned but without Numan, and Billy Currie's pay-packet from his work with Numan, he would have remained a jobbing musician. Don't get me wrong, I *like* Ultravox – not a duff track on their 1980 *Vienna* album – I just wish that they had given Gary Numan some respect. But Midge's opinion of him? The man who never claimed to be an innovator but, beyond question and without any shadow of doubt, made synthesisers popular? The man who gave numerous artists the opportunity to achieve their own success following his pioneering explosion onto the music scene? The man who, indirectly, gave Midge the chance to earn millions, collect classic cars and charm the pants off otherwise completely unattainable supermodels?

His opinion of Numan?

"He's a prat."

There's gratitude for you.

In his autobiography, "If I Was" (surely "If I *Were*"?), he begrudgingly mentions Numan just twice, and then only briefly in passing. The supercilious Midge Ure – the man who, as far as Band Aid and Live Aid go, will forever be preceded by "Bob Geldof and...".

Anyway, of the singles I purchased that day, I have to say that, initially, I preferred the re-release of 'Bombers', the original, faster Punk version of the song that was on the B-Side of 'Complex'. As we've established, the whole Punk thing passed me by but here, with the revolution, such that it was, well and truly over, I was starting to appreciate some of the Punk classics. And 'Bombers', along with 'That's Too Bad', were Punk songs. Compared to these, 'We Are Glass' sounded a bit pedestrian to me. Maybe it was because I'd played the videotape of 'I Die:You Die' a thousand times? That was until I caught a glimpse of a censored version of the video for 'We Are Glass' on a weekday afternoon kids programme. And that was me done, completely captivated once more. The video clip featured Numan in full robotic persona again, animated but an automaton, face bleached white, rarely blinking, often delivering the lyric with belligerence and contempt for his target (the media), his performance augmented by lasers, dry-ice and mirrors multiplying the image of Numan's robotic dancing into infinity. The video was censored due to Numan's wanton destruction of TVs and mirrors, which might have encouraged the more easily-led children of the revolution to smash up their parents' homes. How ridiculous. The banning of the

video hampered sales of what I soon recognised as a classic song and
the single stalled somewhat disappointingly at No.5.

A picture taken during the making of the video appeared on the
cover of *Record Mirror*, with Numan clad in his soon to be signature
black leather jumpsuit, complete with red belts round his waist and
over his shoulder, emulating the red stripes on the cover of the single.
Behind him lasers swirled in the dry ice and Numan looked as coldly
and clinically menacing as ever. The cover took pride of my place on
my bedroom wall, joining the numerous other Numan pictures that I
had Blu-Tacked to the wallpaper, wallpaper that had once been quite
stylish back in 1970 but now looked horribly dated. Dad shook his
head *every single time* he came into my room, completely unable to
understand my fascination with Gary Numan.

The summer of 1980 arrived, full of opportunity and fragrant
optimism but also, alas, my exam results. They were hopeless, the
humiliation compounded by the fact that in some of the re-takes I
had even managed to obtain a lower mark. Dad wasn't at all pleased
but at least I had a job, albeit a part-time one, although I did sign
up for the odd full day here and there during the week for a spot of
overtime. The trouble was, I didn't exactly know what I wanted to
do in terms of a career. The careers advice at school was woeful and
I could never see myself working in a bank, on a building site, or
driving a van. I half-heartedly looked through the jobs pages in our
local paper, *The Surrey Comet*, which in those days was a broadsheet,
but nothing really seemed to call out to me. Nothing really appealed
and, truthfully, my years of learning at Ivywood hadn't really
amounted to anything.

I looked forward to our group evenings at The Toby Jug on a
Saturday after work, and other colleagues, including Jillian, who
Terry seemed very keen on, plus Roger, Jason and Zoë as well as
Kevin from the meat counter joined us, too. One night in the pub
as we all gathered round a table in the smoke-filled Toby, juke box

playing, lagers to the fore, Kevin asked, in his usual broad, West Country accent and quite without provocation, whether any of us had ever given a girl an "organism". There was a moment of stunned, bewildered silence before everyone collapsed into laughter, heaving and gasping, tears flowing, crisp-flecked spittle coughed into the air. I joined in with the laughter as well, if a little uncertainly. The poor man had no idea why everyone was laughing. Terry, almost bent-double from laughing, had to leave the table and went to the bar to get a round in, stopping off at the jukebox to load up a few more songs. I joined him at the jukebox to see what songs they had.

"That Kevin...what a wanker!" said Terry, still flushed red from laughing.

"Yeah, I mean, really...organism, eh?" I said.

I think I knew what an *orgasm* was and was pretty sure there was no so such thing as "organism" during the sexual act, at least none that I'd seen mention of the in the small collection of *Mayfair* magazines that Peter had donated to me recently. I looked back at our table and saw Kevin squirming with embarrassment, still wearing his white butcher's overall under his coat. We dutifully selected 'We Are Glass' to play and while the 7-inch vinyl rack span and the single was selected, we loaded up a few more to play, songs such as:

'Geno' / Dexy's Midnight Runners
'Echo Beach' / Martha & The Muffins
'Mirror in The Bathroom' / The Beat
'The Dreams of Children' / The Jam
'Tom Hark' / The Piranhas
'Love Will Tear Us Apart' / Joy Division

My record collection had begun to swell as I spent more and more of my dwindling cash on singles...but there were still no albums. I don't know why I didn't embrace them. Maybe I was worried that, apart from any singles that had been released, I wouldn't like any of the other tracks but had still had to shell out £5.00 or £6.00 for the pleasure?

"How do you fancy coming down to Littlehampton next Sunday?" Terry asked, suddenly.

"Littlehampton?" I knew this seaside town from my childhood days when Mum, Dad, Peter and me used to occasionally cram into Dad's tiny Austin A40 during the eternally sunny school holidays of the late 1960s and head for the coast. We'd have stashed in the boot a packed lunch of corned beef sandwiches with tomato sauce, a flask of coffee and a bottle of Tizer and head south on what appeared to me to be an epic journey, judging by the maps Dad had and the planning that went into determining the best route.

"How are we going to get down there?" I asked.

"By plane," Terry replied sarcastically.

I looked confused.

"By train, you dildo…how else are we going to fucking get there?"

"OK! Right! Train….got it!"

"I'm thinking next Sunday…what do you reckon? Get a few people from work to go?"

"I'm in."

"OK, I'll sort it out."

True to his word, he did just that and, as it turned out, about 20 people from work said they'd be up for a day by the seaside. The following Saturday we all trooped over to The Toby Jug after work and we had probably the biggest turn out to date, including the semi-moustachioed Steve and, joy, the lovely Katie Webb. There was much excitement about the trip to Littlehampton the following day and it turned into a whole evening of merriment. I didn't drink that much at the time, a couple of pints at most because I didn't enjoy the taste of lager that much. But I enjoyed the company and I enjoyed the music and revelled in the sort of double-act that Terry and I were becoming, making people laugh and laughing at our own private jokes and observations.

"Want a cigarette?" someone asked but I said no. Steve, sitting opposite me next to Terry, laughed derisively.

"Martin? Smoking? Christ, that'll be the day!" he scoffed, intent on inviting scorn directed at me from my assembled friends and colleagues. He drew on his cigarette that he'd just lit and waited to see how I was going to react. I considered my options for a moment (which included hitting him with something big and heavy...like a bus) before I reached over, picked up his packet of Rothmans and pulled out a cigarette. Someone offered me a light and I cupped my hand round the lighter, lit the cigarette and inhaled. There was stunned silence.

Hands up all those who thought I'd fall choking to the floor, or run green-faced to the toilet to throw up? How many? Nearly all of you, I'd imagine.

But, no! I inhaled deeply, and blew the smoke out of my nose in a long, slow, deliberate motion. I tapped the ash into the Charrington Brewery ashtray on the table. All eyes were on me, incredulous as I wordlessly smoked the entire cigarette, finally stubbing out the dog-end, my point having been visibly, obviously and tangibly made. The table erupted in laughter, not directed at me but at Steve who sat there red-faced with humiliation because I'd called his bluff. He was not happy and glared at me as I supped at my lager to take away the god-awful taste. It was no great challenge to smoke the cigarette as I'd inhaled enough second-hand smoke from Peter at home for years. Plus, on the many, many, many times I'd tried to dial Linda Henson's home phone number, Peter had sometimes offered me a cigarette to try and calm my nerves so that I could maybe, maybe this time, complete dialling the number. It never worked.

The evening progressed most satisfactorily and I was overjoyed that I had won one over on the smug, self-satisfied bastard that was Steve, who by now had turned his attention elsewhere, looking for someone else to pick on. I nearly jumped out of my skin when, without warning, Katie Webb came and sat down in a vacated seat next to me.

"Hello, you," she said above the noise of the loud chatter and music in the pub and it was immediately apparent that she'd had a few Bacardi and Cokes.

"Oh, hi," I said, shifting in my seat to face her.

"That was funny," she said, laughing.

"What was?" I asked.

"You…and Steve. Steve and you…and the cigarette. That showed him!" She giggled an impish laugh.

"Oh, that. You don't like him, then?" I asked.

"Not much. I think he's an arrogant big-head," she said and took another sip of her drink.

And there began a conversation where we talked, I made her laugh, and she smiled a smile that I could feel in my pocket. After about half an hour, she beckoned me closer, and her voice dropped to just above a whisper.

"There's something I've been wanting to do…for quite a while actually," she said quietly.

"What's that?" I innocently asked, straining to hear.

She gently eased herself up and kissed me.

My first kiss.

I didn't recoil in horror.

I didn't think, "Oh, blimey…what should I do?"

I didn't flush red with any kind of embarrassment.

And I certainly didn't think about her boyfriend.

The barman made a pre-emptive call to the night-crew at Surbiton Fire Station as, judging by the sparks, he was afraid I might combust right there.

I instinctively kissed her back and gently slipped my arm lightly around her waist and gently pulled her close. Her lips were moist, with the slight tang of Barcardi; I could smell her perfume, I could feel the warmth of her body.

It was pure bliss.

The fire alarm bells rang at the station, the engine throbbed into life, men slid down poles and pulled on their helmets (...no, wait).

After what seemed like forever, we broke the kiss. Katie smiled coyly, and held onto my hand. Across the table sat Terry and Steve...open-mouthed with eyes as big as saucers, pint glasses held motionless in front of them, totally speechless. Katie went to get a drink and I sat there, waiting for a reaction.

"Fuckin' hell, Mart?" said Terry incredulously. "What are you playing at!?"

"What do you mean?"

"Katie!! What you playing at?!" he spluttered.

"Errrr..."

"She's got a boyfriend!" he said, with heavy emphasis on 'boyfriend'.

"Oh, that..." I said, a bit lost for words. "Well, I mean, well, I dunno, really..."

My thrill at my first kiss was starting to wane.

Terry looked disgusted and I really couldn't see why. He made no secret of the fact that he fancied the pants off both Jillian *and* Katie Smith, both of whom had steady boyfriends and, in Jillian's case as it later transpired, a steady girlfriend as well. So what was the problem? Maybe he felt I'd upstaged him. Who knows? I wasn't going to get into an argument about it and I certainly wasn't going to stop flirting, in my admittedly cack-handed way, with Katie Webb, so I ignored him. Katie returned from the bar with a drink for me and another for her and I spent the rest of the evening talking and laughing with her, only barely listening long enough to the instructions from Terry for the meeting time at Clapham Junction the following morning for our trip to Littlehampton.

All too soon, the evening came to an end and Katie said she was leaving with her friends. I desperately tried to make her stay for another drink but she said she definitely had to go. I extracted a promise from her that she would be joining the Fine Fare Summer

Outing the following day and, with a quick kiss on my cheek, she said she would definitely be there. I watched her leave the pub and, with a thousand things swirling round my brain, I too headed off soon after. I half-hoped that she might be outside waiting for me, but she'd gone.

I got home and managed to find my small, white A6-sized Lett's 1980 diary that I'd got for Christmas and which I'd been filling in regularly during the year. I jotted down brief notes about the evening, quite giddy about what had happened.

When I awoke the next morning the sun was blazing in a true, blue, summer's day sky. I was excited beyond belief at the prospect of a day at the seaside with not only my Fine Fare colleagues but Katie Webb, too. How did that happen I wondered? I couldn't stop smiling!

I showered and shaved and opened my decrepit old wardrobe, bought at least third-hand when we'd moved to Princes Avenue back in 1968 and so old it had a shelf marked specifically for 'collars'. I sorted through my collection of hand-me-down aftershaves – Old Spice (the reserve of old men), Aramis (horrible then, still horrible now), Brut (tell me, really, who EVER liked Brut?) and finally opted for a splash from the dregs of a huge ornate bottle of Blue Blazer that Peter had given me. I pulled on a new navy–blue sweatshirt that I'd bought from the new Top Man store, along with a pair of blue jeans and then headed off to Tolworth Station, smiling uncontrollably.

"Will you be home for dinner, son?" Dad asked as I left.

I paused and thought for a moment.

"I doubt it, Dad."

I caught the train from Tolworth to Clapham Junction and sat gazing out onto suburbia as the trees pirouetted past in the sunshine. I couldn't wait to see Katie Webb again. Was she thinking the same about me, I wondered? I alighted at Clapham Junction and went in search of my friends and colleagues who had assembled on the platform for the Littlehampton train. As planned, there were about 20 of my Fine Fare colleagues, all in their summer attire, some smoking, some with backpacks, some with radios, some with footballs and one, somewhat incongruously, with a bucket and spade. Roger was the first one I spotted.

"Y'alright?" I asked.

"Yep. Good, thanks. Should be a good day."

"Yeah."

I looked around.

"Is Terry here yet?"

"Just gone for a slash," Roger replied, his ever-present copy of the latest *NME* rolled up in his back pocket.

"And, er, what about…what about Katie Webb?" I asked cautiously.

Roger squinted and did a 360 degree sweep of the passengers congregating on the platform.

"Yeah…there she is, over there…," he said, pointing.

I turned to look.

"…with her boyfriend."

My heart sank. She was indeed arm in arm with her boyfriend.

"Oh," I said.

I studied her from afar. She was smiling, laughing and didn't seem to have a care in the world. She looked round, caught sight of me and, for the slightest moment, her smile wavered, a look of mild panic on her face. Then she turned and carried on talking to her boyfriend.

I was gutted.

The highest high to the lowest low.

Terry ambled up. "Thought you weren't going to make it, Mart."

"No…no…I'm here," I replied dejectedly and looked back at Katie. Just then the train arrived and we all boarded, slamming the doors shut behind us, finding seats amongst all the other day-trippers. I sat next to Terry and silently fumed during the journey down to the coast, thinking how staged and forced her laughter and smiles had been with her boyfriend once she'd caught sight of me at the station.

Once in Littlehampton, we all regrouped and spent the day on the

open-space lawns just up from the beach and along from the old funfair where, years before, I'd run laughing and squealing amongst
the rides and attractions which then included Dr.Terror's House of
Horror and The Wild Mouse roller coaster car ride that I went on
with Dad. It seemed like a thousand years ago.

I made the best of the day and joined in a massive game of football
while others braved the sea but, all the while, Katie stayed at least
50 yards away from me, clinging on to her boyfriend. I couldn't
help but wonder what had happened since last night. Nevertheless,
photographs were taken; group shots, individual shots and everyone
else seemed to be enjoying themselves.

We found a pub for lunch where we endeavoured to sink a few
beers before the prevailing licensing laws meant it shut at 3.00pm.
On my third pint, while many others played a winner-stays-on pool
tournament, I sat down quite morose, dwelling on recent events.
Katie hadn't joined us in the pub, which was lucky, I suppose.

We were eventually ejected from the pub and returned to the
beach for a final kick-about before we returned to the station to
catch the train home. It was absolutely packed and we had to spread
out along the entire length of the train. I ended up with Terry, Roger,
Clare and Katie Smith plus a couple of others; all of us slumped on
the floor by the doors at the end of one of the carriages.

There was much chatter about the day and, in an effort to amuse
ourselves for the hour and a half journey back to Clapham Junction,
some of the girls started singing. Terry joined in on a few songs and
then prompted me to do one. Fuelled by the lager, I lurched into 'We
Are Glass'. Again, I bet some of you thought I'd make a complete
hash of things but, actually, I had quite a good singing voice having
been in the choir at Tolworth Junior school, under the tutelage of
the wonderful and inspirational Mrs. Corbett (why weren't there
teachers like her at Ivywood, eh?). She had taught us how to project
our then pre-pubescent voices and, more importantly, how to
breathe when singing; all skills that I had retained. What I didn't

have, this late Sunday afternoon as the train rattled back to Clapham Junction, was a clue as to what the words of the song were. Terry manfully joined in as best he could but after the line: "We can take some train down to the sea" (which raised a cheer), he was as lost as I was. Gary Numan has this problem too as, without exception, I have never, ever, ever heard him sing the right words when performing this song live. Never. Not once.

Arriving back at Clapham Junction, we tumbled out of the carriage with the other passengers who displayed mixed emotions regarding our impromptu performance. One old lady clapped and said it was very nice, which was sweet of her. We said some general goodbyes, then Terry and I headed to our respective trains home, he to Surbiton, and me back to Tolworth.

"Well, that was fun," he grinned, kicking his football along the platform.

"Yeah, not bad," I replied, not entirely certain that it had been that much fun at all. Oh, well.

"You up for a beer next Saturday after work? Or bowling?" I asked as we loitered at the foot of the platform stairs. The grin vanished and he looked decidedly sheepish.

"Er, no…next Saturday? No, I don't think so…I'm…er…busy," he said, just about hiding his discomfort at my question.

"Oh…OK…not to worry, then," I said as we went our separate ways. "See you Thursday," I called back.

"Yeah, yeah…Thursday…see you then," Terry replied and was gone.

That Thursday at Fine Fare I was asked to look after the off-licence section of the store, laughingly called 'The Wine Bar'. There were two tills and, as the teens on the endless, anodyne, TV shows shown currently in constant rotation on the Disney Channel these days are wont to say, "Awwk—warrd", Katie Webb was put on the second till with me.

This time I DID recoil in horror.

I DID think, "Oh, blimey…what should I do?"

I DID flush red with embarrassment

And I certainly DID think about her boyfriend.

As it was, the previous Saturday's incident wasn't mentioned once. I struggled for something to say but felt if I said anything 'significant', it'd be couched in bitterness. Why was I so upset though? We'd had one, admittedly delightful, kiss, fuelled by a drop of alcohol on her part. But we *had* kissed and I had enjoyed it and I *did* fancy her and I'd wanted more and had envisioned a romantic walk hand in hand along the seashore in the sunshine, leaving the others behind in the funfair or playing football, just so she and I could be together. Maybe it was because it had never happened to me before? Maybe drunken gropes happened all the time to my peers? Maybe Jack was shagging endless girls all the time? Maybe Ian from The Docs was knobbing groupies nightly after each gig? I knew Terry wasn't knobbing anyone but that all changed the following weekend.

All day Saturday at Fine Fare, *something* was going on. There were furtive whispers, glances and clandestine meetings in the staff room and I couldn't fathom what was happening. Conversations stopped when I appeared and my paranoia went into overdrive. When I asked if any of them fancied a swift half after work, nearly everyone in my circle of colleagues said they had plans that night. The fact of the matter was, they were all going to a party to which I evidently wasn't invited. If only I'd put the '2' and '2' together chalked in 50-foot letters on the gigantic blackboard in front of me, I would have figured it out but, no, I was oblivious.

Clare had organised it and, for reasons known only to herself, she didn't think I was a suitable guest. Terry was going, the Katies were going, Steve was going, Roger was going: seemingly everyone was going. Everyone, that is, except me.

I found out all about the party the following day, a bright, sunny, Summer Sunday afternoon when Terry came round, looking like a bag of dirty washing and stinking of stale beer. He brought his new acquisition, an acoustic guitar that he'd recently purchased from the second-hand shop, The Trading Post, in Surbiton. In this wonderful shop you could find guitars, knick-knacks, half-price Marvel and DC Comics by the boxful and, out the back behind a bead curtain, stacks of old porn magazines. His guitar wasn't exactly a top-name brand and he'd written 'The Music Machine' on it in blue biro. Up in my room, my inner sanctum, cups of tea steaming by a plate of biscuits, we sat opposite each other with guitars in hand.

"I've written a song," he said, kind of embarrassed but clearly suffering with a hangover.

"Really?" I said, dumbstruck. I'd been persevering with my guitar playing as best I could but my repertoire of chords only numbered about a couple of dozen or so. And as for writing a song? Blimey...

"It's called 'Jillian'," he said, nabbing one of my plectrums.

It was a slow, acoustic number, light on words, light on intricate C7 diminisheds but I was impressed nonetheless.

"What do you think?" he said at the end of the brief performance.

"It's good, Tel, really...good. It's about Jillian, then?" I said, as quick off the mark as ever.

"Yeah...she and I were at a party last night...at Clare's."

A penny the size of dinner-table hurtled down and smashed into splinters.

"Oh..." I said as nonchalantly as I could, resisting the almost overwhelming urge to bellow, "*Where was my fucking invite then??!!!!*"

"Was it good?" I said, taking a mouthful of tea to try and suppress the bile and blind anger that was bubbling up.

"Yeah...pretty memorable, Mart," he replied and then paused. "I lost my virginity."

I snorted tea out through my nose.

"Did you?!" I squawked, momentarily reverting to my pre-pubescent high-pitched voice. "With Jillian?" I asked.

"Of *COURSE* with bloody Jillian!"

Yes, of course, hence the song...yes, got it now thanks, Tel.

"How'd it happen?" I asked, not really sure that I wanted all the gory details.

"Well, we were all round Clare's…" he started.

"Not everyone," I interjected.

"No…no, no, not everyone…sorry, Mart," he said sheepishly, "and we were all having a few drinks and I was talking to Jillian…and we got really talking and she said, "Come upstairs."

"And?"

"Well, I said, "Can you promise nothing will happen?" and she said "No," and that was it. Upstairs in one of the bedrooms, on top of a pile of coats."

Knowing my luck, if I'd gone to the party, it probably would have been on top of my coat, requiring a good dry-clean afterwards.

"Blimey, Tel," I said with a mixture of shock and jealously. Without any common ground it was difficult to articulate a wise or pertinent response.

"Are you going out together now?" was the best I could come up with ("Going out"…really, how naive). Terry looked thoughtful.

"Dunno, really…she's got a boyfriend…sort of serious but he weren't there…so, dunno?"

"Oh," I said, distractedly picking out a few notes on my guitar.

I thought for a moment.

"Well, good for you," I said as cheerfully as I could manage.

I wondered when – or even if – I'd ever lose my virginity.

CHAPTER 14

The joy of beer, the lure of girls

July gave way to August 1980 and in the eye of the hurricane, our hero Gary Numan embarked on *The Teletour* of the UK to support the release of his new album *Telekon*. And I *STILL* didn't bloody buy it! And, again, I can't think why! I thought of myself as a massive and increasingly protective devotee of Numan but a *TRUE* fan would buy everything, right? I just didn't buy albums.

Even without my support, the album sailed to No.1 in the charts and the cover, which I saw in music papers and on promotional posters in record shops, continued with the red stripe motif down the left of the cover and across the bottom. Another new single preceded the release and I was overjoyed that, finally, 'I Die:You Die' was going to be released.

I'd scoured the news reports and ads and was satisfied that, again, there would be just a regular 7-inch edition…no picture discs, 12-inch mixes or any kind of release on limited-edition coloured vinyl. I bought it from MJM Records in Tolworth and spared the girl behind the counter any kind of grilling about the release. And I WAS overjoyed that I could add 'I Die:You Die' to my Numan collection. I was dismayed, however, that it wasn't the version that was first aired on *The Kenny Everett Video Show*. This was a new version, much slicker, with more production and, to my ears, had lost some of the anger, which was part of the appeal of the original, which, I suppose, was just an early demo. I'm also dismayed that, to date, the original version has yet to be released.

The video to the song was impressive and this time the narrow-minded TV executives didn't ban it. I managed to record it from a TV show and, as with the Everett version, played it over and over until the videotape started to wear out. It showed a newly shorn Numan with spiky black hair topped off with a blood-red streak. Numan's cherished Corvette Stingray, a corporate gift from WEA Records executive and former 1960s pop star Dave Dee, featured heavily in the video. It was another dark and moody production. I loved the part where he sang:

"Tear me, tear me, tear me…"

This came in the final verse when he then jerked his head stage left to glare, unblinking, at some unseen antagonist. Terry loved it too when he came round to watch it at my place. It became very much our anthem for the remainder of the summer.

The new version was, of course, available for selection on the jukebox at The Toby and, increasingly, Terry and I would go on our own, the crowd from Fine Fare having now started to go their separate ways. Jack had by now left and, sadly, I lost touch with both him and Zoë. Katie Webb left soon after the Littlehampton trip, Clare had left, as had Ian (did The Docs ever get into the studio and make a record, I wonder?), so there were fewer people around for what had become a regular post-work group outing to the pub.

One Saturday, not long before Terry's 17th birthday, we'd arranged to go to The Toby but had each gone home first to get changed. I duly arrived at the pub, leaving vapour trails of Blue Blazer behind me, ordered a beer and waited for Terry. I played 'I Die:You Die' on the jukebox and waited some more. Then another drink. Still no Terry. I was anxious for his arrival. As he was now a man of the world, I'd hoped we might have met some girls. I'd proved I could talk to girls, I'd proved I could be funny and entertaining (my brother always said if you could make a girl laugh, you were half way there…I wasn't exactly sure where 'there' was) and there were sometimes groups of girls at The Toby, so why not?

But Terry didn't arrive and, unable to stomach a fourth pint and never having the confidence or courage to instigate a conversation with a girl I didn't know, I ambled home. I phoned Terry to see where he was but his Mum said he'd gone out earlier and didn't know when he'd be back. Denied an evening of merriment, I decamped to the front room, the house as empty as ever. Dad was out and Peter was rarely home, having hitched up with the girl, Susan, he'd met at his work's 1979 Christmas party. He'd plunged headlong into this new relationship and he and Susan had even gone so far as to put a deposit on a house nearby which needed a massive overhaul and redecoration before it could be considered habitable. But that Saturday night, all on my own and slightly drunk and quite depressed, I put 'I Die:You Die' on the stereo and, wearing Peter's old headphones, I listened to it over and over again, also delighting in the B-side, a beautiful, delicate piano version of 'Down in the Park' which I absolutely adored.

It transpired that Terry 'had to go out' which was all I ever got out of him regarding his non-appearance. This time we were in The Royal Charter at the end of Cleveland Road in Surbiton, playing tabletop Space Invaders, and he kind of mumbled an apology. Then he dismissed the matter, clearly believing it to be irrelevant and of no lasting consequence. I suspect, but I don't know for sure, he'd popped round to Jillian's for a bit more 'how's your father', but he didn't look too happy about it. Maybe she had told him she generally preferred women to men but wasn't opposed to occasionally playing for the other side? She cropped up less and less in conversation so I suspect the latter.

"It's my birthday in a couple of weeks – I'm thinking of having a party," he said, taking a sip from his pint as the image on the tabletop screen flipped 180 degrees so that I could have my turn.

"Sounds good," I said as the screen almost immediately flipped back.

"Me Mum and Dad have said it's OK and I was going to ask some of the old crowd from school…Julie, Suzanne and that, see if they want to come?"

"I am going to be invited this time, right?" I said, still stinging at my exclusion from Clare's party.

"Yeah, yeah, yeah, of course. Don't be so stupid," he said angrily although I still felt a slight sense of betrayal about it all. And justifiably, I thought.

"We can do the music, Mart!"

"Well, why not?" I said. "I'll put some stuff on tape."

"Excellent! That's sorted then," he said excitedly and we clinked glasses to toast the forthcoming event.

Came the day, I got round to his house before the 'official' start time, and was quite resplendent in a crisp white collared shirt, red jumper and blue jeans.

I'd bought some beers from the Peter Dominic off-licence down Tolworth Broadway and, as promised, had recorded some songs onto a C-90 cassette.

"Come in, Martin," said his Mum, Joan, as I arrived. "He's in the kitchen."

Terry's family lived in a tiny terraced house in Cleveland Road with a front room to the left, flight of stairs directly in front, and back room leading to the kitchen to the right. The house always smelled of Falcon hairspray as the kitchen kind of doubled as an overflow bathroom.

"Alright, Mart?" Terry asked while putting the final touches to his appearance, squinting into a tiny shaving mirror over the sink.

"Yep," I said handing over the beer and tapes.

"Oh, good man!" he exclaimed, adding the beer to an already quite impressive stack of Carlsberg. "Joan? Joan?" he called out (he always called her by her name, never "Mum"), "Are you ready to go out yet or what?"

"Just going, Tel. Me and your Dad will be down the pub but if there's any problems…"

"There won't be!" he said, ushering them out the front door. "I'll see you later!"

The door slammed shut behind them and he rubbed his hands together.

"This is going to be good!" he said, popping open a couple of cans of lager. He passed one to me.

"Who's coming?" I asked taking a short sip of beer.

"Dunno," he replied. "I've asked people at work...I don't think Jillian's coming...Roger's going to a Blondie concert...I phoned round some from school so we'll see who turns up, eh?"

We stacked up the record player with about ten 7-inch singles and before long, there was a steady stream of people arriving. The Laine twins, Suzanne with her sister Julie, arrived. I was delighted to see Suzanne! Kyle Lynch turned up, plus Terry's sidekick 'Budgie', as did a long streak of piss called 'Ozzy' who was one of the few people who towered over me. In all, there were about 20 guests, all congregating in the back room and kitchen where the beer and music was. In the front room, there was a plasterboard table with a cloth over it upon which were plates of sandwiches and bowls of crisps.

In the back room meanwhile, my tapes got a good airing and all Numan's hits were a prominent feature. I seemed to have a newly opened tin of Carlsberg in my hand throughout the evening and I was slowly, imperceptibly, getting drunk. The music got turned up louder – I remember 'Cars' being played at an eardrum-piercing volume and everyone seemed to be enjoying themselves. A few other former Ivywood classmates arrived and on the periphery of my vision, things started to get just a little bit blurry.

Much later, the back room was crammed and yet at some point in the proceedings, someone suggested we play Spin the Bottle. I was unclear as to what the rules were until Terry explained them to me – the bottle span, couples retired to a secluded part of the house (tricky as it was so small!) for a snog and/or grope. I nabbed another beer and waited patiently for my turn and eventually the bottle pointed at me. I struggled to my feet and made my way out into the hall and sat atop the stairs waiting patiently. A few moments later, Ellen

Carter, an ex-Ivywooder, emerged from the back room and looked about for me. She finally spotted me grinning inanely.

"Christ, he's upstairs already!" she shouted and I prepared myself for a kiss. She climbed the stairs and all I got was a quick peck on the cheek before she returned to the party.

Dismayed, I bumped down the stairs on my bum and things got decidedly blurrier. It seemed blisteringly hot in the house, despite the fact that the front door was open with people congregating around the front garden smoking. A tiny thought popped into my head, which suggested it might be wise to have something to eat. I went into the dimly-lit front room and was surprised to find that it was empty, all bar Suzanne who was sitting on the sofa. There was only one small table-lamp lighting the room so it took a moment before I saw her. I pushed the door with my foot and it clicked shut behind me.

"You OK?" I slurred, swaying gently from side to side.

"Yes, fine," she said. "It was getting a bit noisy out there so I came in here for a breather."

"Yeah, noisy," I agreed and made my way to the sofa, scooping up a huge handful of crisps as I passed the table.

"How you been?" I asked, managing to get 75% of the crisps into my gaping maw in one go, while the other 25% fluttered to the floor.

"Not bad," she said. "Still looking for a job but maybe something soon, I hope."

"Are you drinking?" I asked, surprised that another can of Carlsberg had found its way into my hand.

"Not really…I've had a couple though."

"Me, too!" I said triumphantly.

I sat down next to her and decided what to do next. What were my options? Should I try and make her laugh? If I made her laugh, I might get halfway 'there'. Or should I just sit and talk? Or should I go back to the party? Or what? Is she nudging just a little bit closer to me? Jesus, my head's spinning.

I weighed up the pros and cons of the situation and decided, finally, that I might just try and slip my arm around her shoulders and ask her if she fancied going out one night. I rested my arm on the back of the sofa, just inches from her slender shoulders and her long blonde hair. Gosh, she's got lovely shoulders. And her hair looks shiny…so long and pretty…. look at all those lovely colours.

"Listen, Suzanne…" I began, "how do…" and that's as far as I got. At that moment, at that precise second… *"CRASH!!"* The door smashed open, clattering against the wall, the main light was switched on and a conga came dancing noisily into the room. There were legs and elbows everywhere and a loud drunken rendition of the conga song. The plasterboard table was knocked flying sending crisps and curled-up sandwiches in every direction and it's fairly safe to say that the moment had been lost. The conga snaked round the tiny room then returned to the hall…I looked round and Suzanne was nowhere to be seen.

Then things got *really* blurry.

Cut to:

Director: OK, luvvie, this is where you decide you've turned into a dog.

Me: Okey-dokey.

Director: Your motivation for this scene is the lure of that girl's legs and feet. See? She's taken her shoes off and you fancy her like anything.

Me: I do! I do!

Director: OK – off you go! Go bite her ankles!

Me: Woof!

Cut to:

Director: Pleasure working with you, luvvie.

Me: Cheers!

Director: Now, you've gone to unleash several pints of fermenting lager in the toilet upstairs.

Me: About time!

Director: Some of it will even find its way into the toilet bowl.

Me: Heh!

Director: On the way back, you're going to pass Terry's bedroom.

Me: (*Hopefully*) Is someone in there waiting for me?

Director: No.

Me: Oh...

Director: But Terry will be shagging Ellen Carter, who, stark naked on the bed, but espying you staggering past, will nudge the door shut with her foot.

Me: Classy!

Cut to:

Director: It's much, much later.

Me: It is?

Director: You're a carpet.

Me: I am?

Director: Yes, you're a carpet and you're face down at the top of the stairs, gradually sliding down, feet first, step by step by step, your head thumping on each one as you descend from the landing down to the hall.

Me: Sounds painful!

Director: It is! Not helped by the fact that Terry's Mum and Dad have come home from the pub and his Dad needs a much-needed slash and you're blocking the stairway.

(Voices off): Tel!? Get this fucking drunken idiot out of the way!!!

Cut to:

Director: You've seen Suzanne leave.

Me: No!

Director: You're angry...

Me: (*Angrily*) Raaarggh!

Director: ...you're sad...

Me: (*Mournfully*) Come back!

Director: ...you're going after her...

Me: (*Desperately*) I have to!

Director: ...alas, you've drunk so much you can't even see, let alone walk.

Me: (*Resignedly*) Ah...

Cue: Drunken oblivion......

I was awoken the next morning by a long, low, *basso profundo* fart. I instinctively checked my pants in case I'd shat myself. But, no, it was 'Ozzy', asleep across my legs, who had let one rip. He hadn't shat himself either but his bowels had moved a good three feet. I was lying on the floor in the front room, caked in crisps and sandwich fillings and minus my jumper. I eased myself up and saw 'Budgie' asleep in one chair, mouth open and drooling. Terry was unconscious in another. At my side was a glass of water and, lo! a washing-up bowl full of vomit. By the taste in my mouth, I concluded that it was most probably mine.

I staggered up and the little sleeping angels started to regain consciousness too. Out in the kitchen, I found my jumper, which someone had thoughtfully rinsed through as, evidently, I'd thrown up all over it. The house was an absolute bombsite...empty beer cans, food, records, cushions strewn all over the place. Terry and the others sheepishly wandered into the kitchen – not too much was said. I put my still damp jumper in a carrier bag, grunted a few goodbyes and headed home. I looked at my watch and saw that it was midday as I caught that rarest of beasts – a 281 bus on a Sunday – and squinted in the bright sunshine. I was relieved that I still had my house key in my pocket but was dismayed that a Tubeway Army badge I'd been wearing had been lost during the vomit incident. Back home, Dad was reading *The News of the World* in the back room.

"You're home then," he said, eyeing me up and down.

"Yeah, sorry, Dad...I should have called."

"Hmmm..." said Dad.

I couldn't really think of anything to say.

"Did you have a good time?"

"Yeah, I think so...I may have drunk a bit too much, and this," I said, opening the carrier bag somewhat shamefaced, "may need washing."

"Leave it in the kitchen, son, I'll sort it out."

"Cheers, Dad..." I replied, the realisation only now slowly dawning on me how worried he must have been when I hadn't come home.

"Fancy some dinner?" Dad asked.

"Yeah...yeah, Dad, that would be great."

CHAPTER 15

Numan 'retires', Noel Edmonds mocks, Beggars Banquet executives wail

Autumn 1980 arrived in an explosion of colour and my life of pure idleness for most of the week, then working Thursdays, Fridays and Saturdays, continued. I'd been at Fine Fare a year and had seen no sign of a permanent, 'proper' job offer. I was still looking in *The Surrey Comet* but, as before, nothing really caught my eye.

Numan's *Teletour* started in September with a nationwide UK tour. All dates were sold out. One Saturday at Fine Fare, I was chatting with Terry at the Wine Bar, a great place to doss because you couldn't be seen from the office and the all-seeing eye of the manager, a huge Jewish man who bore an uncanny resemblance to John Belushi. The Wine Bar was also by the Pick'n'Mix (or Pick'n'Nick) so we were slumped by the counter, idly chewing on our Black Jacks and Fruit Cocktail sweets, doing our best to avoid anything that remotely involved working, thinking or any kind of effort whatsoever. Disturbing our stupor, Roger came scooting up, his face a picture of shock and announced, "I know something you don't know!"

"What's up, Rog?" Terry asked, picking the remnants of his sweet from one of his back teeth.

"Gary Numan is retiring!!" he exclaimed. Roger was a big fan as well.

"What?" I said incredulously.

"Yeah, he announced it on Radio 1 yesterday…"

"What are you talking about, Roger?" Terry said derisively.

"Gary... Numan... is... retiring," Roger said slowly and deliberately.

"Nah!"

"Who says?"

"Honestly! He is!"

"What... completely?" I asked, a bit worried by this revelation, it had to be said.

"He said he's giving up touring and will just concentrate on making records and videos and stuff."

Somewhere in the distance, the executives at Numan's record company, at that very moment, were sobbing in a conference room, fists beating on the table in despair, Phase IV with "The Increasingly Poor Decisions of Gary Numan" just looming on the distant horizon.

"Blimey," I said.

The tannoy in the shop buzzed into life.

"Mr.Howman – office please. Mr. Howman – office please."

"Oh, Christ, what have I done now? Listen, I'd better shoot," and turned tail to head off to the office, pocketing a few sweets as he went.

"That's a bit of a shit then," said Terry. "I wouldn't have minded seeing him live."

"I'm pretty sure that the tour's sold out, Tel," I replied. "Jack always said he was brilliant in concert."

"Hmmm..." said Terry thoughtfully.

His demeanour changed in an instant.

"Oh, well...never mind," and that was that. The matter was no longer of any consequence.

A couple of Saturdays later, I got home from work and there was a note from Peter. It read, "Your mate was on the TV this morning – I taped it. P x"

I checked the Betamax beast and, rejoice, Numan had been on the BBC's Saturday morning flagship kids show, *The Multi-Coloured Swap Shop*, interviewed by the abhorrent Noel Edmonds. This must have been September 1980 as he decamped to America in October that year for the US leg of the Teletour. I watched the tape avidly.

Numan was every inch the rock star, clad in black jeans and boots, plus the leather jacket he'd worn on the Everett performance of 'I Die:You Die' over a white t-shirt. The vicious red streak in his hair was starting to fade a bit. The inevitable question from old Noely was, "Are you really retiring?" Numan, already seemingly mildly irritated at having to explain himself yet again, clarified that he was just retiring from touring, not recording, citing the fact that he didn't enjoy touring as much as he'd thought he would. He made mention of the fact that that there would be some farewell shows in 1981 and then that would be it as far as live performances were concerned.

Other, more trivial questions, some from fans calling in to the studio on 01-811 8055, asked who his favourite pop star was ("Marc Bolan,"), what football team he supported ("I don't really like football much but I used to go and see Chelsea sometimes"), who dyed his hair ("My Mum,"), what the Japanese or Chinese lyric on the *Telekon* album meant ("It means 'I Leave You'"), what make-up he used ("Max Factor") with Noel asking whether he got a lot of stick for wearing it (prompting the weary reply from Numan, "Oh, yeah…the press are great for it!"), all topped off by a competition to win one of the suits he'd worn during *The Touring Principle* (I didn't win) and a clip from the 'I Die:You Die' video.

I must have watched that appearance a hundred times and was so grateful that Peter had taken the time to tape it for me. The fact that he'd recorded over a couple of minutes of *A Hard Day's Night* was neither here nor there.

On the subject of The Beatles, there was another bit of unexpected news. Staggering down the stairs one morning, the house empty as Dad and Peter had gone to work, I focussed on a small piece of paper on the doormat. As I got closer it was clear that it was a newspaper clipping. There was a note attached from my friend, Andrew Burton.

"Thought you might be interested in this," it read.

I looked at the clipping and read the headline:

'LENNON TO PLAY LONDON'

I read on. It seemed that John Lennon, having 'retired' himself in 1975, had emerged from his seclusion and Howard Hughes-like existence in New York and was planning a comeback. I'd read a series of newspaper articles earlier in the year regarding 'The Beatles Today' and was intrigued at just how unrecognisable Lennon was in a paparazzi snap of him and Yoko in a restaurant, Lennon hidden beneath eye-distorting glasses and a thick trailing beard plus unflatteringly greased-back hair. A new single and album were being prepared for release and Lennon had announced that he'd be returning to the UK in 1981 as part of a world tour.

That evening, Dad and I were slumped in the back room in the post-egg, beans and chippy-tea stupor, watching TV. Some inane programme filled the screen, with neither of us really paying much attention as to what was on.

"I saw that newspaper clipping," Dad said from behind his newspaper.

"Which one?" I asked.

"The one about John Lennon."

"Oh, yeah…interesting, no? I'd love to see him in concert. I wonder if he will actually tour?" I said enthusiastically.

"Mmm…" said Dad distantly.

There was a short pause.

"I met him, once," Dad said without warning.

"What?"

"I met him once."

"Who?"

"John Lennon."

"When?" I asked disbelievingly.

Dad lowered his paper and said absently, "Hmmmm, dunno, son. Must have been about 1965 I suppose."

"How could you have met John Lennon in 1965?" I asked indignantly.

"I went round his house!" Dad answered innocently, as if that's what everyone did.

This was just too incredible to believe.

"Bugger off, did you!" I said impatiently.

"I did."

"How?" I asked, demanding to know the full details.

Dad folded up his newspaper.

"Well, I used to run the shoe shop and on Wednesdays it was half-day closing. Les, the chap who ran the furniture shop a few doors along, asked me if I was free that afternoon."

"Go on."

"Well, I said yes I was and he asked if I could give him a hand to deliver some custom-made furniture to one of his customers."

"And?"

"We loaded up his van and drove out to Weybridge, up this private road and up to this big house. Outside there were a couple of Mini Coopers with their windows blacked out and we knocked on the door and it was John Lennon's house."

"Rubbish!"

"No, straight up, son. Cynthia answered the door and we were shown in. The whole place was being decorated and there were gold discs stacked up behind the sofa and chairs and stuff while the work was being done. John arrived and said hello and showed us where he wanted the furniture."

"What was the furniture?" I asked, agog.

"Oh, he'd ordered some custom-built cabinets for his speakers and we installed them for him. Ringo was playing pool in one of the other rooms and little Julian Lennon was running round in his toddler's outfit, looked the same age as you, so, yes, must have been 1965 then..."

"Did you get his autograph?"

Dad winced, embarrassed at the very idea. "Oh, no, no, no, son. I didn't like to ask."

I sat, open-mouthed in complete shock and awe, desperately trying to process this remarkable revelation.

"You *met* John Lennon?"

"Yes."

"John *Lennon* from The *Beatles*?"

"Yes."

"At John Lennon's *house*?"

"Yes," Dad replied, opening up his newspaper again.

"Haven't I mentioned it before?"

"No, Dad, you haven't," I said exasperated.

"Oh, sorry, I thought I had."

I sat there, absorbing all the details of Dad's story. My Dad had met one of the biggest rock stars in music history, from the greatest band ever, actually at his house, and never once thought to mention it? Incredible.

There was another pause.

"Nice bloke," he said from behind his *Daily Mirror*.

So, for a short while, my musical interest slightly diverted towards John Lennon. The prospect of seeing him live in 1981 galvanised me into finding out, come the tour, just how you got tickets for these things. But, don't worry – my gallery of Numan pictures on my wall remained intact, and my press cuttings were still diligently archived in my 'Numan File'.

CHAPTER 16

Terry trashes Fine Fare plus the dawn of Dawn

A few changes occurred at work. It was a Saturday in early October 1980 and I was ambling along Tolworth Broadway back to Fine Fare after lunch, the streets as ever awash with leaves, rubbish and paper. I'd nipped into the Wimpy Bar where I'd had a hamburger with chips and a Brown Derby for pudding (a warm ring doughnut covered in ice-cream and chocolate sauce – hold the nuts though, thanks, as they bring my gums up something chronic). The moment I walked through the staff entrance at the back of the Fine Fare store, I witnessed a state of mild panic with more whispered conversations and a story clearly being hurriedly passed from one person to another. I stopped Katie Smith as she rushed past.

"What's going on?" I asked.

"Terry got sacked!" she said excitedly, before heading off to find someone else to tell.

"Shit," I thought and went to find out what had happened.

Behind the tills at the front of the store, the managers were sweeping up a sea of broken glass. They were joined by one of the district managers, an ancient fossil of a man who looked like the council official from *Dad's Army*, complete with slicked down hair, pencil-thin grey moustache, wire-rim spectacles and a pocket watch on a fob. He was barking orders at the shop managers while guiding the shoppers past the devastation. Outside, a glazier's lorry was backing up across the forecourt. Try as I might, I couldn't find out what had actually occurred.

I went round to see Terry that night and found him still pretty fed-up. We headed to the living room and I asked him exactly what had happened.

"I was out collecting the trolleys from the car park," he began and looked quite upset. "I must have had, I dunno, 15, 20, trolleys all racked up."

"Go on."

"Well, I was just wheeling them back to the front of the shop and the wind caught the first couple of trolleys."

Tolworth Tower created a notorious and often vicious wind-trap – I had seen old ladies literally blown over as they traversed the forecourt.

"Then what?"

"They weren't even going that fast so I didn't even bother to try and stop them. Then the first one just rolled into one of the windows and, fuck me, the whole thing just shattered. There was glass everywhere! I mean, the whole thing just caved in – it didn't break, just shattered." He mimed an explosion of glass.

"Shit!"

"Lucky there was no-one standing in the way but that bastard of a manager came storming over fuckin' shouting and screaming and sacked me on the spot. I couldn't even go and collect my stuff!"

I let out a whistle.

"Bastards, eh?"

"Yeah," said Terry.

"Oh, mate, I'm sorry."

He slumped in his chair but his demeanour gradually changed. "It's unfortunate really as I couldn't pay back the money I'd borrowed from my till this morning," and produced a small wad of notes from his pocket.

"Terry!"

"What? I only borrow a couple of quid when I'm short and pay it back when I've got the money. Everyone does it."

"I bloody well don't!" I said angrily.

"Fuckin' hell, Mart! Calm down!"

He pocketed the cash.

"You got to be careful, mind," he warned. "You know Gill?"

I did know Gill – mid-thirties, blonde and with a mesmerising heaving cleavage.

"Yeah, well her till was short the other day by quite a lot – I don't think she nicked nothing though – but the manager weren't happy."

"He's a miserable git."

"Yeah, ain't he though? Well, she got summoned to the office and he accused her of stealing and she said, 'You can do a strip search because I haven't got the money!' but they didn't."

The thought of Gill slowly stripping naked in the office was definitely one for the Wank-Bank (I didn't spend *all* day in my room listening to music!). I shook the image from my head for another time.

"What you going to do now, Tel?"

"Dunno, really…my Dad says they're hiring at the timber yard in Surbiton so I might go down and see what's what. Apart from that, I quite fancy joining the police."

"You? In the police? How do you reckon that one out?" I squawked in disbelief.

"Well, it's got to be better than nothing. And I'm never going to work in a fucking office so, why not?"

Terry reached for a couple of cans of Carlsberg but I said no, the memory of the aftermath of my marathon drinking session at his party still very fresh in my mind. I did accept a bottle of wine, which was left over from the party so I opened that. Terry drank his beer and, slumped in our chairs, we put the world to rights.

"Oh, I didn't tell you," said Terry, all despair and upset from the sacking clearly now put behind him – he never was one for dwelling on things and I don't think he had a nostalgic bone in his body – "I bought *Replicas* the other day."

"Oh, put it on! I've been meaning to get it for ages," I said, drinking another horribly sweet glass of wine. I could see why it had been left behind.

"It's brilliant, Mart," he said, unwittingly echoing Jack's sentiments from the year before when he'd presented the album to me in Beggars Banquet. The album's opener, 'Me! I Disconnect from You', blared out from the stereo. We listened to the whole album and then, fuelled by more alcohol, played it again, start to finish. I loved the tracks I knew – the opening track, plus 'Are 'friends' electric?' and 'Down in the Park' – but felt that some of the other songs were a bit weak, especially the instrumentals. But it was a good album overall and I decided that, damn it, I'd have to buy it at some point.

I caught the last bus home and reflected on a very pleasant evening. However, I just could not envisage Terry in the police force. Never in a million years.

Terry's squeeze and the person who relived him of his virginity, Jillian, left Fine Fare a few weeks later so, with Terry gone as well, they needed to start a bit of a recruitment drive, especially as we were starting to get some of the Christmas goods in, even if customers would complain as I tallied up their goods that it was "a bit bloomin' early!"

I arrived for work one Thursday evening and was allocated one of the end tills, near the Wine Bar. A steady stream of customers queued up and it was business as usual, generally peaking between 7.00pm and 7.30pm when chaos usually ensued. Maureen, the woman who hired me more than a year earlier, came up along the long line of tills, with a young girl in tow. She sat her at the till next door but one to me and settled her in.

"Martin?" Maureen said, "This is our new girl. She's had her training today but can you keep an eye on her? Make sure she's alright?"

"Yeah, course I can," I replied, probably by now one of the longest serving members of the junior staff.

Maureen turned back to the new girl. "So, are you OK, then? If there's any problem, ask Martin for help, or ring the bell and I'll come down."

"I'm sure I'll be fine," said the girl cheerfully and, as Maureen returned to the office, I saw her properly for the first time.

"Hi," she said with a little wave. "I'm Dawn!"

CHAPTER 17

The venue for my first date: The Wimpy Bar, Tolworth

October tumbled into November and, I kind of lost touch with Terry temporarily, there was so much going on. Peter and Susan were spending as much of their spare time as they could clearing out the floor-to-ceiling rubbish in their new house, which had been left behind by the previous owner and his family of interbred feral step-kids. On Sundays I'd go and help out as best I could, lending a hand to fill up the steady delivery of skips with rubbish, detritus, old furniture, rotten food that had been left in all the cupboards, and, oi-oi!, a stash of pornography. But the excitement was very short-lived. I liked *Mayfair* and *Penthouse* magazines but these were just nauseating, just an ancient collection of fetish magazines featuring young girls being spanked by leering old men. They all ended up on a bonfire in the garden anyway. The more rubbish that got cleared, the more chance Peter and Susan had to start the actual redecorating. This was coming along a treat. One of Susan's friends, Yvonne, also helped out from time to time and overheard me talking to Peter about the new John Lennon single that was due to be released, '(Just Like) Starting Over'.

"Oooh, do you like The Beatles, then?" she asked.

I had to admit that I did. As I've said, Mum had adored The Beatles – one of the last things she'd listened to before going into hospital back in April 1977 was a programme on the radio relating the story of the group. She'd chastised me then, playfully, asking why I hadn't been taping it for her.

"Well," said Yvonne, "I've got their autographs at home."

"Really?" I said.

"Yes, I've had them for years. My Mum's hairdresser's son…"

(I mentally worked out that arrangement in my head)

"…was a photographer back in the 1960s. He took some photos from the wings of the stage in Jersey and he got their autographs afterwards on a magazine."

"Wow!" I said. "My Dad actually met John Lennon once. Did you know that, Pete?"

"Yeah, he told me ages ago," he said, putting the finishing touches to the top coat of paint on a doorframe.

"Oh," I said.

"You can have the photos and autographs, if you like?" Yvonne added.

"Really? Are you sure?" I said, very much excited at the prospect.

"Yes, I don't need them now – I'll bring them along next Sunday."

I couldn't wait!

I also couldn't wait to go to Fine Fare each Thursday, Friday and Saturday. The new girl, Dawn Sullivan, was just stunning and was playing on my mind. She was 16 and a half, short at just over five feet, trim with brown, slightly curly hair and wore just exquisite make-up. I was always mesmerised by her eyes, which were dark with mascara and light eyeliner that enhanced them quite delightfully. She was seriously cute. Invariably, she'd be on a till next to or near mine, and, in the quieter moments, we'd talk. I could make her laugh and her smile was just intoxicating. I anxiously awaited her arrival at work and was left with a dull ache in my stomach whenever she was placed on a till away from me.

Yvonne, true to her word, gave me the Beatles autographs and photographs just as she'd promised and I was thrilled. The photographs showed the group in Jersey 1963 and featured a terrific picture of Lennon on acoustic guitar, an equally terrific shot of George Harrison with Lennon and McCartney in the background, plus a blurry shot of George and Ringo. The audience, at this stage, were all seated! The autographs were on the cover of a souvenir magazine, full of early posed shots of The Beatles, all for the princely sum of two shillings and sixpence. I thanked her profusely and I was really, really touched by her sincere generosity.

Meanwhile, the new Lennon single was duly released and it was… average, at best. It was a bit twee, hardly up to the standards of 'Imagine', 'Power to the People' or 'Number 9 Dream', all tracks on a scratched old "Best of" album someone had bought for me from a scouts jumble sale years before. Interviews with the newly-emerged, reinvigorated Lennon saw him declare that, after five years of looking after his son, baking bread and being a house-husband and not touching a guitar in all that time (all lies!), he'd released his new song as a "thank you" to his generation, all the people that had grown up with him. That was his audience, that's who he was speaking to… but, sadly, he wasn't 'speaking' to me. The song charted (it had to, right?) but loitered round the Top 20 before it started to slowly drift out.

Numan also released a new single, lifted from the *Telekon* album, entitled 'This Wreckage'. As ever I bought it on the day of release from MJM Records – 7-inch only, black vinyl, picture sleeve – but was horrified by the cover. It continued with the lines left and bottom motif but this time it featured duplicated images of Numan, rather than red stripes. But what the fuck was he wearing? He looked like he had a plastic mac and scarf on that my Nan might have once worn. He looked utterly ridiculous. Then I played the single at home…played it again to make sure…and it confirmed my initial thought that it was a turgid, under-whelming song. It was slower than 'I Die:You Die' and 'We Are Glass' but it was just a dirge with no great hook, chorus or any redeeming quality that I could determine, just the clear message to his fans, via the lyrics about "turning off" and "leaving you soon", that he was retiring. I hated it. A lacklustre performance in the studio on *Top of the Pops* did nothing to bolster sales, nor did a brief interview with Numan who, when asked by that week's host, Richard Skinner, "Why are you retiring?", looked completely out of his depth and answered with an awkward, brief and hardly memorable, "I don't know, really." An embarrassing silence followed. I was so disappointed. Rumour has it that the sprightlier Telekon track, 'Remind Me To Smile', was in the running to be the next single. I wonder why that idea was nixed?

By this time, with a couple more weekends of work, the new house was pretty much habitable and Peter started taking all his things, little by little, from Princes Avenue to his new home. On Saturday 15th November 1980, after a day of decorating, there was not much to stop him moving in and so, with a few final suitcases and bags, he left Princes Avenue with Susan. I was lying on the sofa, fully aware that he was leaving. His new house was less than a mile away but this all seemed very bloody final. When he'd moved out in 1978, I barely batted an eyelid. This, though, was something else again.

"Right, I'm off then," he said and ruffled my hair. I didn't move.

"Yeah, cheers then, Pete," I said.

I'm not sure if Peter could tell I was choking up.

"I'll pop in tomorrow. I'll see you later though, yeah?"

"Yep. Yep, OK," I just about managed to say, but I was barely stifling a sob and couldn't see what was on the TV as my eyes were welling with tears.

Thursday 20th November 1980 was an evening like any other and, at the end of another shift, we till staff loitered by the office to hand over our cashed-up takings, plus keys to our tills. One of the new recruits was a guy named Tony and he'd been smitten by Dawn. At every opportunity, he would stop by her till and chat to her. She was just so easy to talk to and laughed often, easily and frequently. I fumed when I saw them together. I thought he was an utter bell-end.

As we loitered, signing over the takings, I talked to Dawn and idly asked what she was doing after work.

"I'm going out for a quick drink with Tony," she replied.

What??!

Oh, this would not do.

No, no, no, no, no, no, no.

Absolutely not.

No way.

"That's a shame," I said, as coolly as I could.

"Why?" she asked.

"I was just about to ask you out!"

Without a pause she shot back, "I can two-time!"

She looked anxious and genuinely distressed.

"Well, maybe we can go out to lunch one day? This Saturday?" I suggested.

"Yes, yes, we can!" she said eagerly. Tony arrived and looked very smug.

"Look, I've got to go but I'll see you tomorrow, yes?" she said quickly. I got the distinct impression she was not actually looking forward that much to her night out.

"Absolutely," I said and headed home.

Dawn's date with Tony was, it transpired, fairly painful and any suggestion from him that there might be a follow-up was sensitively, but firmly, turned down. I deliberately steered clear of inviting her out for a drink, not wishing to come across as too pushy; nor did I feel that confident in pubs yet, so we agreed, fairly innocently, to go for lunch during work. And so it came to pass, that on Saturday the 22nd November 1980, I had my first date.

We managed to get on the same lunch rota and I took her, somewhat less than imaginatively or romantically, to my regular lunchtime haunt, the Wimpy Bar. This was a place I'd been to all my life and had been a standout eatery in Tolworth for years. It had seats at the back by the grill, and booths and tables throughout. It had table-service and served proper burgers and proper milkshakes made with real milk and supplied with paper straws. On one wall was the head of a bull, an artificial one (I think) that glared menacingly at the customers. We nabbed a table in the window, just by the door, and ordered some food. I was mindful that we were on a time limit but savoured every moment of the date. Little did Dawn know that I had been dreaming, literally dreaming, about this rendezvous and had made sure I was showered, shaved and reasonably tidy for this memorable event.

We sat and talked about each other – she had two younger sisters, lived in Worcester Park with her Mum and Dad and was in the 6th Form at Tolworth Girls School. She loved the lisping, sometimes thespian, Toyah and adored The Police. She raved at how much she had loved 'Don't Stand So Close To Me' and I agreed it was a good song. I'd heard it on Radio 1 when it was released whilst I slumbered in my mid-morning hallucinogenic state. As I lay there, listening to the song, I thought to myself that it would go to No.1 and I was right. She also said she was tempted to dye her hair a fiery red colour like Toyah's – I said that it might not suit her!

As she talked, I could not take my eyes off her – I was absolutely mesmerised but all too soon the lunch-hour was up.

"We'll do this again though, right?" Dawn said as we left.

"How does next Saturday sound?" I said.

"Sounds like another date," she said and beamed just the sweetest smile.

And we did have lunch the following Saturday. I spent hours in my room on Thursday afternoons and evenings over the next couple of weeks, lying on my bed and looking out at Tolworth Tower, watching as the sun went down, the crystal clear blue autumn sky growing dark and all the office lights in the tower coming on, knowing that in a few short hours, I'd be seeing Dawn again at work. Every time I saw her, I felt a tingle in my stomach and every time she looked at me, her smile made everything in the world seem right.

I was falling in love with her.

CHAPTER 18

The death of John Lennon

Christmas loomed and Dad had a rare day off from work, Tuesday 9th December 1980. He offered to take me to Kingston and buy me a suit, which he felt might improve my chances, when – not if – I had an interview. He was getting increasingly impatient about my employment status and was not prepared for me to continue "bloody lounging around at home," for much longer.

Monday night I had slept badly and felt like I was coming down with a cold, but nevertheless I still felt up for a trip to Kingston and, come Tuesday morning, I got myself ready.

Before we left, the phone in the hall rang and it was Dad's friend Joan. Joan and her family had become great friends to all of us in the years since Mum had died and Dad was very fond of her. She asked if I was all right and Dad said I was OK.

Joan had heard the news, we hadn't.

"Send him my love then," she said and hung up. It was a very brief phone call.

Dad looked puzzled.

"What's up?" I asked.

"That was Joan... She asked if you were all right..."

"That's odd...how did she know I had a cold?" I asked.

"Um, good point. I dunno, son," shrugged Dad.

Perplexed, we headed off as planned to Kingston, parked up and after visiting a few other shops, headed to a gentlemen's outfitters along Fife Road. It was just after midday. We entered the shop and the bell above the door went ting, summoning the archetypal shopkeeper. He was ancient of years, wore a hang-dog expression and with a tape measure round his neck he emerged from some dark corner of the otherwise empty shop, stepping into the shafts of sunlight that shone through the window, motes of dust swirling as he went. A radio – possibly even a wireless – was playing softly in the background in this monumentally old-fashioned shop that sold suits, jackets, handkerchiefs, cravats, in fact everything the young 1950s gent could need – I wasn't sure it was what I needed though.

"Good afternoon, sir. How may I help you?" he said.

"Yes, good afternoon. Looking for a suit for the boy here," Dad said and before I knew it, I was being measured quite intimately from every angle.

"I've got just the fit for the trousers if the young sir would like to try them on while I fetch the jacket?"

I entered the changing booth in the corner of the shop and pulled the heavy maroon curtain shut behind me, the ancient metal curtain hooks screeching on the metal curtain rail. On the radio I could hear 'Julia' by The Beatles playing, a track from their 1968 *The Beatles* double-album (aka *The White Album*). It was an unusual song to be playing, not one of their most recognisable songs but Dad knew it.

"Not often you don't hear The Beatles on the radio," Dad said cheerfully to the shopkeeper as he came back with the suit jacket.

There was a pause.

"Oh, dear. Oh, dear, oh, dear. Haven't you heard, sir?" he asked.

"Heard what?" asked Dad.

"John Lennon?"

"What about him?"

"John Lennon's been shot, sir," he replied and his voice caught as he said it.

"You're kidding? Is he hurt?"

There was a longer, aching pause before the shopkeeper earnestly replied, "Why, sir...he's dead."

In the changing booth I was nearly sick.

Somehow I found myself back in the shop having changed

unconsciously back into my own clothes. Dad's face had gone as white as mine – he and the shopkeeper exchanged nervous, awkward glances.

"You all right, son?" asked Dad.

I wasn't but I didn't know what to say. Dad didn't know what to say either. We Downhams aren't that good at saying how we feel – a pity, really.

"Will the young sir be wanting to try the jacket on?" asked the shopkeeper trying to fill the awful silence.

"No, no, no, it'll be fine, we'll take it," replied Dad quickly, only glancing at the hand-written receipt.

I stood outside in Fife Road and waited for Dad.

"Bloody hell. That's tragic, bloody tragic," he said softly, shaking his head as he stepped out into the sunshine.

"I'll make my own way home, Dad," I said remotely.

"You sure, son?" Dad said, clearly worried.

"Yes...I'll see you there," I replied and without a further word headed off on my own. I just didn't want to talk to anyone. I don't think I could have done anyway.

I walked down Fife Road towards Kingston Station and it was clear that the news of Lennon's murder was spreading – people looked in a state of shock in what was, evidently, a death that rivalled that of Kennedy's assassination back in 1963. It really was a 'where were you when you heard the news' moment which I can remember with pin-sharp clarity. I bought the early edition of *The Evening Standard* from the newsagent at the station and caught a 281 back to Tolworth.

On the bus, I read the news today, oh boy, about what had happened. Lennon, returning home after a late night recording session to his apartments in the sprawling gothic Dakota building in New York City, had been shot as he entered the lobby by a deranged fan. The police, summoned to the shooting within minutes, controversially elected to take Lennon to the near-by Roosevelt Hospital in their patrol car, rather than wait for an ambulance. Tragically, he was all but dead on arrival. Despite the best efforts of the doctors, Lennon could not be resuscitated and he was pronounced dead in the ER, just after 11.00pm, New York-time. A tragic, unexpected, inexplicable death. Not the first one I'd experienced and, inevitably, the feelings of despair about Mum's sudden death came back to haunt me.

I watched the early evening news and more painful details started to emerge about the sequence of events of the previous evening. Dad and I watched mostly in silence as the whole evening's TV schedule was hastily changed to offer tribute to Lennon. The *Help!* movie was repeated along with Lennon's 1975 interview with Bob Harris for *The Old Grey Whistle Test*. Hurriedly convened programmes on both the BBC and ITV were broadcast with panels of musos, media and critics analysing John Lennon and his legacy. Factory Records boss, Tony Wilson, claimed Lennon was the original Punk, while Paul Gambaccini implored the viewers to listen to the gentler and more thoughtful tracks such as 'In My Life' and 'Norwegian Wood (this bird has flown)'.

Paul McCartney's infamous comment was also broadcast when, relentlessly pressed for comment by hoards of vampiric reporters, Macca, ashen-faced and in state of complete shock, said of Lennon's murder that it was "a drag". He's been chastised for that comment for years but what was he expected to say? Were they seriously expecting the usual, upbeat, thumbs aloft Macca to deliver an immediately quotable, heartfelt eulogy to his old estranged fiancé?

Over the next few days, Lennon's murder took the front page of most of the newspapers with extended reviews and appraisals of his life and work, from people who actually knew or recorded with him, to people who once saw him on a bus in Liverpool. Within days, tribute magazines and specials started to appear in my local newsagent – some were tawdry and hastily assembled, while others, like *The Sunday Times Lennon Special*, were professional and respectful.

Sadly, I genuinely believed that no amount of cajoling or

caterwauling by Kate Bush could make this particular December magic in any way whatsoever.

Returning to work on Thursday, as I traversed the network of subways under Tolworth Broadway, someone had spray-painted 'John Lennon RIP' on the yellow-tiled wall, just under the 'Skinz Rool' graffiti that had been there for years. Lennon's death was the talk of the shop and I witnessed teary-eyed customers in the queues, turning to other equally upset shoppers who, even though complete strangers, were united in their grief for the fallen Beatle.

Dawn could see that I was upset by Lennon's murder and gave me a hug, which nearly broke my heart. She really was seriously cute.

"Are you free Saturday?" I asked, desperately needing something else to focus on.

"What? At lunchtime?" she asked quizzically. "I thought we were going out anyway?"

"No, Saturday…evening…Saturday evening? After work? Do you fancy, I dunno, going to the pictures or something?"

"Yeah, that would be lovely," she said giving me another hug.

We arranged to go and see *The Elephant Man* at the Kingston Odeon – hardly an upbeat, whimsical laugh-fest but it was just what I needed after the overwhelmingly depressing events of the week. I needed something to look forward to.

We finished work and I sped home, showered, shaved and changed into the best my limited wardrobe could offer (I wore the jacket from the suit Dad bought me) and headed down to Kingston. I waited anxiously outside the Kingston Odeon and was thrilled when she arrived, bang on time.

"I was afraid you might not come," I said, escorting her into the bright lights and the warmth of the foyer, as it was a bitterly cold evening.

"Why not?" she asked. "It's our first date, after all!"

Did that imply there would be a second date after this I wondered? Who knew?

The cinema wasn't packed so we found the best seats and sat back and watched the film. And what a great film it was too: a horrible story of brutality and victimisation but by no means a horror film. During the performance, silently, in the dark, Dawn held my hand. I found it completely endearing that, without her glasses, she was as blind as a bat.

Afterwards, I gallantly offered to see her home and we caught the bus to Worcester Park and I walked her back to her house where I was invited in for a coffee. Her Mum and Dad were in the front room and I realised I must have served them a dozen times at Fine Fare. I was formally introduced to her Dad, the ignoble Cliff. He vaguely resembled Bill Oddie but minus the charm, wit and personality (much like Bill Oddie now, come to think of it) and her Mum, Jeanette, who was a dead spit of Morticia from *The Addams Family*. They cautiously eyed me up during the inevitable interrogation about the evening: who I was, where did I come from, what was the film like, how did we get home? I nervously sipped a cup of bitter coffee during the grilling and, although I didn't know for sure at that time, I got the feeling that they didn't like me. As introductions go, it wasn't great.

Having made a less than memorable first impression, I said goodnight and Dawn saw me to the front door. Outside in the freezing cold, she pulled the door to behind her and thanked me for a lovely evening.

"We'll do it again, right?" she said and I said absolutely yes, without question, you name the date, I'll be there, how about tomorrow? She laughed and kissed me goodnight and I was in a heaven. A very cold heaven as, with only a T-shirt and suit jacket on, I was gradually losing the sense of feeling in my extremities. Well, not *all* of them! I waved goodbye as she closed the door and I asked myself two very important questions:

1. Where the hell am I?
2. How do I get home?

I walked back down the road to the bus stop, then, unsure, turned tail and walked back the other way, back past her house. I had no idea where I was. I eventually found a phone box and called Dad who, cursing and grumbling, agreed to come and pick me up after we had established, geographically speaking, where I was. About three quarters of an hour later, as I started to freeze solid in the phone box, replete with that giddy fragrance of stale urine and cigarette smoke, he arrived having had to clear about an inch of ice off the car. The warmth of his Rover was very welcome.

"How was your evening, son?" he asked from beneath his scarf as we headed back to Tolworth.

I sat and thought for a moment.

"Do you know what, Dad? It was great."

Christmas was only a matter of days away and I was determined to buy something for Dawn. I asked Peter for some advice but first I had to come clean that I'd been on a date – he was both shocked and stunned.

"About bloody time," he said encouragingly after I'd given him the full story. "Get her some Estée Lauder "Youth Dew" perfume. She'll love it."

I carefully wrote it down on a piece of paper and headed into Kingston. I circled the perfume counter in Bentall's, the huge department store on Eden Street that, as ever, had been turned into a winter wonderland with animated elves and reindeer between the two main escalators that stretched up to the first floor. Finally plucking up the courage to ask for the perfume, I then headed to one of my old haunts, Books, Bits & Bobs by Kingston Station, which was an Aladdin's Cave of books, comics, magazines, bric-a-brac and music and cinema miscellany, where I bought her a couple of badges depicting The Police. I also nabbed a Gary Numan badge (he does reappear soon, I promise!).

Sunday 21st December 1980, Dawn and I went for a walk round the park in Tolworth then I took her back to Princes Avenue to introduce her to Dad. He was, of course, thrilled that I'd met a girl and was ever the charming host in welcoming her into our home, quite the opposite of how I'd been introduced to Dawn's parents. Armed with cups of tea, I took her up to my room, my inner sanctum, up until now the preserve of my male friends. I'd vacuumed and polished and the room was spotless. I'd even moved all my comics into the now vacant little bedroom. I proudly welcomed her in. She looked round at all my bits and pieces, the books on my shelf, my ever increasing record collection, the knickknacks and keepsakes on my shelves.

"What a lot of pictures you've got," she said looking at the Numan pictures I had tacked to the wall.

"Yeah, I'm a big fan," I said, for some reason a little embarrassed.

"Oh, I like him," she said enthusiastically, "I've got a couple of his records at home!"

We sat and talked, drank our tea and it was all very civilised. Quite innocent. I reached into a bag on the floor and produced her Christmas present, which I had carefully wrapped, plus a card, and presented them to her. Her face was a picture of joy and delight.

"Can I open them now?" she asked.

"No!" I said firmly, "You'll have to wait until Christmas Day!"

She shook the present to see if she could guess what it was and was perplexed by the objects that rattled within – I'd put The Police badges inside the perfume box.

Before long, I had to see her home and there began a regular scenario where I'd either walk her home, having studied the A to Z to find out the route, or take the train one stop from Tolworth to Malden Manor, walk her to her house, a quick kiss goodbye, then run back to the station to hopefully catch the last train home.

I guess we were officially 'going out' now.

CHAPTER 19

The deed is done!

The New Year arrived and unlike previous years, I felt exhilarated, refreshed, excited, optimistic, and deliriously happy and, above all, I was in love. And it was clear that Dawn loved me, too.

How your life could change in a heartbeat.

I'd only met her in November but here, in January 1981, I was seeing Dawn as much and as often as I could, sadly at the expense of seeing my friends. I still saw my Quo-loving mate Chris from time to time but he'd started a full-time job with his Dad, so the occasions when we could meet up were becoming fewer and farther between. We hadn't been up to London for a jaunt round our haunts in months and, as it turned out, we never would again. I was completely obsessed with Dawn and had even made the painful decision to stop buying comics, as I feared she might think I was a bit immature to be still revelling in the adventures of *The Uncanny X-Men* and *The Fantastic Four*. It was a major decision, too, as I'd been collecting comics since 1972 when my brother Peter donated his collection of 1960s DC Comics to me, which I read until the covers came off.

Dawn and I went to the cinema during the first few weeks of January, seeing a range of films, then opted instead to head over to the Charrington Bowl after work for the odd game of 10-pin bowling, heading back to my house afterwards. Dad was always out on Saturday nights, seeing Joan and her husband, so the house was always empty. Peter was fully settled in his new home with Susan so we invariably had the place to ourselves. My relationship with Dawn had become more intimate, with our kisses becoming more passionate.

It was only a matter of time before the inevitable happened.

I'd even paced up and down outside Boots the Chemist in Tolworth before I'd plucked up enough courage to go in and buy a comb, a bottle of Vicks Sinex, some plasters and, oh, while you're at it, can I have a packet of Durex, please?

Chemist: What size?

Me: Size? Oh...oh, just...er...just the, er, just the regular size.

Chemist: You sure? You're a big lad...you sure don't want large?

Me: No, really...thank you.

Chemist: We've got them if you want?

Me: No, no...regular is fine.

Chemist: (relishing my squirming embarrassment as old ladies in the queue behind me tutted their disgust) Fether-lite? Lubricated?

Me: (stifling anger) Just...just, a pack of normal, regular Durex... please.

Chemist: OK, just asking.

Me: That's fine...

(Pause)

Chemist: How about ribbed?

On Saturday 24th January 1981, Dawn and I had left work and decided that we'd head straight back to my house and not bother with the bowling. However, we did pick up a bottle of wine from the off-licence. Dawn had bought along a change of clothes for the evening. Dad was, as ever, so pleased to see Dawn. I opened the bottle of wine while he got himself ready to go out and we sat on the sofa in the back room and had a couple of glasses. Dad finally appeared, sharp as a pin and said his goodbyes. The moment the front door slammed shut, Dawn and I pounced on each other. As we kissed on the sofa, passion rising, steam emanating, I had completely forgotten that Chris had said he was going to pop round. Mid-grope there was a knock at the front door, which momentarily froze our ardour, and I thought for one minute that Dad had come home early. We looked into each other's wide-open eyes, motionless, and waited for the front door to open. It didn't but someone knocked again. I sneaked out into the hall as best I could (there *had* been some pretty heavy-petting after all!) and peeped through the side window and saw that it was indeed Chris, the red tip of his cigarette bobbing up and down in the darkness. The hall lights were blazing so he knew someone was in the house. He banged again, louder and angrier but I kept as quiet as I could. I looked back and saw Dawn, realising that it wasn't Dad at the door, pop her head out from the back room.

"Who is it?" she silently mouthed.

"My mate, Chris," I hissed back.

She paused, smiled and then sauntered cat-like down the hall to join me at the door, slowly stripping off the remainder of the clothes she had just about still been wearing – an exquisite black dress, stockings and suspenders, lovely! Reaching me cowering by the front door, she kissed me passionately. Chris knocked again but, fortunately, didn't look through the letterbox, then gave up in disgust and stalked off. That was probably the last time I saw him.

Dawn and I fell to the floor, Dawn completely, joyfully naked, both of us desperately trying to stifle our near-hysterical laughter. She scooped up her clothes, we headed up to my room, fell into bed and the deed was done.

The first time – awkward, clumsy, embarrassing but eager.

The second time, the following Saturday – fractionally better, with a better idea of what went where.

The third time – OK, so *this* is how you do it?

By the fifth time – I'm standing astride her on the bed, a horned Viking helmet upon my head, a cape billowing about my frame, an oiled six-pack glistening in the candlelight, bellowing, "Be*HOLD*!!!!! I am *MAAAANNNNNNN*!!"

And that became my life for the first few months of 1981, taking us from the bleak mid-winter to the first signs of spring. I'd see Dawn on a couple of evenings during the first part of the week, see her at work, then we'd be together Saturday evening, invariably ending up in bed. Life couldn't be better, although it would have helped if her parents could have made a better attempt at hiding their barely concealed contempt for me. Cliff would interrogate me when I got her home each Saturday night as we often said that we might go bowling after work.

"Did you actually bowl?" he'd ask. He was an utterly cheerless, Volvo-driving, self-opinionated man, supping at his home brewed real ale.

"No, Cliff, I literally ripped your daughter's clothes off the moment we were alone at my house."

I must admit I found it odd to see Dawn at work. I'd often be on the Wine Bar till and I'd watch her on her till, she'd look across and blow me a kiss and I'd think to myself, "I've seen every inch of your naked body!"

I don't know what I'd done to generate this antipathy (apart from often literally tearing off Dawn's clothes the moment we were alone at my house) but I could do nothing right in her parents' eyes. Her Mum used to go along with everything Cliff said and was the embodiment of the downtrodden housewife. I knew they had problems with their middle daughter, Martine, who, only in her early teens herself, was already a sexually active girl and didn't seem that fussy about who her partners were. I'd later learn that Cliff used to beat her regularly for looking and behaving like a slut, which, frankly, she was. She was a mealy-mouthed, bitter, cynical, insidious creature who also couldn't stand the sight of me. The only other sane person in the house apart from Dawn was her youngest sister, Penny, who, then aged eight, was just an absolute sweetheart and soon looked upon me as a big brother.

So, overall, not the ideal family to show off to your own kith and kin! But I was happy – really happy – and Dawn easily, effortlessly supplanted my other friends and, without a pang of regret, it was soon the two of us going to Kingston, going to London and the like. I'd even started buying comics again after I'd carelessly left a couple of issues of The Uncanny X-Men downstairs while getting ready before we went out for the evening. Dawn had read them, anxiously asking for the next issue as she wanted to know what happened! Could she be a better girlfriend?

Early spring, Terry reappeared on the scene, ringing me up out of the blue. We exchanged a few pleasantries and, as he'd intended, he was now working at the timber yard in Surbiton and earning a fair wage. I cheerfully advised that I now had a girlfriend! He invited me round to his house later that week for a full catch-up, although I was careful to ensure that this didn't clash with any arrangements I had with Dawn as, frankly, she would have taken precedence every single time.

"Bring your guitar, Mart. I'll pick you up," he said ringing off.

Excuse me? Pick me up?

It transpired that, not only was he earning a wad of cash each week, he'd also passed his driving test and bought a car. I doubt he'd had more than half a dozen lessons before he passed: I eventually had well over a hundred.

A couple of nights later, he pulled up outside Princes Avenue and even in the hall, as I picked up my guitar and amp, I could hear the music blaring from his car stereo.

"You all right, Mart?" he asked as, with a squeal of tyres, he did a U-turn and we headed back to his house in Surbiton. Saying hello to his mum, we headed into the front room, the scene of the Suzanne/Conga/Vomiting incident at his 17th birthday party. There was no vomit this time, no upturned plasterboard table and no drunken party-goers. No, THIS time there was a bloody great big synthesiser.

"What do you think, Mart?" he said proudly and switched on the full size, polyphonic beast that now squatted in the middle of the room.

"Bloody hell, Tel! Where'd you get that from?" I said enviously as it hummed into life.

"Bloke at work was flogging it so I snapped it up. Good, innit?" he grinned and proceeded to set the in-built drum machine going and played a few notes – very loudly in fact.

"What about your Mum and Dad?" I said.

"Ah, they don't mind...and the neighbour's deaf so we're all right," he said oblivious to the noise, although it was clear he'd been practising. I plugged my guitar in and we had the first of what became an almost weekly event, playing music together. I'd always – always – wanted to be in a band and play music so this was just fantastic. Over the next few years, I'd get the regular phone call:

"You sessioning tonight, Mart?"

"Yep!"

"I'll pick you up in 15."

CHAPTER 20

1981: *My* music, *my*, time, *my* year...

Back in the Numan camp, Gary carried on with his questionable decision to retire from touring, expanding on his decision by saying he wanted to get into video production. He didn't rule out a few guest appearances with other artists and frequently name-checked the group Japan as one of his current favourite performers. He announced two farewell shows at Wembley Arena for April 1981, adding a third night due to overwhelming demand. I was determined to go this time and sent off a postal order for two tickets, which was duly returned a few weeks later, uncashed, as the farewell performances had completely sold out. No mean feat selling out three nights at Wembley. I've heard tell of other groups and artists playing there with reviewers commenting that "there was a lot of orange", indicating that the concerts weren't sold out and that rows of empty unsold orange seats could be seen. But all tickets for these final concerts, the last chance to see Gary Numan on tour, were sold and I missed out again.

Reviewers of these shows were not surprisingly negative with one banner headline, in *Record Mirror* I think, reading: "Aren't ends pathetic?" and, as ever, he could do no right. Management at Beggars Banquet had pleaded with him to reconsider his decision, stating, quite rightly, that although he was popular in America for example, it would be difficult to sustain that popularity without personal appearances and touring. But, no, his stubborn mind was made up and that was it, no more touring. Consumed by his love of aviation, his next project was a heavily promoted but ill-fated flight round the world. The press sharpened their pens in keen anticipation of what they incorrectly perceived as the folly of a very, very rich man.

The flight itself was designed to show that there was more to these "effeminate, mincing, poofy, pop-creatures" (as Kenny Everett's 'Angry of Mayfair' character called them). Lounging around their country mansions bought with the royalties from their first single, hosting drug-fuelled orgies, before being evicted and their sports cars repossessed once the fickle fans with their fivers deserted them, electing to spend their cash on the next big thing - this was not how Numan wanted to be remembered. He wanted to prove to his Dad that he was not one of these fey characters and was capable of taking on such an expedition, a noble endeavour to be sure. Furthermore, he was planning to travel anti-clockwise round the globe, adding the 'hard, hard, lemon, hard' equation to the mix. This was no casual, off the cuff, "let's fly round the world" project. Months of studious and careful planning went into the route, essentially piloting a plane converted into a flying petrol tank, ensuring that they could cover vast distances across the Pacific Ocean without refuelling. Sadly, the flight was beset with technical problems, none of which could have been foreseen and while Numan had a co-pilot on the journey, the ever-hostile British press inevitably blamed solely him for any accidents, delays and unplanned landings – plus the odd crash here and there.

In the absence of any future tours, we fans had to make do with two albums of live material that Beggars Banquet released in May 1981, one album featuring tracks from the *Touring Principle* and one from the *Teletour*, entitled *Living Ornaments 1979* and *Living Ornaments 1980* respectively. They were also released as a deluxe limited-edition box-set, available for one month only, before it was deleted. I had to get this one and duly headed down to Beggars Banquet in Kingston on the day of release and picked up the box-set which was, I have to say, another thing of beauty. This, then, was the first Gary Numan album I bought and it was epic. From the 1979 tour, we'd already had some live performances released in the form of the live B-sides on the 12-inch 'Complex' single, plus the live video. But listening to these other tracks, lifted from his ground-breaking first nationwide tour and his visually stunning second tour, was a timely reminder that, undaunted by the sheer scale of these massive tours, Numan was a first-class performer. I loved the live versions of 'The Dream Police' and 'Metal' from 1979 and absolutely adored the 1980 live versions of 'Down in the Park' (which tied the opening piano version to a breath-taking full-band, version), 'The Joy Circuit', 'We Are Glass' and, of course, where it all started for me, 'Are 'friends' electric?'. I vowed to get *Replicas*, *The Pleasure Principle* and *Telekon* which was an easy decision, now I had heard just what gems could be found on Numan's albums. In the meantime, I listened to the live albums over and over, especially as Dad had now bought a new Hitachi music centre for the downstairs front room, which meant I'd inherited the old Sanyo record player, which now resided in my room. Here, I could play my music on headphones, without interruption, listening to every note, every beat, every nuance of the songs, especially loving, for instance, the almost Buddy Holly-like hiccup when Numan sang: *"Oh, no…oh, no, I turned off the pain, like I turned off you all,"*: on 'M.E.'. What a lyric!

And this was, without a doubt, my music. This was my time when every song in the chart, every magazine on the shelf in WHSmiths, every programme on the TV was aimed at me, just me and my generation. This year, 1981, when I turned 18 with no major celebration, was nevertheless my year and I'd never experience anything like it again.

CHAPTER 21

The Ministry of Defence comes a-calling

What I desperately needed was a full-time job. The idyll of spending time listening to music, sessioning with Terry round his house, enjoying as much time as I could with Dawn, sending her letters every day when she went on holiday for a fortnight to France in May 1981 where I ached, literally ached, at being apart from her for so long, could not continue indefinitely.

I think Dad must have had a word with Peter as, one weekend in the early summer of 1981, Peter came round and sat me down with our local paper *The Surrey Comet* and we went through every vacancy in the job-listings. We dismissed manual labour as we both envisaged me ending up in casualty if I got anywhere near electrical tools, anything sharp or anything hot. So we went through all the other jobs and, apathetic, I shrugged indifferently at all of them. Peter started to get angry.

"What *do* you want to bloody well do, then?" he shouted.

"I don't know, Pete," I said, and I really didn't.

"Well, you can't stay at home forever! You don't actually *do* anything!" he stormed and he was right. I didn't. I didn't help much with the housework, didn't do any chores. Staggering midmorning down from the pit, I'd sometimes espy a lone cornflake, a foil milk-bottle top, a tightly-coiled tube of Colgate toothpaste or an all-but-empty upside-down ketchup bottle lined up on the kitchen table, which I'd interpret as some kind of cryptic shopping list from Dad. He was right. Overall, I did very little. It was a stinging criticism but well deserved.

"What about this one?" Peter said exasperated, looking at the final few jobs listed. It was a vacancy at the Civil Service as a clerical assistant in Chessington, working for the Ministry of Defence in fact. Peter read through the job spec.

"They need two O-levels...you've got them, right?" said Peter. His tone implied "you've just about got them, right?" and again, I was embarrassed at my woeful examination results, even after the re-takes.

"Yeah, I have," I mumbled.

"Right, you're going to send off for an application form and you're going to fill it in and you're going to bloody well apply!"

"I will, Pete, I will," I said, desperate to escape from this painful confrontation.

I sent off for the application form, dutifully and studiously filled it in, sent it back and was surprised when, a few weeks later, I was summoned for an interview.

The interview was held at RAF Chessington and Peter, who had the day off, said he'd drop me off at the RAF base. I was dressed in the suit Dad had bought me and I was as nervous as hell. Dawn gave me a 'good luck' card. The RAF base seemed vast and even though I'd been dropped off in plenty of time, I still took ages to find the block where the interview was to take place. This was my first proper interview and I faced a panel of three people: an old army officer, a middle-aged civil servant and an ancient, decrepit, cheerless woman from Personnel. They asked me about school, what I was good at, what I enjoyed doing, what I thought the job might entail ("Filing and stuff?"), what my political leanings were ("Dunno, really. I've never voted.") and how I felt about working for the Army ("Yeah, good, I guess."). After an hour or so, they told me they'd be in touch and I left as quickly as I could. I found Peter waiting for me and he asked me how it went as he drove me home.

"Alright I suppose?" I said, not thinking for one moment that it would go any further.

A couple of weeks later, I received an A4 envelope in the post, and, bloody hell, I was offered the job. I had mixed feelings about it… this all seemed very grown up, very responsible. Dad was quietly pleased but made it clear, in no uncertain terms, that I *had* to accept the job offer. And I *did* have to. Of course, I did.

I phoned Dawn that night and she was delighted. It just seemed, oh, I dunno, so fucking terrifying! I sent the acceptance form back and I promptly received my joining instructions where I read that I had to attend a meeting at the Ministry of Defence in London on the morning of the 10th August 1981, before heading back out to Chessington to the sprawling site of government buildings a few miles along from RAF Chessington. I had about a month of freedom left.

I handed in my notice at Fine Fare and Dawn was upset that she wouldn't be seeing me Thursdays, Fridays and Saturdays anymore. I even got a leaving card and a present, which I wasn't expecting. My colleagues had clubbed together and bought me some record tokens. One of my colleagues was a new girl named Joanne who I had trained and who was the daughter of Maureen, the assistant manageress. Joanne was tall and was the spitting image of Joanne Catherall from The Human League. She had signed the card and, amongst the many messages of good luck, and one saying "good riddance" from Steve, she'd written, "I'll miss you!" and had drawn a little sad face under a row of ten kisses.

The record tokens were ideal as I was spending more and more on singles. I now had two or three 7-inch record boxes and was recording my purchases on Dad's new music centre as soon as I got them. I can listen to those old tapes now, or their equivalent playlists on iTunes, and each one is like a musical diary, hearing songs that bring back bittersweet memories, each song forever locked into a specific time frame. A couple of key examples would be the singles I bought with one of the record tokens: 'Tempted' by Squeeze and the other 'Stormtrooper in Drag' by, ostensibly Numan's former bass player, Paul Gardiner. I'd seen the latter advertised in one of the many magazines I was buying. I was a regular reader of *The Face*, *New Sounds/New Styles* and even *Smash Hits* as they seemed, for the most part, to be quite supportive of Numan.

'Stormtrooper in Drag' was the same tempo as 'This Wreckage' but couldn't have been more different. It was sparse, driven by bass with a simple, steady drumbeat, plus an effects-driven guitar, drenched in echo. There was no question the vocal was delivered by Numan and I loved it!

The B-side, 'Night Talk' ("from the forthcoming album *Dance*"), was superb. The lyric, double-tracked in places, remains one of my favourite mid-period Numan songs. The production, the whole essence of the song, was astounding. And that, I think, is one of Numan's overlooked abilities – he's a great producer, not necessarily in the same mould as, say, George Martin, but it's more how he can create a mood, a texture, a feeling and an image. Others may well deliver lyrics of such profundity and social relevance, holding a mirror to society in an attempt to elicit self-analysis and provide an alternative to the accepted norm and unite humanity in global peace and harmony (as with 'Rabbit' by Chas'n'Dave). But I don't necessarily have to know what Numan is singing about to fully embrace and enjoy his great songs, 'Are 'friends' electric?' being a case in point. I didn't have a clue what he was singing about – not a one, but I loved it nevertheless. The song spoke to me even though, aside from the science-fiction elements of the lyrics, it was a deeply personal song by Numan. If the rest of this new album, *Dance*, was as good as 'Night Talk', then it was going to be a classic. And I wondered whether the lyric, "An office in a side-street is no place for you" would turn out to be prophetic.

The Friday before I started at the MoD I went and got my haircut at Dad's barbers on Ewell Road, then walked back home, seeing Tolworth Tower in the distance and feeling a small pang of regret that I wouldn't be seeing Dawn at Fine Fare anymore. I also felt a smaller pang of regret that I wouldn't see Joanne either as she really was a cutie.

Came the day, with a squadron of butterflies in my stomach, a lengthy crap behind me but an imminent bout of the squitters a distinct possibility in the very near future, I made my way up to London to the Ministry of Defence. I was dressed to the sevens in my suit (I could never quite manage the nines but I was working at it) and I even had a new briefcase in which I had an apple, a KitKat plus my old school pencil case, with 'MARTIN IS A MORON' written on it with a thick black marker pen by someone at Ivywood, possibly Miss Morrissey, my maths teacher.

I signed all manner of documents, including the Official Secrets Act, which means, even now, I can't say exactly what I did at the MoD otherwise there is still a real possibly that I'll be dragged away unconscious and wake up in Portmeirion, surrounded by penny-farthings and Mini-Mokes.

What I can say is that my job was working as a clerical assistant and working for the Army, which was a shock to the system, and very soon I learned that the opportunities to doss about were virtually nil as, from day one, I was in at the deep-end. It wasn't anything I couldn't do given time but it was a steep learning curve. Everything was urgent, everything had to be done now and all hampered by the fact that I was replacing a very popular woman who was moving to another department. So, whereas previously all the pipe-smoking Colonels, Lieutenant Colonels and Majors had a nice young filly to chat-up each day and flirt with at the Christmas party, they now had me; long-limbed maybe, certainly virile but definitely not their type.

Dad could, at long last, relax a bit as I was now gainfully employed, when it had looked at one point that I might end up whitewashing walls after all, just like some of the Neanderthals I'd left far behind me at Ivywood School.

The MoD was a strange place, and not in an interesting way. It was, as you would expect, steeped in protocol. There were forms that had to be completed in triplicate, all following due process, due deference was expected at all times towards seniors, and tea had to be made three times a day at 9.30am, midday and 3.30pm on the dot: I didn't remember that being in the job description. This being the early 1980s, there was obviously not a computer or word-processor in sight. Instead, in the latter half of the 20th century and completely incongruous now, there was a typing pool where 20 women sat at their electric typewriters, all of them lined up in long rows of desks not unlike a classroom. I had to run down to the typing pool with urgent jobs, pleading with the monosyllabic woman in charge to put my priority documents at the top of the pile:

She would finally notice my presence, as I loitered hopefully by the typing pool reception desk. Only the very foolhardy would ever venture past the desk and into the actual inner sanctum of clattering typewriters. The supervisor, a rippling bulk of a woman who stank of Rothman's, would begrudgingly amble over, but only when she was damn well good and ready. There was never any "Hello", or, "How are you?" or even a cantankerous "What do you want?" Just silence. I'd have to instigate the conversation.

"Hi, how are you?" I'd ask cheerfully, offering her a foolscap folder, breathless after my sprint, desperate to ingratiate myself to the point where I hoped she might take pity on me.

Finally, the beast would speak.

"What?" she would grunt.

"Isn't it a lovely day?"

"Not in here it's not."

"Gosh, that's a nice...er...cardigan you're wearing. Beige – such a commitment to colour, don't you think? I was wondering if you could see your way to putting this at the top of the pile?" Then I would gingerly push the foolscap folder towards her across the reception desk, as if this were some clandestine meeting in Cold War Berlin.

"Why?"

"Because it's really urgent?"

"Has it got an "immediate" ticket?"

"Yes, yes – look…it's pinned to the top of the folder," I'd plead.

"It's not signed," she'd reply and shove the folder back to me.

"But it does say immediate though…"

"If it's not signed, I'm not doing it," she would bark, then turn round without another word.

Indifferent, belligerent and wielding absolute power, I am sure she secretly hoped that this mere slip of a lad would challenge her authority so she could unleash hell. But no, I just turned tail, initially defeated, and ran back to the office, silently fuming all the way. I'd have to face the explosive wrath of the requesting army officer as to why I hadn't been able to convince the supervisor to type my documents, get the 'immediate' ticket signed, then run back to the typing pool so the whole process of beseeching and pleading could begin again. A monumental waste of time, it more than adequately demonstrated how the Civil Service ran in those days.

Each lunchtime, the army staff would head over to the Mess and sink a few liveners (sometimes quite a few liveners). This left me in the clerks' room with my colleagues, three very old women who chattered about the most inane, inconsequential subjects, all the while eating their home-brought sandwiches out of Tupperware boxes or tin-foil. There was nothing for me to do and I was never, even if I'd wanted to be, included in their endless prattling. I was probably the youngest person in our division, if not the entire site.

Once the officers had decamped to the Mess, I'd whip out the latest copy of *Smash Hits* and read it, with feet up on my desk, from cover to cover. As we've established, Numan's round the world flight had not proceeded as planned and there were regular updates about the problems he'd encountered. The press had a field day. He was, after all, an easy target – their perception was "arrogant, rich, pop star decides to attempt round the world flight to satisfy ego but fails miserably". I think it was the micro-talented Paula Yates in her column in one of the music papers that started a 'Get Numan Grounded' campaign. Let's remember that he actually completed the flight round the world – not without problems, not without technical hitches, not exactly to plan but he *did* complete it, not thinking as they flew over the Isle of Wight at the beginning of the expedition, "Do you know what? Bugger this, let's turn back!" This fact was ignored by the mainstream music press but at least in *Smash Hits* Numan got fair coverage. It was here that I saw a full-page advert in a late August issue alerting me to the fact that Numan's new single, 'She's Got Claws', was due for release, with a 12-inch limited-edition version available at a special price from Beggars Banquet stores.

This was very much a new era for Numan. I bought the single one Saturday from Beggars in Kingston and was struck, once again, by the imagery used on the cover, showing a deathly-pale Numan, his face partially hidden by a doffed trilby hat. The half of his face that was visible featured a grey eye, almost like a shark's in that it was completely devoid of emotion. Most shockingly, his cheek was bleeding from three slash wounds. The android Numan was dead, it would seem. It was mesmerising. The song itself, about the perils of being a celebrity in the 1980s, and a vulnerable one at that, was a slower, moodier song than anything from the *Telekon* phase. It was almost soulful in places, augmented by a fretless bass, so totally different from the clinical effectiveness of his former bass player Paul Gardiner's style. I had the video for it recorded on a compilation of *Top of The Pops* shows, tacked onto the end of an edition hosted by the effervescent Peter Powell, a man I'm still surprised managed to walk down a crowded street without being beaten to a bloody pulp. The compilation featured some of the great songs from that summer, including Dexy's in the studio performing 'Show Me', Kate Bush, on video, singing 'Sat in your Lap' (yes, please!), Spandau Ballet performing 'Chant No.1 (I don't need this pressure on)' and Numan with 'She's Got Claws'. The video, with Numan's new persona - this was very much the Humphrey Bogart look with double-breasted suit and a trilby hat - saw him being stalked by a cat-woman, while wearily denouncing the trappings of fame and the betrayal of certain women in his life. Hardly anthemic, the song was certainly another mouth-watering taster for the forthcoming *Dance* album.

I anxiously awaited the album's release and bought it from MJM Records one Saturday in September 1981, using the last of my record tokens. Feeling nostalgic (can you actually feel nostalgic at 18?), I popped in to see my old colleagues in Fine Fare and was greeted with a hug by Dawn. Quite by chance, Terry was there too, chatting up Katie Smith. It was apparent that he'd already been introduced to Dawn.

"Whatcha got there then, Mart?" he asked.

"It's the new Gary Numan album – bought it just now," I said, handing the bag to him.

"I didn't know he had a new album out," he said, reviewing the titles of the album tracks. He scoffed at one.

"What's this then?! 'Boys *LIKE* me'? What's that all about, Mart?" he said handing my precious purchase back. Katie squeaked with laughter.

"I think that's 'Boys Like *ME*' Tel," I said, although not entirely sure myself.

"Yeah, well, whatever. Listen, I've got to shoot. I'll see you soon. You sessioning next week?" he said to me, giving Katie a quick squeeze as he left.

"Yeah, should be. See you then!" I called as he disappeared into the car park.

That evening, Dawn came round straight from work and, once Dad had gone out, we retired to my bedroom and I finally had the chance to play *Dance*. From the opening, stuttering bass line of 'Slowcar to China' played by Mick Karn from Numan's oft-mentioned favourite band, Japan, to the soaring fade out on the final track, 'Moral', I was absolutely, slack-jawed in awe. It was a magnificent album from start to finish. Dawn and I listened to it in bed, with only a small table light to illuminate the room. I played the album again and we made love to the slow rhythms of 'Slowcar...'. It became 'our' album and over the next few months, we played it until we almost wore the grooves off the vinyl, not to mention the pattern off my duvet. We both loved the punching 'Night Talk', the delicate frailty of 'Cry The Clock Said', the plaintive regret in 'Stories' and the Son-of-We-Are-Glass, 'You Are, You Are'. Fans often say Numan peaked with his trilogy of electric albums but I could not disagree more. *Dance* is by far and away my favourite album – it's one of those albums that I wish I could hear again for the first time. Maybe it was what I was feeling, what I was going through, what I was experiencing for the first time. It still, even now, has that resonance. Dawn and I were young, we were in love, we lived inside our own little universe and, at the time, I couldn't imagine a life without her.

The rest of 1981 passed without any major incident, apart from Dawn also quitting her job at Fine Fare, stating that it wasn't the same without me. Besides, she wanted to spend more time studying but this still gave us more time together and we'd go out shopping on a Saturday, either to Kingston or up to Oxford Street where we'd buy books, or records or posters or comics and just loved being together. My record boxes were swelled in the lead up to Christmas 1981 with the purchase of some classic singles, including:

'Under Pressure'/Queen & David Bowie

'Bedsitter' (12-inch version)/ Soft Cell

'The Voice'/Ultravox

'It Must Be Love'/Madness

'Don't You Want Me'/The Human League

Add to these a weird oddity that briefly tickled the charts, 'Love Needs No Disguise' by Dramatis and Gary Numan. Numan's old backing band had formed their own group following Numan's decision to quit touring and this was their first release which featured Numan on guest vocals. I found out about it by accident when Dawn and I were in Books, Bits & Bobs in Kingston and saw someone leafing through a photo album on the counter that appeared to show Numan live in concert. I looked closer and saw they appeared to be fan photos of Numan on stage, dressed in the suit he wore on the Dance album cover.

I asked the girl behind the counter, who I'd known for years having bought my Marvel Comics from her Dad's stall in the mid-1970s, where the photos were taken.

"Oh, they're taken from his latest video," she said. "Someone in the audience had a camera and she's let us sell copies."

"It's with Dramatis," interjected the girl who'd been looking at the photos and who was clearly an absolute Numan devotee, wearing a 'Teletour 1980' T-shirt covered in Numan badges. "It's his old band," she continued, with Dramatis consisting of Rrussell Bell, Ced Sharpley, Chris Payne and Dennis Haynes. Bassist Paul Gardiner had elected to go solo.

"Beggars have got it in. I just bought it," she said, showing me the single.

So I added that to my growing Numan record collection – it was an OK song but didn't match the sheer, peerless quality of the Dance album.

At work, there was the office Christmas lunch, which was organised, as you might expect, with military efficiency. It was at a pub called The Cricketers in Chessington where a full spread awaited us. I wasn't that fussed about going but non-attendance was not an option. At the table, where I had a full Christmas dinner, I was seated next to the Colonel in charge of our division. He was military through and through and was not a man to be trifled with. He was bald, square shouldered, with huge arms like matured hams and could probably drop-kick me the length of a football field. However, as the wine flowed (and flowed) and the port and brandy were passed round the tables, he mellowed a bit.

"How are you getting on, Martin?" he asked in his usual deep sonorous voice, a large brandy in hand, smoke from the post-meal cigars and pipes clouding the pub.

"Not too bad, thanks," I beamed, quite a lot of wine, brandy and port by now sloshing round my head.

"How are you finding it working with the Rottweilers?"

I was confused. Who did he mean?

"The women in the office!" he guffawed. "Can't be much fun, eh?" he added but fortunately my colleagues were out of earshot.

"Oh, them? Right! Well, it's all right, I suppose. Not much in common but there you go," I replied, not wishing to badmouth the women in question.

"You're a bright lad, have you never thought of enlisting in the Army?"

I nearly choked on the latest glass of port that had appeared in my hand.

"Me? In the Army? Christ, no! You've got to be bloody kidding me!"

Director: No, no, no! Cut! *CUT!!*

Me: What's wrong?

Director: You've gone off script, luvvie!! You've gone off script!!

Me: I have?

Director: Yes! You should have said, "No, sir, but it's an interesting proposition and an option that I will give full consideration to and thank you for your sincere interest in my career and prospects."

Me: Ah!

Director: We'll dub the line in post-production. Now *TRY* and keep to the script!

Me: Sorry!

Back at the table, in absolute silence, all eyes turned to me. The Colonel drew himself up in his chair, shoulders back. He placed his brandy glass down on the table, dabbed at the corners of his mouth with a napkin and, without parting his lips, ran his tongue over his teeth to remove any last vestiges of food. He was clearly about to say something momentous – I didn't feel like it was going to be good.

Slowly and coldly he demanded, "And, may I ask, why not?"

I had clearly badmouthed the Army – his passion, his career, his life, his very *raison d'être*. I doubt he could have looked angrier if I'd told him that I thought his wife was a hairy fat pig.

Everyone watched me as I flushed red with embarrassment.

"Well…well…well…er…well…" I spluttered as the Colonel glared at me like James Finlayson in the old Laurel and Hardy movies.

My brain froze.

"I'm waiting!" the Colonel demanded.

"Well," I squawked, as the room span and I desperately tried to jump-start some of the brandy-soaked brain-cells in my head.

"I'm waiting!" the Colonel demanded again.

"Well….well…well…it's because…it's because…I'm a devout coward!"

All eyes turned to the Colonel for his reaction, some anticipating a swift right hook. I closed one eye and braced myself for impact.

There was a moment's silence before he erupted in laughter, clapping me on the back with his huge, bear-like hand with a mighty "whomp". Those around us laughed too, relieved that I'd got away with such insubordination.

"Do you know what, Martin? You're alright!" he said, wiping away tears of laughter. I tried to shift some of the dislodged intercostal segments of my spine back into place.

"I'm sure you're going to go far!" he said, getting up from the table and, still laughing to himself, went to circulate amongst the rest of the staff.

Christmas was great fun although I elected to spend the big day itself with Dad rather than Dawn. Dad and I had decorated the house with the ancient Christmas decorations we'd had since, like, forever. These included the tree lights that lacked a plug which Dad, for some strange reason, was reluctant to buy a plug for, even though they probably only cost something like 15p. He instead insisted on wrapping the bare wires round the prongs on the plug for the TV, placing the household in mortal danger. I don't think Dad was intentionally a spendthrift but had, in the past, looked to save a few bob here and there. The classic example was when we moved into Princes Avenue back in the winter of 1968 and we were flat broke. That first Christmas, it was freezing with only a single fume-belching paraffin heater to warm the entire house. Santa Claus only made a cursory visit, leaving a second-hand portable record player for Peter (a homemade kit-built one at that!) and a few annuals for me. My Uncle John suggested to Dad that there was a way to gimmick the electricity meter by carefully removing the security wire from the lead seal, opening the meter itself and wedging a match in to stop the wheel from turning, thereby stopping the units clocking up and giving us 'free' electricity.

"Just do it at the weekend, otherwise the Electricity Board will get suspicious," Uncle John sagely advised.

Against Mum's protestations, Dad had crouched at the bottom of the stairs in front of the open cupboard revealing the slowly turning wheel inside the securely fastened electricity meter. With a match in one hand, Dad set about easing the wire out of the lead seal.

"Oh, be careful, Jimmy!" Mum pleaded, unable to watch.

"Will you shush!" Dad said impatiently.

Peter and I were, however, quite happy to watch as Dad gently worked the piece of wire – this was far more entertaining than anything on the three channels on our black and white TV! All we needed was the theme from *Mission: Impossible* and we'd have an afternoon of great entertainment.

Dad sweated over the wire and lead seal for what seemed like hours.

"Ah!" he said finally, sounding very pleased with himself. "That's got it!"

A second later, there was an almighty bang accompanied by a flash of light so bright that, even through our eyelids, we could see our skeletons illuminated through our skin. There was a horrible electrical smell, coupled with the unmistakable stench of burnt hair. We looked blinking round the hall through the smoky haze and thought for a moment that Dad had been completely vaporised as all that seemingly remained of him were his slippers in front of the cupboard. Our gaze was slowly drawn to the top of the stairs where Dad was sitting on the top step, still crouched in the same position, looking vaguely like Ken Dodd and largely missing an eyebrow. In his hand, where his fingernails had turned a little grey, the match had somehow been ignited.

In a quivering voice he finally said, "Best not then, eh?"

CHAPTER 22

Peter gets married, I get engaged

At the beginning of 1982 I looked back on what a momentous year 1981 had been. A girlfriend, a new job, earning a reasonable wage. Dad was pleased about the way things had turned out and absolutely adored Dawn.

I was still managing to see Terry though and still enjoyed our musical sessions, although I was frustrated that we never actually played any songs as such, just endless improvised tunes based around a riff on the synth. I wouldn't have minded actually doing a cover version or something but Terry was adamant that we wrote our own material.

We amassed dozens of cassette tapes of our epic improved masterpieces, tunes that took on an extra dimension when Terry bought a Westone V1 Thunderball active bass guitar with a huge floor-mounted bass amp. I loved playing bass, even though my expertise was limited.

At home, Dad was still working five, six or even seven days a week but was trying to cut back on his hours. Peter, meanwhile, announced that he was getting married to Susan with the date set for April 1982. He asked me to be the Best Man. I didn't really know what a Best Man did exactly but I graciously, if nervously, accepted.

March 1982 brought the first Numan product of the year, a new single called 'Music for Chameleons'. It followed the more soulful tone of the *Dance* album. For the first time, there was an extended mix on the 12-inch single, which Dawn and I adored. I made up tapes of all the singles we bought and the songs became the soundtrack of our life together. Terry had the extended mix in his car, pumped through a stereo that, at full volume, could quite possibly have burst your eye-balls.

Numan, meanwhile, decamped to America for mainly tax-reasons and, perversely, planned a US tour for autumn 1982, barely a year after his 'farewell' concerts at Wembley. Numan always says he regretted his decision to 'retire' from live shows in 1981, claiming that, after the emotional and seemingly last ever show, after the crowds had left the Wembley Arena, he went and sat on the edge of the stage, surveyed the vast empty venue and thought, "Oh, shit!"

The press had another field day. Even old Noley had said during the 1980 *Swap Shop* interview, "Is this *really* it?" clearly intimating that he thought it might have been just a huge publicity stunt. When the US shows were announced for autumn 1982, he was derided in the music papers and branded a hypocrite, accused of getting fans to unnecessarily pay thousands of pounds to attend the 'farewell' shows, further accusing Numan of knowing full well he was secretly planning to tour again. I doubt that was actually the case but that's how it was reported in the press. There was a cartoon of Numan in one music paper showing him running to the bank with his pockets stuffed with £5 and £10 notes, with money trailing behind him. The press perception of Numan was still that he was a very rich, vain pop star who got lucky. I doubt Numan ever made a single cent in profit from any of those shows.

Peter's wedding was a huge gathering of the Downham Clan and was a memorable day. I undertook my duties as best I could, never liking the public speaking aspect but it was OK. During the afternoon, after endless photo sessions and as the guests drank and danced, I sat with Dawn in the corner of the banqueting room where the post-wedding party was being held, surveying the room as the family quite rightly placed Peter and Susan at the very centre of the celebrations. The pair of them looked deliriously happy. Dawn held my hand.

"Do you think we'll ever get married?" she asked quietly.

I was stunned.

"I don't know, do you want to get married?" I asked. The thought had never even crossed my mind.

"I don't know. I think I'd like to though."

My heart swelled and I kissed her.

"Who knows then, eh?" I said and hugged her tightly.

On the way home in the car, after Dad had dropped Dawn off at her house, we reviewed the events of the day.

"What did you think then, son?" asked Dad.

"Oh, it was great, Dad. Good to see everyone. I think I've taken about four rolls of pictures!"

He paused.

"Mum would have loved it," he said, sadly and for a moment I thought he was going to cry.

"Yeah, she would've done, Dad," and I rested my hand on top of his on the gear stick.

I loved my Dad.

Life was good, Dawn and I had been going out together for over a year and everything was fine. Well, nearly everything. At work, the Colonel did indeed have words with me. I was summoned into his office, replete with maps on the wall dotted with map pins, a plan press filled with architectural drawings in one corner and badges and flags from his regiment adorning the other walls. On his desk were a brass angle-poise lamp, an 'In-Tray', an 'Out-Tray', a finely-tooled leather blotter and an ornate fountain pen set. I loitered uncomfortably in front of his desk while he signed endless documents with a flourish.

"Sit down, Martin," he said without looking up.

I sat in the leather chair opposite, which farted and squeaked as I lowered myself onto the cushion.

"How are you getting on?" he said finally, looking up from the documents, which he placed in the 'Out-Tray', replacing the cap on his fountain pen.

"Yes, good thank you," I said sitting upright in the chair.

"Enjoying the work?"

"Yes, very busy but all OK, thank you."

"Good," he said, studying me over his arched fingers. "Remember our chat at Christmas?"

I nodded.

"Well, you will have seen the situation down in the South Atlantic - it's getting a bit tense, to say the least."

It was, indeed. The Argentineans had invaded The Falkland Islands which, until someone showed me on a map I had assumed, like most of the inhabitants of the UK, were somewhere off the coast of Scotland.

"What I need now is someone to be seconded to the Falkland Islands department here to provide administrative support. I want you to be that person."

"Oh," I said again, processing the information.

"It's a temporary posting and it involves a temporary promotion to senior clerical officer. Only acting SCO, though. There's no money involved, just a nominal title. Are you interested?"

Director: For pity's sake Martin, say the right line!

"Well, absolutely, thank you," I said, not entirely sure that I wouldn't be actually based in The Falklands Islands. He went through what the job entailed and confirmed that I *wouldn't* be based in The Falklands. Either way, I agreed that I'd be up for the challenge. The carrot dangled in front of me, as an incentive, was that if I completed the task satisfactorily, there would be an interview, "just a formality", and I would get promoted automatically.

"Good, man. There's no need to get Personnel involved as it's only an informal secondment, but you start Monday week. Dismissed."

"Thank you," I said standing up to leave, the leather chair farting and squeaking again as I stood.

Just as I got to the door, the Colonel spoke again.

"And, Martin?" he said. I turned back.

"The occasional "Sir" wouldn't go amiss?"

"Oh, yes, right, thank you, sir," and I left his office to return to my colleagues.

Back at my desk, I told them what had happened in the meeting and I naively expected them to be pleased for me but, no, quite the reverse. After a stony silence, one of the crones spoke when I asked them what was wrong.

"So, you expect us to be happy for you? Only here a few months and you're getting promoted over us? Is that it?"

"Pretty much, yes."

"Well, we're not."

And that's the last time they ever spoke to me. For the rest of the week, before I moved to my new department, they sent me to Coventry.

Dad and Dawn were delighted with my news and it seemed that I'd made the right decision to join the MOD. Again, I can't say exactly what I did but if I thought the work I'd been doing up to this point had been busy, this was a whole new level of 'busy'. Long hours, lots of running about, lots of time-critical tasks to be undertaken, everything stopping if Parliamentary questions were asked so full replies could be typed for the Prime Minister, with even the monosyllabic woman in charge of the typing pool turned a blind eye to the typewriter we had secretly appropriated for our office. It was exciting and terrifying in equal measure. We knew, for example, that the Argentine warship the 'General Belgrano' had been torpedoed only an hour after the event. For the duration of the mercifully short but nevertheless bloody Falklands War, I was run ragged.

The summer of 1982 rolled round and what Dawn had mentioned at Peter's wedding played on my mind. Could I imagine actually being married? Did I want to get married? Where would we live? Would we have children? But, like I said, I couldn't imagine being without Dawn so my thoughts began to turn to "Yes, I would like to get married."

This meant that I had to ask Dawn's Dad for permission to take his daughter's hand in marriage. Not an enviable task. We avoided Dawn's house and ergo her parents as much as possible, preferring the unconditional liberty and freedom of my house. The persistent questioning by her Dad and the sarcastic, caustic comments from Martine meant it was not generally a happy household.

Back at Princes Avenue, as we spent so much time in my room, Dad said he'd redecorate, giving the room its first lick of paint and new wallpaper since about 1968. Dawn helped me move all my things out of my bedroom so they could be temporarily stored in the small bedroom. These included all my records, the latest of which was Gary Numan's new single, 'We Take Mystery (to bed)'. I had this epic monster on 12-inch single and:

It.

Was.

Awesome.

A throbbing, relentless juggernaut of a song, the personnel on this track were Numan's US touring band, most of whom would play on the forthcoming *I, Assassin* album. While his old band were trying to forge their own career, Numan had employed the services of Pino Palladino on fretless bass, Roger Mason on keyboards, plus Chris Slade, a veteran of numerous groups from the 1960s and 70s, on drums. His percussive performance on this song was stunning, with the drums almost as a lead instrument. My inner Numanoid also noted that the typeface for the lettering on the cover was the same as used on *Replicas!*

A special promotional film for the single was shown on *Top of the Pops* featuring the now Stateside Numan in New York performing the song in a stark, white studio. Clad in a completely black suit topped off by a black trilby, the film, featuring an animated performance, showed he was blonde again. I loved it! I loved the B-Side as well, which featured 'The Image Is' which could have, and should have, been a single in its own right, along with an early version of the title track.

As we cleared out my bedroom, Dawn lifted a particular box and out tumbled the stack of men's magazines Peter had donated to me a few years before. She was shocked.

"What have you got these for?" she asked, visibly upset.

"Oh, shit! I've been meaning to throw them out for ages," I blustered, hastily putting my well-thumbed copies of *Mayfair* back in the box. Dawn looked close to tears.

"Am I not enough?" she said.

I leapt towards her and wrapped my arms around her, saying that of course she was enough and that I loved her with all my heart. She was hurt though and I felt wretched.

"I'll get rid of them! I promise!" I said desperately.

A few days later, once Dad had finished the decorating and a new carpet had been laid, Dawn came round bringing with her a small carrier bag. Up in my newly decorated room, and before the furniture was all moved back, she opened the bag.

"What's this?" I asked.

"It's a Polaroid camera," Dawn said playfully.

"What for?" I asked, puzzled.

"Well, we can take our own photographs now!"

"Oh?" I said.

"Like in your magazines!"

"Oh!" I said, rising to the challenge.

And over the next month or so we *did* take photographs! Lots of them, all very artistic, costing me a small fortune in Polaroid film!

The thorny issue of asking her Dad about marriage had to be addressed, whether I liked it or not. My Dad was, of course, overjoyed at the prospect but how would Dawn's parents react? When I did have to see them, they treated me with the same amount of contempt and disdain as they'd done from the outset but kind of tolerated me, like you would a stray cat that keeps coming into your garden. I think they'd hoped by now that Dawn would have gotten fed-up with me and given me the elbow. The deed had to be done.

One glorious Sunday afternoon at Dawn's house, Cliff was sat in his garden in a deck chair drinking a frothy homemade beer.

"I'll leave you to it," whispered Dawn and retreated indoors.

Cliff barely looked up as I sat down in a vacant chair.

"How are you?" I asked cheerfully.

"Yep. Good," he replied. There was no attempt to continue the conversation, just a yawning chasm of awkward silence. I wondered whether to just come right out and say Dawn and I wanted to get married.

Cliff just sat there, occasionally supping at his ale, staring vacantly at the flowers in the garden.

"Do you want a beer?" he asked half-heartedly, waving his half-empty pewter tankard at me. The thought of drinking lager still made my stomach turn, even after all this time and the prospect of imbibing one of Cliff's cloudy, noxious concoctions didn't appeal in the slightest.

"No, thanks," I said. Cliff looked at me disdainfully.

"No…I don't suppose you do," he said and carried on drinking.

It was time to bite the bullet.

"Listen, Cliff…I've been seeing Dawn for quite a while now…"

Cliff groaned and shifted uncomfortably in his chair.

"…and we've been thinking that we might like to make it a bit more serious, like, you know, a bit more permanent?" I was struggling to find the right words even though I'd gone through what I'd wanted to say a hundred times in my head. I blundered on.

"And, at some point, we were thinking that we might get engaged…"

Cliff muttered something unintelligible under his breath. I can't imagine it was anything positive. Then the yawning silence returned. I could see him going through the implication of what I'd just said in his mind and he wasn't pleased.

"What are you going to do for money?" he finally spat.

"Well, I'm not doing too bad at…"

"Have you got any savings?"

"Well, no, not yet, but…"

"And where are you going to live?

"Er…"

"Have you thought of that? Hmm? Have you?"

"We've looked at…"

"And don't think you'd be living here, either!" he said, cutting me off again. "Dawn's not working, houses cost about twenty or thirty grand, if not more and you think you could afford one? On what you earn? What are you…a…a clerical assistant? Is that likely? Is it?"

This wasn't going well. Cliff was a senior manager at BT where he earned a considerable salary and their 4-bedroomed house in Worcester Park wasn't exactly small.

Director: You can punch him, if you like?

Me: Tempting, but I'd better not.

Director: Are you sure?

Me: No, really. I'm good, thanks.

"Look, I've got a temporary promotion…"

"Temporary…" he snorted in derision.

"…and all being well, I'm hoping that I might get a better job at the MOD. I've been told there's a special project I'm in line for so, maybe, I might get that."

Nothing I said seemed that positive. It was all "if" and "maybe". Cliff looked at his now empty tankard. I tried to say something a bit more definite.

"I've also been thinking about going to night school as well to see if I can improve my qualifications. It might help with my career."

"What are you going to study?"

"Er, not sure yet. But if I get another O-Level, it'll all help."

The interrogation continued but Cliff showed just the smallest sign that he wasn't going to forbid our engagement outright and throw me out of the house.

"When will you be starting that?" he asked suspiciously.

"This September, I guess, for the autumn term."

More silence.

"Hmm…" Cliff looked marginally, fractionally, less angry than he had been a few minutes ago. "What does your Dad think?"

"Oh, he's all in favour of it!" I said enthusiastically.

"Hmm…"

Silence.

"September, eh?"

"Yeah, that's the plan."

Silence.

"Well, let's see how that works out," he said, making it implicitly clear that he wasn't going to discuss the matter any further at this stage.

I went indoors to find Dawn who had just told her Mum of our plans. Her Mum, with hands shaking just ever so slightly, was pouring a large sherry – she didn't offer me one. We said some quick goodbyes and headed out the front door.

"What did my Dad say?" asked Dawn excitedly.

"Well, he didn't say no."

A few days later, Dawn rang me and was very excited.

"Mum and Dad want you to come on holiday with us!"

Resisting the urge to vomit, or to go and find a gun to blow my brains out, I asked her what they had in mind.

"They're going to Butlin's in Pwllheli with Penny and they want us to go along with Martine."

I wondered whether we actually had a gun.

"Oh! Great!" I said noncommittally.

But I couldn't say no to the offer, as it appeared that her Mum and Dad were making an attempt to get along with me and had offered this olive branch, this peace offering. So I eventually said yes.

The week away was planned for August 1982 but I can't say that I was looking forward to it, not helped by the fact that, a few days before we travelled, Martine announced she wanted her new boyfriend, Mark, to come with us. In an effort to pacify their middle daughter – and hopefully cheer the miserable, spiteful bitch up – Dawn's Mum and Dad had agreed. It was going to be a tight squeeze in a three-room chalet.

The journey started off OK but the closer we got to Wales, and after a tortuous journey in two cars, the weather closed in and it started to rain.

And rain.

And rain.

And rain.

It rained every day of the week we were there. It was utterly miserable in every measurable way. We tried to make the best of it but it was awful. Dawn's Mum and Dad with Penny were in one bedroom; Dawn and Martine were in single beds in another, while Mark and I were in the lounge on campbeds. There was no room to do anything and we were all crammed together into one intolerable, bad-tempered, argumentative tangle. We attempted to do things together but it was no use, hampered by the gales that blew constantly. I tried to be upbeat but the caustic, cantankerous comments that effortlessly poured from Martine's bitter and twisted mouth made that almost impossible.

The bad weather was relentless. Even walking to some of the camp's facilities or the on-site cinema was nearly impossible. Other guests wandered round the camp like ghosts; everything was a rain-washed grey with the colour bleached out of every surface. Flags and bunting flapped frantically and forlornly in the unyielding gales.

After a couple of days, Dawn and I made ourselves scarce and left the rest of the family to it, which, in Martine's case, was humping her boyfriend at every opportunity in her Mum and Dad's double bed while everyone else was out. This I discovered when I unexpectedly returned to the chalet one morning as I'd forgotten my wallet. It was hellish.

The only ray of sunshine, figuratively speaking, was that Dawn and I got engaged. We went out of the holiday camp one night, dodging the security, baying hounds, barbed wire, night-time patrols and spotlights, and found a local restaurant where, having secretly purchased a ring a few weeks before, I produced the box from my pocket and formally proposed to Dawn. She cried, said yes a dozen times in quick succession and we bought a bottle of sparkling white wine to celebrate.

So, I thought, that's what getting engaged feels like?

It felt like a bit of an anti-climax.

CHAPTER 23

Carrie, and my own momentary lapse of reason

I had to sort my life out, to prove that I could achieve more and aim for bigger and better things and prove to the cheerless Cliff that I was not a waste of space. Things got off to a reasonable start at work where I had been seconded to another department, on the proviso that, if I succeeded in completing the special project that the Colonel had mentioned nearly a year before, I'd get promoted permanently to senior clerical officer. If I wanted to go any further, with the next step being executive officer, I really would have to improve my qualifications and, as I'd promised Dawn's Dad, I looked into booking some night school classes. None of them really appealed but I narrowed the search down to learning German or studying sociology. I went for the latter and sent off an application to the Adult Education Board.

Back at home, after the soul-destroying holiday in Pwllheli, I tried to catch up with Terry but when I rang his Mum, I was in for a shock.

"Oh, he's at Police Training College," his Mum, Joan, said casually.

I was speechless.

"When did that happen?" I asked, barely able to contain my disbelief.

"He's been there for a good month, I s'pose... he's really enjoying it."

"Does he come home at all?"

"Not much."

"He never mentioned it to me! That he was actually going through with the idea!" I felt a bit betrayed to tell the truth.

"No, he's like that with everyone. Once he's made his mind up, that's it."

"Well...tell him I said hello and to give us a ring," I said uncertainly.

"I will. Quite like the peace and quiet to be honest. You two don't 'alf make a racket when you get together."

"Yeah, I know," I replied sheepishly.

"When you going to make a record and make some money and get rich and famous?" she mocked good-naturedly.

"One day, Joan! One day!" I said and hung up.

Blimey.

Terry in the police force?

Unbelievable.

But what of our hero? There was good and bad from the Numan camp. The "good" was that his club tour of the US was well received and there was a rumour – just a rumour – that he might tour the UK again. And, falling most definitely into the 'excellent' category, the video of the last night of his 'farewell' (hah!) tour in 1981 had been released and had been tempting me on the shelves in HMV and Virgin for months. I had just been so busy with work and Dawn and the holiday and getting engaged, that I hadn't had a chance to buy it. The distributors, Palace Video, had an offer where you could send a blank video and, for a reduced fee, they'd run off a copy of the show and send it back. But even though I was going to have to watch what I spent and start saving – I was going to get married and buy a house, right? – I couldn't resist the proper, off the shelf product and bought it one Saturday from a small, short-lived record store down Oxford Street. It may have actually been a Palace Video store come to think of it.

And what did the performance show? Loaded up into the Betamax beast and with the bass control turned up on our new TV from Radio Rentals, it showed Numan at the very top of his game – confident, assured, arrogant – against a breathtaking light show that put the lights from The Touring Principle to shame. It was epic. I loved, as ever, the live versions of 'Down in the Park' with Numan in the Numan-Mobile emerging from beneath the drum risers, and 'Are 'friends' electric?' Equally amazing were the live versions of 'The Joy Circuit', 'Everyday I Die' and 'I Dream of Wires'. I also loved the fact that Numan almost came in too early at the beginning of 'This Wreckage', inevitably cocked-up the words to 'We Are Glass' and that the drums over-ran on 'She's Got Claws', as Paul Gardiner on bass did his best to try and emulate Mick Karn, prompting a bemused "whoops" from Numan. Paul Gardiner was a *good* bass player – solid and rhythmic – but he was no match for the peerless genius of the underrated talent that was Mick Karn. I vowed to myself that if – IF – he toured again, I would move heaven and earth to get a ticket, even if I had to go and queue at the box office and get one.

That was the good – what of the bad? Well, the third single from his forthcoming new album, *I, Assassin* was released and, as ever, I bought it on the day of release. The cover showed Numan in an outfit that had the critics holding their sides with mirth. 'White Boys and Heroes' had Numan dressed with a new take on his gangster image which, while successful on the cover of *Dance*, was a complete misfire here. This time he was wearing a white suit and a white beret. It was not a good look *at all* – he looked like one of The Rubettes.

But what of the song itself? Well produced – maybe; liquid bass lines and soaring sax – check; soaring synths and vocals – all present and correct. But it didn't move me, didn't excite me and was another dud as far as I was concerned. Not even the 12-inch mix could make me like the song. Even a special promo film of Numan in LA did little to help sales. It was shown on *Top of the Pops*, on a Thursday night when Peter had popped in for a cup of tea and a packet of chocolate biscuits, and was met with derision.

"I bet he's got a fucking hat on," Peter said, positively dripping with scorn, not to mention biscuit crumbs. Numan's hair had started to recede noticeably and he was wearing hats more and more in videos and promo photos. Dad sat beside him on the sofa, chuckling at Peter's Wildean wit. The two of them were like two peas in a pod sometimes.

"Ah, shut your face! You're going bald as well!" I said angrily.

"Maybe, but it runs in the family. If I'm going bald, you will too, mate!"

Dad sat there quite smugly, his head covered in his usual thick, well-coiffured barnet. I instinctively ran my fingers through my hair. Did it feel like I was going bald? Nope, no...plenty there, thankfully. It seemed that, maybe, baldness skipped a generation.

And then, continuing the 'bad' theme, alas, the *I, Assassin* album came out and it was a massive dud. Aside from the three singles, of which I only liked two, there was nothing on there to compare to the supreme, majestic quality of *Dance*. Only one other track, 'The 1930s Rust', was remotely listenable to. I played the album to Dawn one Saturday night up in the sanctuary of my room and once was enough.

"It's not very good, is it?" she said, almost apologetically.

I had to agree. New Numan product had previously been something to look forward to, like a combination of Christmas and your birthday. But this? No, it wasn't very good and, expecting something as good as *Dance* where every song was memorable, I was massively disappointed. Worst of all, there was not one sensual, soulful track on *I, Assassin* that we could make love to.

In time for the September 1982 term, I started evening classes at Tiffin Girl's School in Kingston, studying sociology.

I soon realised I should have chosen something else. It was dull beyond belief. The class started off with 20 attendees but the number dropped off week by week until only about 10 regulars remained. Maybe they found the subject as boring as I did? Maybe they struggled with doing a full day's work, going home and briefly stopping off for a fish-finger sandwich and a quick crap before heading out again for three hours of adult education in the evening? I know I did. I was knackered.

But there were a couple of people I got on with. One of whom, Den, it transpired, was a massive Gary Numan fan. During the tea breaks, we chatted excitedly about Numan and his career, discussing lyrics, symbolism, exquisite bass-lines and how Den had got tickets for the Wembley shows in 1981 and what a mind-blowing, emotional show it had been. If he toured again, I was bloody well going to get tickets! One hundred percent! No question! Tickets, I say! Tickets!!

There was another attendee who sat quietly on her own and, initially, didn't really talk much. She fascinated me – her name was Carrie Waterstone and every time she came to the class, she looked like she'd just stepped out of a salon. She looked, at the very most, in her late twenties, dressed exquisitely, wore perfect make-up and had a lithe but shapely figure.

Eventually I got chatting to her and, as we talked about jobs, we realised that we both worked on the same sprawling government estate in Chessington. We exchanged stories about the unidentifiable food that was served in the canteen if you dared brave the fetid, acrid smells that emanated from within. I made her laugh and when she laughed back, it was just wonderful.

As the weeks passed, she invariably came and sat at the desk next to me in the classroom but when she didn't turn up for a couple of lessons, I felt the same dull ache in my stomach as when Dawn had been placed on other tills at Fine Fare, only a couple of years before.

Carrie started to play on my mind.

Lyrics from 'The Image Is' seemed apt:

"You dance around my head. They say it's illegal but I'm sure it's… OK"

I thought about her a lot. She seemed a lot more mature, more self-assured and more worldly-wise than Dawn. Dawn was still lovely, now in a kind of geeky, college student sort of way. No bad thing, to be sure – but compared to Carrie, she seemed a bit, I don't know, immature. So when I started to constantly fantasise about Carrie in my room, slowly taking her clothes off, then naked in my bed, I knew Dawn and I were in trouble.

CHAPTER 24

Tempted by the fruit of another

Christmas 1982 was looming and, on the surface, everything was fine. I was working hard, plus I had started a savings account to demonstrate to Dawn's Mum and Dad that I was serious about getting engaged and had the wherewithal to plan for the future. Dawn and I still saw each other at every opportunity, although we didn't dive straight into bed with such regularity as we'd done in the past.

But underneath, buried deep so nobody knew, buried so deep that I couldn't give away the slightest hint of the feelings of doubt and uncertainty that I had, I was in turmoil. Carrie was the first person I thought of when I woke up in the morning and the last thing I thought of when I went to sleep at night.

On one occasion, at night school, Den didn't show up, so at tea break, after another mind-numbing hour or so of sociology, it was just Carrie and I sat at our usual table. We sat chatting about life in general and I asked her what she was hoping to gain from studying. She paused before answering.

"I'm not sure, really," she replied absently. "I'd like to make something of my life before it's too late, and I need some extra qualifications. I wasn't that interested in lessons at school. I was far more interested in having fun!"

I nodded in agreement.

"Plus," she added, "it's nice to meet new people. You know, get out of the house a bit."

She sounded sad.

"Oh, you'll be fine," I said encouragingly. "I mean, Christ, you're only young...you've got your whole life in front of you, surely?"

"Really? I'm 36 next year."

I nearly fell through the floor.

"No way!" I said, absolutely astonished.

"It's true…couple of years after that, 40… then downhill all the way," and she mimed a rollercoaster reaching its apogee then plunging down.

"Well, you don't look 40…or 36…or 35…or anything," I said clumsily.

"Oh, that's really sweet of you, and she laughed. She really didn't look like she was in her mid-thirties.

"We should go out for lunch," she suddenly announced.

"What? Not to the canteen! We'll go back to the office with crippling stomach-pains!" I joked.

"No, what's the name of that pub opposite the entrance at work?"

"The Harrow?"

"Yes, The Harrow – we can go there."

I feigned embarrassment and coyly said, "But I'm engaged to be married."

She paused.

"I know," she said and didn't seem the least bit bothered.

We met up as planned on Tuesday 9th November 1982 and, as I loitered by the main gate, with the security guard eyeing me up suspiciously, she arrived looking even more glamorous than she did at night school. Her smile when she saw me was stunning. I escorted her to the pub and we ordered a couple of drinks. On the jukebox, 'Mad World' by Tears for Fears was playing, a song I will forever associate with Carrie. We found a table in the corner and chatted idly about life and loves but, throughout, she didn't take her eyes off me. Eyes that were a crystal blue set off by her short, blonde hair. She was stunning. I savoured every moment but all too soon we had to return to work. She gave me a little peck on the cheek and said she'd see me at night school. I headed back to the office, mind spinning.

Over the next few weeks, we saw each other for lunch at least once a week and I looked forward to it with immeasurable excitement each time. She was funny, experienced, really was worldly-wise, and we effortlessly flirted with each other. When I saw her I was one person, but when I was back among my family and friends and, obviously, with Dawn, I was another, a schizophrenic existence, to be sure.

On Monday 20th December 1982, the last night of term, we finished the lesson and went for a drink in Kingston. We found a pub that was full of Christmas revellers, with glittery foil decorations hanging from the ceiling and 'Merry Xmas Everybody' by Slade inevitably playing on the jukebox. An office Christmas party was in full swing and it was clear that a lot of the people had been in there since lunchtime. People danced about, some wearing paper party hats, but nearly all drunk as skunks. An older man from the office party, shirt untucked and tie askew, had a perfect imprint of red lips planted on his bald head, everyone laughing and joking. It was packed, smoke-filled and noisy but, as we loitered by the bar, a couple left and we managed to nab their table. We sat knee-to-knee and, over a couple of drinks, talked about plans for Christmas, Christmases-past and life in general. After an hour or so, I had to make a move and we walked out into the cold, frosty night, the sky full of stars stretching into infinity. She held my arm as I walked her back to her car and I said I hoped that she would have a nice Christmas.

As we got to the car, she pulled me close and kissed me, her tongue moist and probing. I unbuttoned her long, dark blue coat and slid my arms around her and returned her kisses, passionately. We said goodnight for the next ten minutes. I half expected her to invite me back to her flat in Norbiton and was bent-double with frustration when she didn't. We finally broke the embrace and my heart was thumping. I stopped short of saying, "I love you," but that's exactly how I felt. She gave me one last kiss, promising she'd see me in the New Year. I watched in a daze as she drove off, dazed partially due to the alcohol but mostly due to steaming lust. I wondered how I was going to cope without seeing her until January.

I struggled with these thoughts – the fact that I really enjoyed seeing her, my fantasies becoming more and more intense – and given our secret rendezvous, my fantasies looked like they may very well become real. I effortlessly suppressed any guilt about the betrayal, helped by the fact that Dawn didn't have the slightest idea what was going on, even though our relationship had been a bit strained of late. She was in the final phase of her studying and would sit the last set of exams in the spring of 1983 where there was every indication she would breeze through them all. I loved Dawn, I really did but Carrie was just a completely different person and I could not stop thinking about her.

This may have soured Christmas 1982 a bit. Invited round to Dawn's house for Christmas Day and Boxing Day, I was surprised that her Mum and Dad had agreed to Dawn's request. I was going to stay over on Christmas Day night too, although it had to be on the sofa in the living room.

On the day, Dad dropped me over at Dawn's before heading off to spend the day with Peter and Susan. Dawn's house was brightly lit, nicely decorated but no amount of tinsel, fake snow and fairy lights could mask the fact that Dawn's sister, Martine, was sucking the whole Yuletide spirit from the household. She'd dumped her boyfriend Mark and was now seeing someone called Andy who she clearly wanted to be with on this festive day for some personal pork stuffing with a liberal dribbling of bread sauce. Not only that, she had a streaming cold and had now decided she was fat and was barely eating anything. I tried to make the best of things and Penny, Dawn's little sister was as delighted as ever to see me. But Martine just skulked about the house scowling with her arms folded and when she did speak, it was invariably to utter some sarcastic comment. She clearly hated – HATED – being at home, with all the forced smiling faces, the twee well-rehearsed family anecdotes and fake Christmas cheer. All merely a veneer of happiness hiding a very dysfunctional family. Dawn smiled throughout but it was all a bit of a strain.

Among the gifts I'd bought Dawn was a set of David Bowie picture discs in a white wallet entitled *Fashions*. It was a limited-edition set and featured key singles from his career to date. It really was rather splendid and her face was a picture when she ripped open the paper. Dawn, meanwhile, bought me the new 'Best of' album from Gary Numan, *New Man/Numan*, which collected most of his singles making a rather nice addition to my collection. Beggars Banquet could have done a far better job with the packaging, which showed a picture of Numan with his current gangster image opposite another that appeared to be of Numan from the cover of *Replicas*. Both images were pixelated and indistinct so it wasn't the greatest of album covers but it was, I suppose, nice to have all his hits in one place.

We sat down to Christmas dinner at the long dining table and, alas, I got to sit opposite Martine. Cliff, seated at the head of the table, drank his homemade brew, while Jeanette drank glass after glass of wine in order to try and numb the pain. I had quite a few glasses, too. Dinner was served and Martine pulled a face of pure revulsion at the turkey with all the trimmings that was placed in front of her. I watched, with increasing anger, as she picked at the food, moving bits around the plate, visibly and audibly gagging at each reluctant mouthful.

"Come on, eat up," Jeanette said as cheerfully as she could, trying desperately not to upset her middle daughter. Martine, her eyes heavy-lidded, slowly turned to her mother with a look of absolute hatred and contempt. She looked back down at the dinner plate, hunched her shoulders and made a disgusting, guttural snort of snot and phlegm, swallowing the lot in one vile, stomach-churning motion.

"Fucking hell, Martine, do you want ice and lemon with that?" I blurted out.

The table went silent. Cliff glared at me on the point of apoplexy, Jeanette retreated to the kitchen and Dawn burst into tears and ran upstairs. Penny looked about innocently; unable to comprehend why everyone was so angry. Martine looked at me; her mouth twisted into a deeply unpleasant, sneering smile, that all but said, "That's *you* fucked, then." I fully expected Cliff to explode – and who could blame him – but he just silently got up from the table, ripped off the paper hat he'd been wearing and went into the front room, shutting the door firmly behind him.

I went to find Dawn. She was face down on her bed, her shoulders shuddering from great heaving sobs.

"I'm sorry..." I started to say as gently as I could but she wasn't having any of it. She swung round, eyes red and shouted, "Get away from me!"

"But..."

"You've ruined *everything*!!"

"I didn't mean to," I said feebly.

"Why did you say it? Why did you have to say that?"

I got defensive.

"It's your bloody sister – she doesn't like me and to tell the truth I can't stand her either! She's a bitch!"

"I KNOW! I don't like her either. No one bloody well likes her! But you didn't need to say...didn't need to say...*that*. And in front of Penny as well! She's only nine for Christ's sake!"

"I..."

"Nine years old! What were you thinking?!"

"I...I...dunno...it just came out. I'm really sorry."

"Just...just go away," she said and hid her face back in the duvet. She was crying again.

I went back downstairs and sat in the backroom. Martine had retreated to her room, Cliff was still secluded in the front room and Jeanette sat with a visibly upset Penny on her lap. Nothing was said.

"Look, I'm really sorry about what I said to Martine."

"I know," said Jeanette, gently rocking Penny in her arms. "She's not an…" she chose her words carefully, "…easy girl to like."

The house eventually calmed down. Cliff finally emerged from the front room, Dawn came down but Martine stayed in her room. Not a fantastic Christmas Day, it has to be said, and it pretty much spelt the end of any hope of endearing myself to Dawn's family. Any suggestion that I was still going to sleep over on the sofa that night was pretty much knackered and I ended up walking home.

Dawn and I had a few days apart after Christmas as we dealt with the fallout from my outburst. I phoned her every day though, and apologised again and again and asked for forgiveness. But, in my heart of hearts, I didn't know what I was asking forgiveness for. Martine was just horrible and delighted in driving a wedge between Dawn and me. For the most part, her parents tiptoed round her, desperate not to upset her, with only Cliff erupting from time to time to give her a good hiding.

However, by New Year's Eve, Dawn and I were just back to normal, whatever passed for 'normal'. We went up to Trafalgar Square in the afternoon and saw in 1983 with thousands of other revellers, a noisy mass of people celebrating the New Year in the capital. We strolled back to Waterloo Station arm in arm and caught a packed train back to Worcester Park. I still felt that I'd let her down on Christmas Day and it had crippled me to see her so upset, even though I had been leading a schizophrenic existence by seeing Carrie as and when I could and fantasizing about her in erotic detail. I really hadn't meant to say what I had but Martine had just got under my skin. I walked Dawn home but declined her offer of a coffee and walked the mile or so back to Tolworth in the early hours of 1983, the last train having long-since departed.

As I neared home in the freezing cold, I noticed that a toyshop on Tolworth Broadway that I'd been going to ever since I could remember, Black & Lowe's, had abruptly closed down. Its windows, where I had once pressed my nose and longingly gazed at assorted

Action Man equipment and vehicles, where I had been entranced by the Major Matt Mason astronaut figures and had pined for the sheer beauty of the Matchbox Motorway figure-of-eight slot-car set, were now concealed beneath several huge posters advertising a song, 'New Year's Day', by a group called U2. I felt desperately sad that a small part of my childhood, a shop that I could remember going to with Mum, standing hand in hand at the window and carefully choosing what to spend my limited money on, was gone.

CHAPTER 25

The downward spiral

January 1983 was cold and bleak. The decorations in our house came down and were put back in the soot-covered loft and life returned to its usual rhythm of work, rest and, if we were lucky, play. The new term started at night school and I was apprehensive about seeing Carrie again. Inevitably we sat next to each other and we talked about how our respective Christmases had been. I kind of intimated that mine hadn't been great but didn't go into specific detail. I asked how hers had gone.

"Oh, not so bad. Saw some friends but quite quiet," Carrie said but, again, seemed a bit sad.

"I thought about you a lot, though," she added.

And I really didn't know what to do. On the one hand, I loved Dawn – I really did, but the struggle of trying to ingratiate myself with her family was just becoming just too much of a bloody chore, thanks all the same. Dawn was studying hard and so I'd been feeling a bit ignored and side-lined for the past few months. We rarely went out and, while I was no oil-painting myself, Dawn had let herself go a little bit as she was so intent and single-mindedly focussed on passing her exams. As a result, she was looking more and more like your archetypal student and when we did go out, she didn't dress up or wear the exquisite make-up that she once did. So life didn't seem to be that much fun. Not that any of that excused in the slightest the clandestine relationship I'd been having with Carrie or what happened next.

"Do you want to go out for a drink again?" Carrie asked and I agreed without hesitation, remorse or guilt.

We went out for a drink after night school the following Monday 10th January 1983. This time we met at a pub near her flat in Norbiton where, after half an hour and a couple of drinks, I walked her home.

We barely made it through the front door before she leapt on me, almost tearing her clothes off and in a heartbeat we were writhing on the floor in her hallway, making love – hot, passionate and urgent.

We didn't even make it to the bedroom.

Afterwards we lay in the semi-darkness of her hallway using her coat as a makeshift mattress and my coat as a blanket. Carrie was curled up naked next to me.

"That was nice," she said dreamily then added quickly, "You did enjoy it, right?"

All the bravado and lust from earlier had now been replaced by a voice that sounded small and vulnerable.

"Yeah...yes, of course I did," I replied as I glanced around the hallway at all the discarded clothes, Carrie's having been literally thrown all over the place. I noticed that her Christmas decorations were still hanging from the ceiling.

And just one thought crossed my mind.

"Fuck, what have I done?"

I didn't see her at work over the next few days, crippled by an overwhelming feeling of guilt about the whole situation, guilty feelings that were arguably long overdue. It's sometimes difficult to deal with things when a fantasy becomes reality and it's not necessarily what you wanted. All this meant that I ducked out of night school the following week. I didn't see her again for a fortnight and I was apprehensive about seeing her long before she arrived at the lesson. When she did, she looked awful. She didn't have a scrap of make-up on and it looked like she'd been crying.

At tea break I escorted her to our usual table in the corner of the canteen and I asked her what was wrong.

"I'm late," she replied.

I was stunned. I couldn't think of a thing to say.

Not immediately anyway.

"How late?" was the best I could do.

She didn't look up, didn't make eye contact.

"Few days. Nearly a week."

Fuck.

Using a contraceptive when she jumped on me at her flat hadn't really been an option.

Of course she was late.

Of *course* she was.

I felt my stomach churn.

Fuck.

"What do we do?" I asked pathetically.

"We'll have to see, I guess," she replied absently.

Over the next few days I barely ate, barely slept and went through a thousand possible outcomes.

What was Dawn going to say?

What was Dawn going to do?

What was Dad going to say?

What was Dad going to do?

Did Carrie want to be with me?

Did she even want to keep the child?

Could I actually cope with being a father?

What the fuck was *I* going to do?

One thing I was sure of and that was that there was no happy ending as far as I could see.

At the end of the week, when fortunately Dad was out, I got a phone call in the evening. It was Carrie – she obviously had my number so we could talk about 'things' and what was going to happen next.

"Are you OK?" I asked.

"Yes," she said.

There was a long pause.

"I came on today...so I'm...I'm not pregnant."

I couldn't tell whether she sounded relieved, sad or disappointed.

"Well...that's good? Isn't it?" I said.

I couldn't be sure if this was what she wanted to hear either?

"Yes... yes, I suppose it is," she said slowly, flatly and monotone.

There was another long pause, before she continued.

"So…what happens now?"

I didn't know.

I tried to say something positive – anything – but I just stammered and mumbled incoherently.

"I see," she said and by her tone, she knew there wasn't going to be a happy ending for her either. "So, that was it then, was it?"

"I think so," and I sounded like a schoolboy again – embarrassed, immature and useless.

"I see. OK. Fine, then," Carrie said and sounded bitter.

I started to say, "I'm sorry…" but she'd hung up.

And that was the last time I spoke to her and I never saw her again – she didn't come to any more lessons at night school, which, as it was only a 16-week course, was coming to an end anyway. I also confined myself to the office of a lunchtime to avoid seeing her at work.

A few months later though, she rang when I was out. Dad looked perplexed when I got home from the pub late one night.

"There was a phone call for you earlier," Dad said and it sounded like an accusation.

"Really? Who from?"

Dad picked up a small piece of paper, straightened his glasses and read the message he'd carefully written down in his usual, schoolboy longhand.

"Someone called 'Carrie'."

Oh, shit.

"Who's she then?" he asked suspiciously.

"Someone from night school…a friend," I stammered.

"Hmmm…"

"What did she want?"

"You tell me, son. Is she on drugs or something?"

Despite living in respectable suburbia for most of his life, Dad was still a London Boy at heart. When he got cross or angry, the

London Boy resurfaced and "something" was virtually spat out as "summink."

"I...I don't think so?"

"She must have been drunk then." He went on, "She said 'It was the best sex she'd ever had' and she wants you to call her."

I doubt that it actually had been the best sex she'd ever had but hey.

I took the number Dad had written down even though I still knew it off by heart. I stood there and wondered what to say. What could I say?

"Does Dawn know?" he asked. It was definitely an accusation this time.

"No, Dad...it was...it was a one-off," and I felt like a complete bastard, which, to be honest, I was. "Don't worry...I'm not going to call her," I said as reassuringly as I could.

"Hmmm..." he said again but seemed satisfied with my reply.

"I'm sorry, Dad."

"Don't apologise to me, son...it's your life."

"Don't tell anyone though, will you? Not Dawn or Peter or Joan or no-one?"

"I won't."

I turned to leave when he spoke again.

"Listen, son...listen," he said, softer, more gently, his anger dissipated, "I don't blame you. Look, life's not a rehearsal and you're a long time dead after all but, for Christ's sake, please, son, please, just be careful!"

After that scare – and I *WAS* scared, believe me – I craved "normal", I wanted normal, I wanted a return to the normalcy before my deceitful but short-lived affair with Carrie. I wanted everything back to what it was and to pretend that nothing had happened. See? All normal! Complete denial! Me? Have an affair? No, you must be joking...not me. I'm a good boy.

I saw Dawn that weekend, prising her away from her studies, and we spent Saturday night in bed where I lavished every kind of attention upon her. It was all fuelled by guilt but it did the trick. As we lay in bed immediately after, Dawn breathlessly said, "Christ, you hit all the right buttons there!"

The rebuilding of my life before the affair continued apace, brick by brick, and with exquisite, almost perfect timing, Terry called to see if I wanted a session round his house. I nearly bit his arm off. He was back from Police Training College, was now out on the beat and was ready for some semblance of 'normal' himself. He picked me up in his new car – a new series gold Rover 3500 – which was a beast.

"Fucking hell, Tel, how can you afford this?" I asked as we sped back to his house in Surbiton.

"Wait until you see what else I got!" he cackled.

In the living room, he'd also bought a brand new Roland Juno-6 – a top of the range synth that would not have been out of place on stage with Gary Numan. He'd hooked up his old synth to some kind of drum machine and the two of them belted out metal rhythms like I'd never heard at our ragged sessions before.

"Bloody hell, Tel…got anything else to show me?" I asked in disbelief. My salary was OK – but this? Blimey.

We had an excellent session that night and Terry introduced snatches of a track that he adored, 'Blue Monday' by New Order. I don't think it had been released as a single yet but he championed it weeks before I heard it on the radio or saw it on Top of the Pops. I did a fairly competent approximation of the bass-line and I really wished that we could do more cover versions rather than the 20-minute, often rambling, self-penned songs that we usually did, such as the epic 'The Swan and The Fox', which was a hybrid of "Christian" by China Crisis and Numan's "Complex".

Afterwards we drove to a pub and had a full catch-up. Police Training College had gone well and he loved being a copper. I asked why he hadn't let me know he was joining the force.

"Dunno really. Didn't seem important..."

"You could have given us a heads-up, I replied, gingerly sipping at a pint of Foster's as he refused to buy me a Coke or a glass of wine.

"Ah, don't fret, Mart. You've been busy with Dawn and stuff so..." he shrugged and left it at that.

We caught up on all the other things that happened, me getting engaged for one and for a moment I was tempted to tell him all about what had happened with Carrie but decided against it.

And with this rebuild of 'normalcy', where was our hero? This odyssey from troubled teen to adult is supposed to be set against a backdrop of Gary Numan songs and the effect that he had on me and he's been sadly missing for the past few chapters. So where was he in the early months of 1983?

Nowhere to be seen.

He arrived back in the UK in April 1983, fresh from his sojourn across America plus time spent off-shore as a tax-exile in Jersey, returning to a hero's welcome from his fans when he landed his plane at Surrey's Blackbushe Airport. He promptly vanished into the studio to start work on his new album. No photographs appeared in the press, no interviews that I recall – nothing.

I had to make do with playing all his old albums but made a few important purchases. One was the original *Tubeway Army* album, which, while sadly not on the original, strictly limited-edition, blue vinyl, was a revelation. Pre-major use of synths, it showcased Numan's song-writing skills – still decidedly Punk in places ('Listen to the Sirens', 'Something's in the House') but also featured, perhaps unexpectedly, more mature, more reflective songs such as the chilling 'The Life Machine' and 'Jo the Waiter', neither of which would have been out of place on Bowie's *Hunky Dory* album. For the first time I got to hear the original album versions of 'The Dream Police' and an acoustic version of 'Everyday I Die', before it was turned into the multi-layered, almost torch song epic at his farewell shows.

I also bought a couple of bootleg records from the record dealer in Kingston Market. This was during a shopping trip out with Dawn, an event that I was so glad had been reintroduced. She had finished studying, had completed all her exams and anxiously awaited the results. I knew she would not be receiving a brown envelope with anything less than a complete set of passes, unlike mine. I still had to take my Sociology O-Level exam but knew it would amount to nothing. I hadn't studied, hadn't revised and had, to say the least, been a bit distracted. But that was then, most definitely, and this was now and Dawn and I were back on track.

We rifled through the singles and I was pleasantly surprised to find two bootleg EPs, volumes 1 & 2 of the John Peel Sessions, featuring tracks that Tubeway Army and the fledgling solo Gary Numan had performed live on the influential DJ's iconic radio show. I was amused that the song tracks were pseudonyms, presumably to avoid being sued, with, for example 'Down in the Park' re-titled 'Over the Way'.

Handing over the two EPs, I asked the dealer whether, on the off chance, he had a copy of 'Down in the Park' on 12-inch, possibly secreted amongst the other rarities he had under his stall. Bagging up my EPs, he let out a long, theatrical yawn, accentuated by patting his hand over his mouth. Unnecessary, I thought.

"No, I don't have it," he said, holding out his other hand, waiting for my hard-earned cash.

"No?"

"Nope…it came and went a couple of years ago and, to be honest, not much interest in him now."

I didn't believe that for a minute and prepared to argue my case for the defence but he'd turned away, pocketing my cash and serving an eager punter who was after the 'Spiral Scratch EP' by the Buzzcocks. That was my last visit to the dealer who, until 2012, was still eking out a living selling second-hand DVDs in Kingston Market.

One Friday night, soon after this shopping trip, I got home from work and discovered that someone had tried to deliver a package. There was a 'while you were out' card on the doormat. I had to pick it up from a warehouse near Norbiton Station. The warehouse was fortunately open until 7.00pm so I persuaded Dad to drive me there when he got home. I presented the card at the reception window and five minutes later, some men in brown overalls brought round a huge package. It was guitar-shaped.

"Sign here," said the woman behind the counter although I could barely take my eyes off the parcel. It weighed a ton with all the packaging but I managed to get it back to Dad's car.

"What you been buying now, son?" Dad asked despairingly.

Dad never really liked the thought of people frittering away their money on non-essentials. Dad's ethic was work and save, work and save, so any suggestion of buying something for, oh I dunno, fun, was frowned upon. But this wasn't anything that I'd ordered and I told him so.

"Nothing, Dad. Honest!" I said although I could barely contain my excitement.

At home, I took a pair of scissors to the wrapping and a small card fell out. I opened it up – the printed message read:

"This is for looking after me for the past few years while I've been studying. I love you! Love, Dawn xxxxxxx"

The rest of the package revealed a brand new guitar. It was a Kay Les Paul Copy with built-in special effects: Phase, tremolo, fuzz, wah and whirlwind. I was astonished, overwhelmed, excited and actually speechless. I ran to the hall and phoned her immediately.

"I thought you'd be pleased," she giggled.

"It's beautiful!" I stammered. "Where did you get it?"

"Oh, I ordered it from Mum's catalogue and I'm paying off a bit each week. Do you like it though?"

"Like it? I LOVE it!"

I went upstairs, plugged it into my now woefully small practice amp and tried out the special effects. It was awesome – the 'fuzz' controls finally made me sound like a proper guitarist. I couldn't wait to take it to the next session and show it off to Terry.

That opportunity came the following week when, for once, it was me showcasing a new musical instrument. Even with my small practice amp, it made me sound pretty good and as I'd been practicing quite a lot, Terry and I were really starting to gel with an instinctive, almost 6th sense between us as to how the songs and melodies should go.

In the pub afterwards, Terry reflected on what had been a very good session.

Supping his pint, he announced, "Do you know what? You should get a flanger."

I didn't have a clue what he was talking about.

"A what?"

"A flanger." He went on, with sagely wisdom. "It's an effects pedal…loads of guitarists have them."

"What's it do?" I asked, completely none the wiser.

"Well, you know the guitar bit in 'Are 'friends' electric?", the bit between verses? There's a distorted guitar…it sounds like a kind of falling note."

I knew it well!

"That's a flanger, that is, and I think you should get one."

"Really?"

"Yeah…they don't cost much."

The following weekend, I went down to Hand's Music Store in Kingston and found to my horror they *did* cost much. Sixty-five quid much! But I wanted to sound better as a guitarist and if it was good enough for Gary Numan, it was good enough for me, so I charged the purchase of my Boss Flanger to the new Barclaycard that I'd got (how I'd rue getting that!) and headed home. Dad was out, so I got my new guitar, amp and leads and set up in the living room and plugged the pedal in. My God, I sounded great! Even with my limited skills, the sound that came from my amp sounded awesome and by adjusting the levels on the pedal, I could emulate the guitar effects on 'Are 'friends' electric?' perfectly, just as Terry had said I would. I was absolutely thrilled.

Dad came home about an hour later, stood in the doorway to the living room and surveyed the scene.

"What you got there, son?" he asked.

"It's a flanger, Dad! Good, isn't it?"

"A what?"

"A flanger? It's an effects pedal for my guitar..."

"That's nice," he said but, just as confused as I'd been the previous week, he had no idea what I was talking about.

"What's it do?"

I demonstrated the pedal by playing the guitar part from 'Are 'friends' electric?'. Dad was clearly unimpressed.

"Hmm," he said, nonplussed as I switched off the amp and unplugged the pedal.

"Hmm," he said again, "how much did it cost?"

I winced.

"Sixty-five quid..." I answered. I sounded guilty but I didn't know why.

"And that's all it does?"

"Well...yeah...pretty much, I suppose."

"And it cost sixty-five quid?"

"Er...yeah."

"Hmm," he said finally before turning tail and heading for the kitchen, clearly aghast at how much I'd spent on such frippery.

I said, "But it's my money, Dad..."

My pathetic protestations were drowned out by the sound of water filling the kettle. I retreated to my bedroom with all my gear, angry that I'd tried to include Dad in something that clearly meant something to me, but had been belittled. As I've said, Dad never meant to be mean but he could be quite thoughtless from time to time. I guess in his mind, £65.00 still represented a fortune which, back in the 1940s and 1950s, could have probably bought a house.

My anger was short-lived and over the coming weeks, as I got to grips with my new guitar and new *Boss* Flanger, my guitar-paying improved and I looked forward to sessions round Terry's house more keenly than ever.

So, as Summer 1983 breezed in bright on the horizon with its white clouds blowing eastwards on a zephyr breeze, with sunshine and blue skies, life was pretty much back to normal and everything looked rosy, right?

Wrong.

CHAPTER 26

I fall...down,
no control somehow

Just as everything was starting to go right, with the whole Carrie saga put firmly behind me, things started to go wrong. Nothing major, no life-changing catastrophes, and no threat of famine, war, pestilence or death... just a slowly encroaching malaise and with it a sequence of events that dismantled my cautiously rebuilt life over the course of the year, brick by brick.

First off, I failed my Sociology Exam – no major surprise there but it meant that in Cliff's eyes it just served to reinforce his opinion that I was an abject failure. And I HAD failed. I'd made a promise to Cliff but also more importantly to Dawn that I would better myself, improve my prospects and get a career. That certainly didn't seem to be an option this year. On the flip side Dawn sailed through each and every one of her exams – again, no surprise – and achieved A and B grades almost with impunity. There was a party to celebrate which was probably one of the last times I went round Dawn's house. As with Christmas, there was fake cheer, false smiles and well-rehearsed family anecdotes with endless photographs taken. Martine tried again to sour the event but was outnumbered by friends, family, aunts and uncles all united in the celebration of Dawn's success. I was really pleased for Dawn who could now take the pick of whatever job she wanted but there was not enough alcohol flowing for Dawn's parents to show even the slightest bit of goodwill towards me.

Even though I had failed the exam, I was still on secondment at work. The whole Falkland Islands exercise had long-since finished and I was eventually seconded to another department, still as acting CSO. There was just the matter of holding the Colonel to his word about the 'automatic promotion' to permanent CSO with the appropriate increase in salary (plus, who knows, maybe a bit of back pay?). Nothing seemed to materialise so I bided my time and waited.

I took two weeks off in late summer of 1983 and spent them with Dawn. We toyed with the idea of going away but she was sending off her CV and applying for jobs – well-paid jobs – so she wanted to be available for interviews if she was called. We mooched about and had days out along with a few trips up to London visiting our old familiar haunts.

When I got back to work, I made my way through my In-Tray and caught up on events over the past fortnight. One document that I read was the regular summary of departmental news and I was stunned by the announcement that the Colonel who had promised me the CSO job had been promoted to Brigadier. Furthermore, he'd already left the division and his successor was already in place.

Fuck.

What about my job?

I stewed over this announcement for a few days before booking a meeting with the new Colonel via his Secretary. I nervously waited outside his office before I was summoned in with a terse, "Come!"

The new Colonel, a bad-tempered, ginger-haired man, had no idea who I was and looked completely baffled when I mentioned the long-promised permanent promotion.

"I'm sorry, I know nothing about this. I'll get my secretary to contact Personnel."

"I don't think it actually went through Personnel..." I said feebly. "It was just a secondment..."

"Well," he harrumphed, "there's nothing I can do then!" he said angrily and the matter was pretty much closed. I left the office utterly dejected. I'd worked my balls off and for what?

Can you hear those bricks crumbling? One by one...

The following weekend, Dawn came round to my house, obviously upset about something. In the sanctity of my room, she burst in to tears. I asked her what was up.

"It's Mum and Dad." she cried, "They don't like you…"

"I know they don't – they never have done!" I replied, confused to say the least.

"No, they *really* don't like you…" she sobbed.

I asked her what had happened.

"Well, the other night, Dad slapped Martine round the face for wanting to go out wearing a dress that revealed everything…"

This wasn't going to end well…

"…and he was in a real bad mood. A bad one. Worst I've seen him, ever. Martine was crying upstairs and I said he shouldn't be so hard on her and he just went for me…"

"Did he hurt you?" I demanded, anger rising.

"No, he didn't touch me but he launched into one and said I was wasting my life with you, that you're immature and lazy and wasn't getting anywhere…"

"And?"

"He just went on and on, shouting in my face. I went to Mum hoping she'd step in as I thought she'd be on my side but she just repeated everything Dad had said," and she cried some more.

I got really angry.

"Well, if they didn't like me when I was trying to be nice, they sure as hell won't like me now!"

"Please don't do anything," she begged.

"Oh, I'm not going to do anything!" I shouted defensively. "In fact, I'm not going to do a *thing*! I'm not going round to your house anymore… I'm not going to speak to them… I'm not going to phone… And, I'm not going to anymore of your bloody oh-so-nice family parties!! Martine should have been drowned at fucking birth, Penny should be taken into care!!! Your Mum's just a mealy-mouthed bitch!! And your Dad is a fucking bully and should be reported to the Police!!! I fucking *hate* your parents and I wouldn't piss on them if they were on fire!!! And you can tell them that from me!!!" I bellowed in one long, seamless tirade.

I hadn't realised just how loudly I could shout as the neighbours started banging on the wall. It seemed I'd inherited Dad's red-mist temper.

Dawn just cried and cried.

I was furious.

Not a lot else was said that night and, looking back, it's difficult to see how we could have hoped to recover from this event. I stood by my word though and never went round to Dawn's house ever again.

By the Autumn, Dawn started to get interviews and it was clearly only a matter of time before she got offered a job. One that really appealed to her was as an Executive Officer working for a government department up near Waterloo Station where, following a successful interview, she was duly invited to join the ranks of the Civil Service, in a senior role that appeared to be forever denied me. I was happy, if begrudgingly, for her but also immensely fucked-off at the same time.

Why was everything a massive struggle for me? Why didn't I get the breaks?

The first anniversary of our engagement passed without any ceremony.

After the best part of a year, and just when I needed him, Gary Numan emerged from the studio and released his new single. One Sunday night in early September 1983, up in my bedroom as I sulked about my lot, I was listening to the Annie Nightingale show on the radio and she announced that she was about to play Numan's new single, 'Warriors'.

I literally leapt from my stupor and turned the radio up, anxious that his last single and album releases had not exactly been classics by any definition of the word. What was this one going to be like? Soulful? A ballad? Something anthemic? Back to his electronic roots? I listened tentatively as the song started – a machine-gun like

drum track, a mournful chiming of synths, a pounding bass. Hard.
Industrial.

Numan had me at the opening line:

"I fall – down.

No control, somehow.

No help – now."

He was talking to me again. Directly to me as the bricks continued
to fall. I sat and listened as the guitar solo punctuated this new,
thudding, menacing song. He sang to me again:

"She's gone.

Gone.

I won't look back.

She's gone."

…and once again, he seemed to be articulating what I was secretly
thinking.

The song faded out with the machine-gun like drums and the hard
but fluid bass and I was gob-smacked. Annie Nightingale added that
the single would be released the following week, followed by an
album of the same name plus, oh, kill me now, a UK tour.

I could scarcely wait to buy the single, snapping it up from the
ever-reliable MJM Records along Tolworth Broadway and flew home
to play it, on 12-inch naturally.

I played it over and over again, mesmerised by the haunted,
disillusioned vocal from Numan. He sang once more of isolation,
betrayal, loss and the fear of becoming the fallen star he'd always
dreaded as evidenced by the lyrics he added to his live performances
of 'Me! I Disconnect From You'. The 12-inch version featured an
extended mix with a long fadeout that showcased the bass and
drums. I loved it!

And the B-side? Oh, my God – 'My Car Slides', Parts 1 and 2.

"And here am I.

Sad and lonely.

And here am I, quite by chance I slide."

I fell in love with the whole package, with a still blonde Numan
having thankfully ditched the Rubettes-like attire from his last single
and instead gone for the Mad Max look, or, as the less-sympathetic
music press referred to it, the "Mad Max Factor" look. I added the
tracks to my almost weekly compiled tapes, by now a literal music
diary, and waited impatiently for the album.

Dawn hit the ground running in the Civil Service and was soon
immersed in her new job, effortlessly fitting in with her new
colleagues and the new challenges of working full-time. Whereas
she had spent virtually the last three years without exception at my
side and going out with me – my partner, my fiancée – she started
to go out for drinks and nights out with her new workmates. And
why shouldn't she have done? She was young and gregarious and I
wasn't exactly a great deal of fun these days. We still saw each other,
still went out, still had a sex life, but even that seemed perfunctory
at best. I tried to think of things to look forward to and couldn't come
up with many.

One by one, the bricks continued to fall until there was virtually
nothing left.

I nabbed the *Warriors* album on the Saturday after its release
and played it from start to finish up in my bedroom, where I again
seemed to be retreating more and more, slowly becoming enveloped
in creeping melancholy. I had my fingers crossed, and hoped against
hope, that it was better than *I, Assassin*…and thankfully it was.

The light, harmonic, soulful, sax-driven 'The Iceman Comes',
the bitterness of 'This Prison Moon', the vivid terror evident in
a tale of a perilous flight in 'My Centurion', the Bowie-influenced
'Sister Surprise' (with a few lines half-inched from Dame Dave), the
plaintive 'Love is like Clock Law' and the jaunty closer, 'The Rhythm
of the Evening'.

Every track was a killer. I loved every single one of them. If I had
been a journalist, the headline of my album review would have read,

"A triumphant return to form". Sax figured throughout the album, as did the percussive slap bass. Numan's previous bass player, the sublimely talented Pino Palladino, even though on Numan's retainer, had jumped ship to join the new soul boy on the block, Paul Young. Pino had suggested a replacement in the form of the man who actually taught him to play bass, one Joe Hubbard.

On Thursday 15th September 1983, HMV in Oxford Street hosted an afternoon signing by Numan of the *Warriors* album. I asked for the day off from work but was refused point-blank as we were in the middle of a huge project. I was told that, under no circumstances was I to be out of the office, even if there was a bereavement, even if I was ill, even if was at Death's door, because we were facing an imminent and immovable deadline where, if we missed it, heads would roll, having been given a bloody good kicking first. If I'd pulled a sickie, I am reasonably sure they would have marched round to my house to drag me into the office! I remember looking at my official Civil Service/MoD leave card with my leave request carefully written out, all crossed out in red Biro and "DENIED" written in capital letters entered in the comments column. This enamoured me to my boss at the MoD - an utterly cheerless, put-upon, ineffectual man - no end. I wondered why I stayed there and decided I needed to look elsewhere for another job. As for the HMV signing itself, although I couldn't get there to meet the man in person, 3,000 of my fellow Numanoids did, bringing the West End traffic to a temporary halt as the queue snaked out of the shop. Damn, what a missed opportunity!

I saw in *Smash Hits* that *The Warriors Tour* would take in the whole of the UK in a massive 40-dates and I sent off a cheque for two tickets at Hammersmith Odeon in October. I didn't hold out much hope as the last time I'd tried to get tickets, for his 'farewell' show at Wembley in 1981, it had completely sold out. But, a week or so later, the envelope arrived and, lo, there enclosed were the tickets, the first time I'd get to see my hero live in concert.

The date was Saturday 15th October 1983 and Dawn, who was

quite looking forward to it, had a hangover from the night before. She'd been out on another office jolly and had started to mention a guy in her office, Mike, with increasing regularity and seemed very fond of him, but "only as a colleague", she insisted. I started to doubt her every word.

We caught the tube over to Hammersmith Odeon and I was astonished, as we queued outside, at the number of people dressed as Numan – from his Punk beginnings, through the blonde *Replicas* period, to the be-suited *Dance*-era image. A few brave souls even managed the full Mad Max semi-bondage look, which Numan was currently sporting. Dawn and I, in our jeans and sweatshirts, looked quite tame and boring in comparison. We had a drink in the packed upstairs bar and I sank a few plastic beakers of lager. Lager and me had become firm friends again of late...very good friends in fact.

I was bewildered by the clothes, outfits and the sheer effort nearly everyone had gone to. There were some people who were absolutely the spitting image of Numan in their black suits, black shirts and blue and red ties, complete with black hair and pale skin.

We made our way downstairs to the stalls and we were about halfway back. My excitement mounted. Not only was this the first time I'd seen Numan live, it was also the first concert I'd ever been to, quite pathetic really as you'd think by the age of 20 I would have been to a few more by now. My mate Dave Okomah probably had a hundred tickets stubs if not more.

The support act – Tik and Tok – were rubbish (all image, no substance), so I waited for the main event. The stalls slowly filled as the anxious audience gradually filed in from the bar. The atmosphere was incredible, the anticipation immense. I wondered how many fans in this audience had seen him before or how many, like me, were seeing him live for the first time. The house lights finally dimmed, the first 10 rows of people bolted for the stage and the curtains opened to reveal the *Warriors* stage set – a bombed out, post-apocalyptic cityscape with the synth players top left and top right in derelict rooms, drums in the middle, bass left and guitarist right...and then, fucking hell, Numan dead centre.

The roar was deafening, the drums pounded right through me and the bass – the bass! – was phenomenal – loud and hard. The light show, pivoting above the stage saw Numan, completely at ease in this, his natural environment, tear straight into 'Sister Surprise'. My heart soared and I screamed my approval at the end of this first number. Numan stalked and prowled around the stage, a seasoned performer, frequently surveying the audience with a penetrating stare, almost daring them to confront him, which was downright chilling. I honestly felt like he could see me in the audience, unlikely given the lavish, blinding light show that he had employed for this truly magnificent tour. I was overjoyed to see 'that weird creature', Ced Sharpley, back on drums, and Chris Payne and Rrussell Bell on synths, live and in person; people I'd only ever seen on TV or on my Numan concert videos. Joe Hubbard did not look like a man to mess with, knees bent, crouched over his fretless bass which he wielded almost like a shotgun and looked like he would have probably ripped your lungs out at the slightest provocation. The final musician in the backing band was John Webb, Numan's younger brother, who played keyboards and sax – I was astounded at how he sounded almost exactly like Dick Morrissey, who'd played sax on the past few Numan albums. Amazing! Surely no backing tapes were used? Surely?

I heard live the songs that had literally changed my life – 'Are 'friends' electric?', 'Cars', 'Down in the Park', 'I Die:You Die' – along with other classic such as 'Metal', a re-arranged 'Remind Me To Smile' and possibly the highlight of the show, 'We Take Mystery (to bed)'. This featured a lengthy bass solo from Joe Hubbard that saw Numan standing aloft and aloof on the derelict building centre stage, nonchalantly drinking a can of Coke, while Hubbard ripped his fingers to shreds up and down the fret board of the bass, no note seemingly being played twice. At the end of the solo, as the rest of the band joined in for the finish, Numan leapt from the top of the building – a good eight feet up – and sang the final chorus without missing a step. The triumphant show closed with a mighty version of 'We Are Glass', and my voice was pretty much shot by the end of the concert, which had seemingly passed in a heartbeat. It was exhilarating.

Much as we'd enjoyed the show, and Dawn really had enjoyed it, the concert was only a much-needed lift in an otherwise downward spiral of despair. We tried to make things work – we still went out, we still did things together, we still were, ostensibly, engaged to be married but I was dismayed that Dawn didn't seem to be contributing any money into our joint-savings account that I'd set up the year before. In fact, when I started having driving lessons and I mentioned that I might spend the money that I had saved on a second-hand car, Dawn hadn't batted an eyelid.

I thought more about Carrie, even though I shouldn't have done, but I couldn't help it. I was tempted to call her but I never did. That didn't stop me from frequently reliving every second of the night in her flat: sitting getting dressed alone in her tiny front room after the deed while she was in the bathroom; looking at the small Christmas that tree she still had on her sideboard, with lights wrapped round it that looked even older the ones we had at Princes Avenue; strangely feeling melancholy by the fact the top of the tree was buckling under the weight of an oversized and seemingly home-made angel; overjoyed when she returned from the bathroom, still naked, and sat on my lap, trying to persuade me to stay for the rest of the night but, racked with guilt, leaving her alone.

Deciding I wanted to see Numan again, I sent off for tickets for his show at the Dominion on Tottenham Court Road. At the time they arrived, I was still planning to go with Dawn but by when Saturday 5th November 1983 came around, the end was in sight. For this concert, we were going to dress the part. Dawn, without any consultation with me, had dyed her hair dark maroon. Not so long ago, this might have involved a discussion with me as to what colour she might dye it but, no, she just went ahead and did it. Not to be outdone, I dyed my hair jet-black, hiding the once snow-white towel in the back of my wardrobe, as, post-dying, it looked like I'd mopped up some sump oil from underneath Dad's car, much as my burr-burr had done years before!

We stayed with her grandparents, who lived in Putney and who just about tolerated me. The night before the show Dawn, sleeping in the single bed in the spare bedroom, left her handbag in the living room where I was sleeping. It's clear to me now that she meant to do this – no woman leaves a handbag lying around, do they? And, rising to the bait, I opened it up when everyone had gone to sleep and found, to my horror and confirming my doubts, several notes from Mike to Dawn about how lovely she was. There was also a credit-card sized card with soppy, sentimental words on it about how much he loved her. I felt like tearing them all up. Instead, I had to put them all back where I had found them, knowing full well that I was about to lose her.

We went to the show and, as planned, we dressed up – Dawn wore a figure-hugging red dress which I'd never seen before (when did she get that, I wondered?) along with a black hat and black high-heels. She certainly didn't look like a student now. I went in a skinny black suit, white shirt with button-down collar and a red tie plus black shoes that glistened in the darkness. The Dominion performance was even better than the show at Hammersmith Odeon. As we had dressed up, we felt like we really belonged to, and were genuinely a part of, Numan's dedicated fan-base, rather than the seemingly casual attendees we had been at the last show. We even managed to get down to the front of the stage where, with my head next to one of the main speakers. I was deafened by Hubbard's 'We Take Mystery' solo and for the next few days thought that a phone was ringing somewhere.

The knowledge that Dawn may well have been having an affair, the fact that I had had a brief affair, the overwhelming feeling of despair, punctuated my surges of bitter, all-consuming jealousy, and the overall feeling that nothing was going my way, all contributed to a bittersweet evening. Listening to the *Warriors* album now brings back some very, very unhappy memories.

We continued this lie, this sham of a relationship through November 1983, with me in a right state, veering as the mood took me between desperation, anger and frustration. Matters were not helped by the fact that things at work weren't going well, either. I was bitter and angry that I had been promised a promotion, and had worked my nuts off and had delivered my side of the deal but the MoD had reneged on theirs. Despite my feeble protestations, I could do nothing to overcome their decision and so, secretly, I applied to British Telecom in Wimbledon for a job. I received a letter from them saying they were interested and would I come for an interview. Came the morning of the interview, Wednesday 7th December 1983, I threw a 'sickie' (the deadlines we had been facing at work back in September had long since passed) and went up to Wimbledon for the interview, which was a breeze. Afterwards, I thought to myself that I would go and meet Dawn for lunch as a surprise.

What a surprise it was going to be.

I made my way up to Waterloo and along to the nearby offices where she worked. I popped into a phone box opposite her building and telephoned her number. One of her colleagues picked up the call and told me that she had just left.

"Good," I thought, "I'll wait until she comes out."

A few minutes later, she duly emerged, arm in arm with the oft-mentioned Mike, all smiles and laughter. I'm not sure who spotted whom first, but the long streak of piss that was with her realised they'd been rumbled and made his very awkward excuses and did a runner, literally running away down the street, looking anxiously behind him in case I was in pursuit. I may have been more of a lover than a fighter but at 6' 2", I presented quite an imposing figure and I really was tempted to go after him and beat the shit out of him. Instead, Dawn ushered us towards a nearby pub. I was shocked and speechless. I cannot remember exactly what we talked about, what we said, what accusations were made, but it was clear that this was just about the end of the line for us. She did say that she was very fond of Mike and liked him a lot and wasn't sure how she felt about me anymore. I was angry that she could do this to me – oh, the hypocrisy(!) – and tears were shed by both of us. An hour of arguing left us both exhausted. Eventually, defeated and impotent, I walked her back to her office and then caught a train home from Waterloo. As I sat in a virtually empty early-afternoon train, I searched through my wallet and found the small photograph of Dawn that I had kept with me for the past three years. It was a small black and white photo-booth picture that Dawn had given me back in 1980 and it showed her back then – young, smiling and exciting. With tears welling in my eyes again, I tore it up into tiny little pieces and threw them out of the window as the train thundered through Vauxhall.

Christmas was coming and I felt wretched – I was on my own for the first time in years and it felt like I was missing a limb. I was reluctant to go into any of 'our' shops, or visit any of 'our' haunts because it would have just crippled me if someone had said, "What? No girlfriend today?" I was morose, numb and heartbroken.

The last time I saw her was just before Christmas on Sunday 19th December 1983 when I met her in The Manor Pub just outside Malden Manor Station. Dawn had called me and asked me to meet her for a drink so that we could talk properly about what had happened. It was another freezing cold night and the pub was virtually empty. Rather than rationally talk about what had happened, I instead lurched into a self-pitying, "I'm so alone", "Come back to me", "I can't live without you" routine that was pathetic to say the least. Pathetic because it clearly showed on Dawn's face, as I pleaded for a second chance, and pathetic because we had no other option but to split up. What prospects did we have? None. It would take me several months to finally come to this realisation but splitting up was the best, indeed the only, thing we could do. Not surprisingly, Dawn was non-committal, saying that she needed "more time" but really – really and truly – she now only wanted me as a friend. That I couldn't be. And so I left the pub, my one-time fiancée, and my partner for the past three years, and went home in freezing fog. I got home, sad, angry and confused. I slumped on my bed and looked out of the window where, even despite the fog, I could still just about see a few lights on in Tolworth Tower, remembering the time when I would watch those same lights back in 1980, excited at the prospect of seeing Dawn at Fine Fare. I put a tape on, and listened to tracks from *Dance* and *Warriors*. When the delicate sounds of 'I Sing Rain' played, I cried and cried and cried.

The next day, I took down all the pictures of Gary Numan from my bedroom walls, all the now sun-faded covers from *Record Mirror* and *Sounds*, along with the few posters that I'd bought from shops down Oxford Street. They just didn't seem necessary any more.

So, I entered 1984, alone, confused, unhappy and churning with bitterness. How could she have done this to me? I was desperately hurt by how it had all ended and how Dawn had dumped me. It was a pretty miserable time spent in my room, headphones on, listening to all the songs that seemed to reflect how I felt – 'Hold Me Now' by The Thompson Twins, 'Never Never' by The Assembly, along with the Dance and Warriors albums by Gary Numan. I sat and wallowed. I envisioned camping outside Dawn's house to show how much I wanted her back, I considered waiting outside her office again for that never-to-be-had second chance – I also visualised pushing her under a train, so confused was I. What was I going to do?

Hitching up with my old mate Terry Easton soon into the New Year, I told him my woes. He was well ensconced in the police force by now and was living a very different life to mine – long hours, unsociable hours – so it took a while before we could meet up. When I poured my heart out to him in The Royal Charter in Surbiton, he couldn't have cared less – the upset it was all causing me was of no interest to him whatsoever. In fact, he mentioned that he had happened to see Dawn shortly after Christmas in The Southampton pub that was then outside Surbiton Station and later demolished in the early 1990s.

"She looked really fat," he said, not realising how much this was further upsetting me.

"Oh?" I said, creased up with mixed feelings.

"Yer," he continued, "she was wearing a stupid hat and was with some miserable-looking fucker." The hat was what she had worn to the last Gary Numan concert. The miserable fucker was, I presumed, Mike.

"Oh?" I said again.

"She looked so stupid, I tried to pull it off her but didn't realise it was pinned-on so I pulled a whole load of 'er hair out." Terry collapsed into fits of laughter.

"Oh," I said.

We eventually decided that the best thing to lift my depression was to get me out and about and, as Terry was by now a master of pubs and clubs, having enjoyed the social life in the police to its fullest, elected to take me out to a club he knew in London, Buzby's, on Charing Cross Road. I was apprehensive about this visit to a club and was as nervous as hell. But with a few drinks inside my thin frame (and whatever happened to that, I wonder now?), after a quick visit to The Bonesgate Pub in Chessington, we sped up to The Smoke in his Rover, the night dark and the lights bright. And thus began a few months of regular clubbing where we would drink ourselves stupid, dance like maniacs, and chat up any woman we could find. And even though I went on these club visits with such great expectations, I never scored once. But, man, I danced the night away and that, for the time being, was enough.

CHAPTER 27

What Numan did next, and the birth of my group, The Rumble Brothers

After the *Warriors* tour, relations with Numan's record label, Beggars Banquet, rapidly deteriorated, compounded by the fact that Beggars, with a sizeable lump sum in the bank (due in no small part to Numan's global success), made it clear that he was no longer the number one artist on their roster. Justifiably hurt by this snub, he effectively told them to fuck off and then set up his own label, Numa Records. His naive but well-intentioned belief that it would be relatively easy to make, distribute and sell not only his own records but also singles by his own roster of recording artists proved to be quite the opposite. Not one of their singles or albums made the slightest dent in the charts while his own releases suffered from poor distribution and lack of promotion. They also suffered, sadly, due to lack of interest. Numan's superstar status was clearly on the wane, never to really recover. The idea in itself was a good one, but, ultimately, a poor one.

My own poor decisions included jumping ship from the MoD when, perhaps, I should have stayed put and stuck it out and waited for the next opportunity. My mindset at the time was that after the whole issue of the long-promised promotion, I didn't really have a future at the MoD and after the less-than memorable day of the interview I'd finally got a job offer from BT where I started in March 1984. I took a pay cut and a demotion but felt I had no other choice but to leave the MoD where I firmly believed, with some justification, that I had been badly betrayed and let down. Ensuring I had a holdall full of nicked stationery on my last day, I headed to the giddy world of the newly privatised British Telecom plc.

I got into some dicey relationships with other girls, some of whom I thought would be 'The One' but they all turned out to be bitter, miserable failures. I was a serial monogamist and got engaged a few times more but they just didn't work out. I spent a lot of the late 1980s and early 1990s more often than not on my own, except for one memorable summer where I was engaged again, this time to a girl called Debbie. She was tall, blonde and quite lovely but for reasons unknown other than sheer lust and bedevilment, I also started seeing, on the sly, Laura, a divorcee at work. It was kind of a Dawn/Carrie scenario all over again as Debbie was younger than me while Laura was 38. Laura seemed so demure in the office but in the bedroom she was something else (and, come to think of it, in the living room, and the kitchen, and on the stairs, and in her car). She taught me a lot, I have to say. I lost over a stone in the process trying to keep them both happy, both blissfully unaware of each other. And, yes, they both dumped me when they found out what had been happening.

But throughout this time, I steadfastly refused to abandon Gary Numan, becoming even more of a devotee. Each year from 1984 to 1997 I went to every Numan concert at least once, usually with my friend Andrew Burton or my cousin Tim when Numan played the Guildford Civic Hall. I bought every single and album Numan released, often buying them in multiple formats. Whilst his superstar status may have faded, he released some excellent songs during that time, with some I personally considered to be latter day classics, such as 'Your Fascination' (1985), 'This Is Love' (1986), 'I Can't Stop' (1986), 'New Thing From London Town' (1986), and 'The Skin Game' (1992). I loved the *Berserker, The Fury, Outland* and *Metal Rhythm* albums, and finally joined the Gary Numan Fan Club (Fan Club Membership Number: 12160!), buying all the back numbers of the Fan Club newsletters, all bar the long-out of print issues 1, 2 & 3 (if anyone has these for sale, let me know!), faithfully renewing my membership each year until the club folded a few years ago. It was never easy being a Gary Numan fan in the 1980s and 1990s, with each of my purchases generally ridiculed by my friends and peers. I remember one lunchtime back in 1984, when I was working for BT in Kingston, returning to work clutching an Our Price Records carrier-bag which contained my latest obligatory purchase, Gary Numan's latest single, 'Berserker' on 12-inch. On the cover sleeve, Numan sported his new 'ice-man' image – thick white make-up and blue hair and blue lipstick. One of the girls in the office demanded to see it and paraded the single around for everyone to see.

"Is that Gary Numan?" she mocked.

"Yes, that's him…it's his new single."

"What's he wearing?" asked one colleague.

"And why is he blue?" asked another.

"It's his new 'ice-man' image," I replied, snatching the single back and securing it back in the carrier-bag.

"He looks like a bloody clown!" said another colleague as they all returned, laughing, to their desks. It wasn't a good look, I had to agree.

Of those friends and peers, I gradually lost touch with Terry Easton around 1988. His work in the police force meant that he socialised within the clique of his colleagues and, to be honest, we had less and less in common. He and I did finally get to see Numan live on the 1984 *Berserker Tour*, featuring Numan's 'Ice Man' image which consisted of white make-up and blue hair as featured on the 'Berserker' single and album – I thought he looked ridiculous. Sadly, bassist Joe Hubbard didn't sign up for the tour and was replaced by Andy Coughlan who, while competent, was no match for the menacing Hubbard. Coughlan's bass solo on 'We Take Mystery' was adequate at best. As far as our own musical leanings went, I didn't get that much out of sessioning anymore. The rambling self-penned epics that we produced were all well and good but just didn't do it for me. Our band, named The Tall Boys, then Serious Drinking, then finally Tone It Down, had expanded to include a couple of Terry's mates from the police on synths and guitar which was great but it just wasn't what I wanted to do. When your hobbies become more like hard work, it's time to stop. Terry played a significant part in my life though and that's not something I'll forget.

Also in 1988, Dad finally retired, much to Peter's relief and mine. He was offered the opportunity to take early retirement and he jumped at the chance, facing the humiliation of a policewoman stripogram on his last day. I found his goodbye card years later, signed by all his colleagues and there were hundreds of signatures in the card and on dozens of sheets of A4 paper stuck inside, all wishing him well. He asked us what he should do with his spare time as he was contemplating taking up lawn green bowling but, fearing that that would *really* turn him into an old man, we persuaded him to take up golf instead, which he did with great enthusiasm, if not much ability. Dad became the centre of the family, content with his lot, enjoying a well-earned retirement, his red-mist tempers a dim, long distant memory and he was very, very happy.

We would sometimes playfully chide him about his infamous red-mist temper and he'd cackle along with us, questioning whether he really was as bad as we made out.

"Sometimes, Dad!" we'd chorus. But now he was fully content with his lot; a lifetime of hard graft behind him, surrounded by family and friends that loved him unreservedly.

And let's take a minute here to catch up with my brother, Peter. He's been vilified in the early chapters of this book but, as we got older, our relationship blossomed. After he married Susan in 1982, he'd set up home, studied hard and eventually got a job in The City, successfully working his way up the corporate ladder, getting better paid and more responsible jobs in the process. His first son, James, was born in 1986 and their second, Eliot, in 1991, both fine lads. By the mid-1990s, Peter was earning a sizeable wage in the banking industry, earning a salary that increasingly looked like a telephone number. My salary, even today, looks like a short SMS number you text from your mobile to enter a competition. But even though his success was the mirror opposite of my career shortcomings, he stood by me and has done so ever since, especially with what happened a few years later.

During my ten years at BT, I gradually worked my way back up the management ladder as I journeyed through the more routine, mundane departments of customer service and billing complaints. Given that we both worked for the same company, I only encountered Dawn's Dad Cliff Sullivan once, quite by chance at the BT sector-switching centre where I worked in Birkenhead Avenue, Kingston. I was dressed in my suit for a meeting and was in the bog having a slash when Cliff ambled in. He looked old, fat and dishevelled in an ill-fitting suit and he couldn't have been far off retirement.

We cautiously eyed each other up and as I rinsed my hands in the sink, I said, "Hello, Cliff."

With what appeared to be a Herculean effort, he finally, begrudgingly, managed to say, "Hello, Martin."

As ever, even after all these years, there was no effort to carry on the conversation, although I was tempted to ask, "How's the family, then? All dead I hope?"

A few years later, in 1986, I transferred to the brave *new* world of Prestel, BT's videotex service, a kind of forerunner of the internet, with text and images transmitted to suitably-equipped PCs, with the data resembling TV teletext services but downloaded via a modem. The office was based in Temple Avenue, within spitting distance of Fleet Street which was in its death throes as the centre of the British newspaper industry, with the last few remaining dailies about to uproot and move to modern offices in various anonymous steel and glass business centres elsewhere. I loved working in the old, and probably haunted, Victorian building Prestel was then headquartered in, dodging the picket lines at lunchtime outside the old Sun newspaper offices after Murdoch had led the mass exodus from Fleet Street by controversially moving his entire operation to Wapping, smashing the grip of the unions in the process.

Seeing Numan on the *Exhibition Tour* in 1987, I nearly wept with delight when, in the back of the tour book, it was announced that Beggars Banquet were finally releasing on CD a 'Best of Gary Numan'. I waited for weeks because the release date kept getting pushed back – and ended up ringing the Beggars Banquet office at least once a week for updates until, one memorable lunchtime, I found it in the CD racks in WHSmiths up at Holborn. The shop was opposite the then towering symbol of opulence, The Daily Mirror Building, housing the Machiavellian schemes of Murdoch's arch-nemesis, the boot-black haired, pension-raiding, fat fuck, Robert Maxwell.

That evening, I sat before my new CD player – part of a Marantz music system that I'd treated myself to – and tentatively placed the shiny discs in the tray and sat back to listen to, for the first time, Numan's songs without the buzz, hiss and crackle of *every single* vinyl copy that I had, and without the wow and flutter of the various cassette tapes that I owned (blimey, couldn't Beggars do *anything* right?). The first track that blasted through my headphones was the live version of 'Me! I Disconnect from You' which I played two or three times in succession; the powerhouse drumming from Ced Sharpley absolutely driving the whole song. There followed a trip through Numan's singles and selected album tracks across two discs. To hear the songs clear and note perfect, without any blemish or distortion, was incredible, enabling me to hear for the first time little nuances and song elements that I hadn't been able to appreciate before. To listen to the fadeout of 'We Are Glass' without any crackle or hiss was amazing; to hear the untarnished clinical essence of 'I

Die:You Die' was memorable, with the strange muttering over the
closing notes only now audible to me; to revisit the song that started
it all, 'Are 'friends' electric?', with the bass, drums and synths much
higher in the mix, was (no pun intended) electrifying.

Working in London was handy as you were 20 minutes from
anywhere. If someone said, "I'll meet you for a beer at Bank", you
were there in 20 minutes; if someone said, "I'll meet you for a beer at
Tottenham Court Road", you were there in 20 minutes. It was great!
I also loved the walk from Waterloo each morning to the office,
especially in the autumn when, crossing Blackfriars Bridge, the City
in the cool of the early-morning sunshine glowed gold. At lunchtime,
I'd do huge circuits of Fleet Street and the environs, once chancing
upon an old-fashioned record shop in Chancery Lane, which, losing
its passing trade, was closing down. In the window, amongst dozens
and dozens of sale items and classical music box sets, I espied,
somewhat incongruously, CDs of the first of Numan's own releases
on the Numa label, *Berserker* and *The Fury*. I nabbed them for a fiver
each and added them to my collection where, for a few years, as
limited first edition copies, they were quite rare collectors' items.

Looking through my Numan collection today, I'm horrified to find
that I have *The Fury* in no less than six incarnations: the original vinyl
LP, the original LP picture disc, the "Extented (sic) Mixes" cassette,
the original Numa release on CD, the Eagle Records re-release on
CD with extra tracks, plus a later Numa CD re-release featuring the
extended mixes. It featured some great tracks ('The Pleasure Skin'
for one) but it's just a shame that the cover featured Numan in a
white lounge suit with a red dickie-bow – he couldn't have looked
less furious if he'd tried. Another poor decision.

Working in The City (or near enough) I was able to make regular
visits to what was to become my spiritual home, The Old Bell pub
by St. Bride's church. So it naturally broke my heart when a few
years later, the powers-that-be decided to move the business from

London to the suburbs of Hemel Hempstead and the utterly soulless town of Apsley, which had a garage and a pub and bugger-all else. A huge media centre had been built and the powers-that-be, who all conveniently lived near Apsley and could probably walk to work in less than five minutes, decided that this was to be our new HQ. Which meant for me to get to work, I either had to drive 10 junctions round the M25 for a near 100-mile round trip there and back, or rely on public transport where I had to get a bus and a train and a tube and a train to get to the new offices.

But it wasn't all bad. At the new Prestel offices, named Network House, I met three people who became almost like brothers to me.

Eric Watson: A huge, bearded, real-ale swigging, bear of a man from Sunderland. Eric was a joy to work with and, during the course of various lunchtime conversations in the pub, he said that he played bass and suggested that we should have a jam round his gaff one day.

Ben Nicholas: A force of nature, someone I should *not* have got on with as he pretty much got the job I was coveting. But how can you dislike a man who was loud, irreverent, manic, loud, possibly insane, as lecherous as me, clumsy and loud (did I mention loud?)

Gary Smith: A member of one Prestel's clients who were going to share the same building. He liked comics, had a self-made *Watchmen* smiley face screensaver on his PC and liked The Beatles too so it was pretty much guaranteed that we'd get on.

From 1989 to 1992, I worked in Apsley, and was delighted when, true to his word, Eric invited me round for a session at his house. It was Wednesday 24th April 1991, the morning after a massive pub-crawl in St Albans and I'd kipped in his spare room. Nursing killer hangovers, and after his wife, Ros, had gone to work, we got all our kit out – my Yamaha SG guitar and new amp, while Eric fetched his Fender Jazz bass and rolled in his huge 4x12 fuck off bass amp – "I'll keep it turned down a bit, Mart," he said reassuringly, realising that it towered over my amp. He played left-handed so, sat on the floor, mirroring each other and, consuming tea, biscuits and Paracetamol, went through some 12-bar numbers. We then reached for our respective songbooks – I'd bought my *Beatles Complete* along with *Gary Numan: The Official Songbook Volume 1*. Eric demurred on Numan but we went through some Beatles tracks followed by songs from Eric's Free and Bowie songbooks. It was great fun! THIS was what I'd wanted to do all along. It was all very well sessioning with Terry back in the day but this? Proper songs, with words, middle-eights, guitar solos and meaning: this was what I wanted to do.

We had another session round his house on Friday 31st May 1991, again nursing killer hangovers and do you know what? We weren't bad. Word got round at work that we were sessioning and Tony Sweet, the boss of our section, announced that he played drums and that we could have a rehearsal round his house if we liked. I also suggested to Gary Smith that he come along as I knew he had a good singing voice. I'd heard it after a weeklong residential BT Practical Management course in Brighton which he and I had attended, where we had spent the week upsetting the course tutor, rolling our eyes in disbelief at some of the 'new age' techniques of modern management, ogling the doe-eyed vision that was June Biggs during the day and getting spectacularly drunk in the bar each night. Gary drove me home from Brighton at the end of the week, along with Anna, another Prestel colleague who had also been on the course. Anna was an enigma to say the least. She was 43 (looked 33), lived in a squat in Lambeth Walk, had a Punk Mohawk hairstyle, adored angry Punk songs (and angry Punk sex probably), had numerous piercings and was a habitual drug-taker. Slumped in the backseat, as we left the sunny environs of Brighton, she said, "You don't mind if I smoke, do you?" and when Gary said he didn't, she proceeded to light a joint roughly the size of my leg. As the potent fumes billowed round the car, even with the windows open, Gary and I got a bit mellow to say the least. I had The Beatles' *Sgt. Pepper's Lonely Hearts Club Band* cassette with me, which we played several times. Gary and I sang along to every track, note perfect from start to finish, with me taking the Lennon vocals and Gary effortlessly taking McCartney's. I'm still surprised we made it home in one piece.

The first session that we had round Tony's was Friday 21st June 1991, when Gary was coaxed into singing Cream's 'Sunshine of Your Love'. After he'd finished, when he asked, "How was that?" I said it was fantastic!

I really enjoyed singing with Gary. Our voices matched each other perfectly and I loved harmonising with him. We even started gigging and played our debut on Saturday 6th July 1991 at Tony's wife Barbara's birthday party. We were ragged but I think we surprised a few people.

Soon after, the line-up expanded to include another colleague, Steve Hughes, on guitar. My God, we were a band! Eric christened us The Rumble Brothers for reasons I sadly no longer recall. I couldn't get them to play any Numan songs though, despite my best efforts, with Eric always vetoing the suggestion: "We are *NOT* fookin' playin' any Gary fookin' *NOOMAN!!*" he would often opine in his soft, gentle, lilting, sing-song Sunderland accent.

From that point on though, nearly every Thursday night after work, we'd have a session round at Tony's house. Gary and I sat side by side singing into the one microphone that we possessed, Eric standing by his big fuck-off bass amp, occasionally hitting it when the valves started overheating, Tony in the corner of the living room on drums, and Steve Hughes on guitar. I played guitar, too, but not to Steve's standard. It was fun and there would be times when everything just clicked and we sounded like we knew what we were doing. Our set mostly consisted of Beatles, Free and Stones numbers, plus a bit of Cream and Bowie, and I still have boxes of tapes from those sessions which I keep planning to convert to mp3 files. Each evening would finish off with a huge pizza, a few beers, a brief discussion about what songs to practice for the following week, then a long drive home round the M25.

But then another guitarist joined, Liam, who was one of Eric's mates from Sunderland. He was a very good guitarist but a total perfectionist so insisted we got it right, each and every time. As we were a strictly amateur band, his controlling nature could *really* grate. The slightest error, fluffed vocals, or messed up guitar chord and he'd stop the rehearsal and make us start again. His intent was no doubt to make us a better band but, blimey, he could get on your nerves. More often than not, he'd bring along his girlfriend, Katherine, to each session in Tony's back room and she'd sit and watch us rehearse, occasionally joining in on backing vocals.

It was not long before Liam effectively took over the band which, even with the best intentions, didn't sit that well with the rest of us, and kind of took the enjoyment out of the sessions. Whereas once there was much laughter as we tackled new songs, we all started to argue, Gary and me in particular.

Liam felt, quite rightly, that Tony's backroom was becoming just a bit constricting so, with Tony, conspired to find an alternative location, just to see how we fared in a bigger environment. Early in October 1991, a rehearsal was arranged for a weekend. Instead of Tony's back room, we had booked the Gossoms End Scout Hut in Berkhamsted. It also transpired that we were going to play a Christmas gig there, scheduled for the 7th December 1991. It was clear that we needed all the practice we could get so I dragged my carcass out of bed to drive up there for midday. Arriving at the venue, I saw that Eric, Gary and Liam were already there. Also there, I was delighted to note, was Katherine.

We set up the instruments and equipment and powered up the new PA system we'd all invested in. Steve Hughes couldn't make it so it was just the four of us – and Katherine. We were soon joined by Patrick Reilley, a colleague from work who had appointed himself as our official band photographer, who took various snaps during the course of the afternoon. We went through our repertoire, such that it was, a few times and I had to admit Liam was a pretty good guitarist, if somewhat loud. But after a few good-natured songs, his perfectionism manifested itself again and with the slightest glitch in any song, he'd make us start over again. And again. And Again. We were only amateurs for Christ's sake. So, after a couple of hours, Gary and I got fed-up, left Eric and Liam to it and played football in the other half of the hall with one of Tony's sons, Tom. After about four hours we'd all had enough and packed up the gear in the cars with the next session arranged for the following week.

We reconvened at Tony's house as arranged, which was the first time that we all played together – me, Eric, Tony, Gary, Steve and Liam – in the short-lived line-up of The Rumble Brothers Mark II. Katherine was there too and I wondered what she was doing with Liam as they seemed so mismatched. What I didn't know, what I had absolutely no clue whatsoever about, was that, after only a few rehearsals, she had completely fallen in love with me.

The next session was on October 30th and again we assembled at Tony's house and again Liam demonstrated what an excellent guitar player he was and what a pig-headed swine he was too. After countless takes of Lennon's 'Jealous Guy' he kept picking the tiniest fault in whatever we were doing, be it the drums, my singing, Steve's guitar, Eric's bass, Gary's vocals – basically anything but what he was playing (Hey! He was good but not that good!). He complained more and more and I'm afraid that the red-mist started to come down. Reaching a critical point, I closed my music book shut with a loud crack and slammed it on the floor.

"Do you know any instrumentals?!" I snapped at him. He nodded wordlessly.

"Then fucking well do them, then!!" I shouted and stormed out into the kitchen, shaking with fury. I was more than a little surprised, not to say shocked, when I found Katherine in tow.

"You mustn't worry," she said gently in her sweet Geordie accent, "he's like this with everyone."

She calmed me down and I eventually rejoined the rehearsal. At this point she was sending out all the right signals but I was still just too stupid to see them.

I don't know how I survived the next few weeks intact. The first big upset came on the 1st of November. Liam had suggested that we practice round his house in Watford where he lived with Katherine. Tony brought along a couple of drums, I brought my guitar and amp, Eric brought his bass and amp and Gary brought untold misery. As we sat there in Liam and Katherine's front room, we chatted about the progress we'd been making. Gary, meanwhile, was slumped in the corner, unspeaking, unsmiling, not getting involved and clearly sulking about something. The practice broke off while Liam went to fetch Katherine from work. While he was gone we tried a few other numbers. I suggested one to Gary who snapped, "No! I can't sing it! It's too high!" We tried it without him but he was clearly not happy. But all I was doing was trying to include him in what we were doing in case he thought he was being left out, as he didn't play an instrument. I suggested another one, 'Back in the USSR'.

"You know you do that one, not me!" he shouted.

Not wishing to get involved in another argument I merely sighed and tried to carry on but this was the final straw for Gary. Whatever he had been seething about he now finally erupted. Out came an angry tirade against me, and a full-blown row ensued where we had to be virtually hauled off each other by Tony as it looked like we might do serious damage to each other. Tony 'escorted' Gary out of the house and took him back to the office to pick up his car.

In the aftermath it was unbelievably quiet. I looked at Eric. He sat there, his eyes wide behind the heavy magnification of his glasses and looked stunned.

"What the fook 'appened there?" he asked, unable to quite believe what had just occurred.

I didn't know then and I'm not entirely sure now. Was there something I'd unwittingly said or done to Gary that massively pissed him off? I know at the time I was angry and ultimately I was very sad because I really enjoyed singing with him. But for the time being, as far as I was concerned, Gary was out of the band and the days where we would sit and rehearse songs on our own, or sit in my car in the downstairs car park at work listening enthralled to the band tapes from the previous session, or indeed the entire camaraderie we once shared, were over. Even though Gary rejoined the band again in the New Year, this evening marked, at the time, the end of our friendship. Mostly down to my pig-headedness, it was a friendship that would take years to fully recover.

We carried on rehearsing for the Christmas gig without Gary. The gig loomed large but now none of us really seemed that enthused about it. And all the while, Katherine continued to drop hints about how she felt about me. I was still oblivious to the signals she was sending out. A lack of perception I suppose... one of my failings.

Example: After I'd broken up with Dawn back in 1983, I had ventured down to Kingston one Saturday in spring 1984 to buy some new clothes from Top Man as I was going out clubbing with Terry that night. I shopped for a suit as my black one was starting to get just a little bit tight. My increasingly regular visits down the pub were starting to take their toll, and I now resembled less Tony Hadley and more Tony Hancock. As I wandered round the store I was vaguely aware that the girl behind the counter was closely watching me, and was smiling as well, as opposed to shouting out, "There he is, officer!! Get him!!" I tried not to stare but she was stunning. I took the suit to the counter to pay for it.

"You're Martin, aren't you?" she said, with just a gorgeous smile.

"I am," I replied, somewhat taken aback.

"You don't remember me, do you?"

I had to confess I didn't.

"I used to go to school with Dawn," and it finally clicked. She had been in Fine Fare several times with her.

"How are you? Are you still with Dawn?" she asked as she bagged up my suit. I gave her a brief summary of the events of late 1983 and she looked sad.

"Oh, I'm so sorry," she said and brushed my hand sympathetically. "I thought you two were going to be together forever?"

"So did I," I said, even after all these months.

She changed the subject.

"Nice suit! Is it for a special occasion?"

"Yeah, I'm going out tonight. Going up town to a club."

"Which one?" she asked eagerly.

"Buzby's? Charing Cross Road? I'm going up with a mate of mine."

"Ooo, I've never been there! Is it any good?" she trilled enthusiastically.

"Yeah, well, we like it. Music's pretty good."

"Sounds great!"

She paused.

"I wish I was going…I've got nothing to do tonight," she said coyly.

"Haven't you?" I asked.

"No, I finish at 5.30 though…"

I paused.

She looked at me expectantly.

"Oh, well…see you around then," I said cheerfully and headed off with my new suit, leaving her standing open-mouthed behind the counter.

When I told Terry that night, he punched me so hard on the arm it left a bruise.

It seemed I was as still as slow on the uptake as ever. Despite some huge clues and massive hints that Katherine not only liked me but was falling in love with me, I missed them all until a few weeks later when she made it absolutely clear what was going on and that she wanted to be with me, not Liam. Pat had scheduled another of his famous Pizza Parties for Friday 15th November at his tiny cottage in Berkhamstead for all his work colleagues. They were renowned and eagerly anticipated as pizza played only a small part. Inevitably, all those attending would get drunk as monkeys on the copious amounts of beer and gin. The band was invited as well, but Liam thought he had to work a night-shift.

"Katherine can still go, I don't mind," he said.

At work the following day, I checked with Pat to see if it was still OK for me to crash at his house after the Pizza Party. The answer was a resounding "No!" He now had a couple of old college friends coming and they needed to be put up too. Damn! Where was I going to sleep? I couldn't even stay sober and drive home because my car, at that minute, was sitting outside my Dad's house in a pool of oil. Eric wasn't going so I couldn't crash at his place – I could probably get back to London but wasn't prepared to pay my monthly salary to a licensed bandit in a taxi to take me all the way south of the river to Tolworth. I decided that I'd probably have to leave the party early and catch a train home but it wasn't something I really wanted to do.

That evening I tarted myself up as best I could and joined my colleagues in the trek up to Pat's Pizza Party VI. As usual, the attendees separated into two groups – one upstairs at Pat's tiny cottage, the others downstairs. I went upstairs with Ben and a few others and settled down for the evening. Pizza was ordered, video films played, beer cans popped open and the merriment began. Ben, as ever the life and soul of any party was reducing one of the young girls who worked in the canteen to fits of giggles as they played, quite boisterously, on Pat's bed. I sat bemused by the whole thing as I genuinely thought the girl from the canteen was going to wet herself, she was laughing so much.

About an hour later, I heard the door open downstairs as a latecomer arrived. I nearly choked on my pizza when Katherine climbed the stairs – I DID choke on my pizza , when I saw what she was wearing – short black skirt, the sheerest of tights, black high-heels, a light black crocheted jacket and subtle make-up. She sat down opposite me, produced a bottle of wine and smiled. I looked at Ben. All shenanigans on the bed paused momentarily as he mouthed, with eyes as big as saucers, "Who's that?!"

"Katherine," I silently mouthed back and realised I'd been caught out as she had been watching my every move.

After a little while, I leaned across to pluck another beer from the eight-looped pack and remarked how pleased I was to see her. She said she'd gotten directions from Pat and had been picked up at Berkhamstead Station by a friend of Pat's called Sean. He must have thought he was on a bit of a 'cert' but had been firmly put in his place when Katherine had discarded him at the front door. She also said that Liam was definitely working that night so wouldn't be coming.

"Oh," I said and carried on drinking.

The evening's fun and frolic continued with Ben hooting and howling in the background, the film long since forgotten by everyone.

At about 10.00pm I said, somewhat reluctantly, that I'd have to be going.

Katherine was visibly upset by this. She thought for a moment and then announced, "We've got a spare bed - you can sleep on that?"

I felt awkward about this, but before I could protest, she had disappeared downstairs to phone Liam to see if it was OK. She reappeared a few minutes later – he had said yes. The poor, blind fool.

The evening started to wind down with all the videos watched, all the pizza eaten, all the beer drunk. Most of the other guests had gone leaving me and Katherine on the bed upstairs. We sat side by side in the semi-darkness. I pleaded with Pat to put on Sting's latest album, the magnificent *The Soul Cages*. Pat duly obliged – Katherine sat up with a start.

"I've got this," she exclaimed. "I don't have many CD's but I bought this one a couple of weeks ago!"

We sat and listened, unsure as to what was going to happen next.

The album finished and the silence was broken by Pat ascending the stairs.

"Come on you two – bugger off!!" he said in mock anger. "I've got to get some sleep!"

Katherine ordered a taxi, which arrived about ten minutes later. As Friday night slipped into Saturday morning, we said goodbye to Pat, climbed into the taxi and sped off in the dark back towards Watford.

Once we'd arrived at her house, she escorted me into the living room and disappeared into the kitchen to make coffee. I put her copy of *The Soul Cages* on and sat back and surveyed the room – there were pictures and keepsakes of Liam and Katherine together that screamed at me, "We're a couple and YOU'RE an intruder!!" And I was an intruder. What was I doing here? What was I possibly thinking?

Before I knew it, however, Katherine had returned with the coffee. We sat and chatted idly, the album playing softly in the background. I can't remember what we talked about – I know for certain that Liam did not crop up at all.

And then the inevitable happened – at what point I don't know. Everyone else just didn't matter. No words were spoken, no doubts voiced or guilt expressed…

The following morning, I awoke alone in the spare bed and my memories of the previous night came flooding back. After we'd gone too far and done too much, Katherine and I had sat a while, drinking the remainder of the wine we had somehow, somewhere opened. We tidied up as best we could, then I had retired to the spare bedroom and crashed out. A short while later, Liam must have returned home from work, but by that time I was oblivious.

I sheepishly got out of bed and went to the bathroom. Every sound I made – running taps, splashing water, cleaning teeth – seemed to echo noisily around as if to magnify my guilt. I felt awful. I felt nauseous too, but it wasn't from the drink of the previous evening.

I quietly dressed and went downstairs to the kitchen, every step creaking on the way down, wondering what on earth Katherine was going to say. I wouldn't have long to find out. As I sat in the living room drinking a cup of tea, she came down dressed and looking quite radiant. I had been expecting her to emerge, dishevelled with a hangover saying, "I don't remember what happened?" But no – here she was, all smiles. I followed her out into the kitchen.

"Did you enjoy last night?" she asked brightly. My words – a clumsy combination of agreement, guilt and haplessness – tumbled out.

"I did enjoy last night and I'm so pleased you remembered and no I didn't hear Liam come home and you look lovely Katherine and, oh fuck, what are we going to do?"

"Don't worry," she said stroking my cheek, "it'll be alright, I promise."

We sat and had breakfast and decided we were going to spend the day in London. She left a note for Liam saying she'd be back later and then we made our way to Watford Station and caught a train down to The Smoke. As the carriage was pretty full, we stood and talked. I still couldn't believe what had happened and told her so. We recapped the events of the past month and I was lost for words when she told me how she had fallen in love with me the moment she had met me. She admitted that she and Liam had been living a lie for months but she didn't have an alternative. Although they were officially a couple, recently they had become almost flat-mates.

The next few hours we spent walking and talking around the sights of London. We went to St. Paul's Cathedral and wandered round, hand in hand, in silent awe of the hallowed and magnificent building. I still could not believe what was happening and how unexpected it had been. By early evening we were hungry so we went to a restaurant called McArthur's (long since gone) next door to The Crown Pub on New Oxford Street. It was here that we decided what we were going to do next. She and I were going to carry on as normal, as if nothing had happened (oh, but it had, it *had*!). Katherine was then going to gradually let Liam know that she was leaving him. We agreed that it was going to be difficult but we toasted our future together.

Our first day together came to an end and I reluctantly saw her off on her train at Euston. We agreed that we'd speak to each other in the next few days. However, it was going to be far sooner than that. Having returned home on Clouds 9 through to 15, I got a call at quarter past midnight. It was Katherine. She had already told Liam she was leaving him. I nearly fell through the floor. It wasn't that she felt she had to tell him, it was because she didn't want to hurt me. He'd come in from work, had sensed something was wrong and they'd had a major heart-to-heart complete with tears, anger and frustration. No mention of me was made, just that she didn't want to live with him anymore. Resigned to the situation and upset beyond consolation, Liam packed his bag and headed home that night to the north-east of England to County Durham to get away for a couple of days.

Eric got a call at work on Monday from Liam. He told Eric what had happened and that he needed to get away from everything for a few days. However, he said he'd still be at the rehearsal planned for Thursday 21st November. As he hung up, Eric looked across the office to my desk and said, "What have you been up to, Mart?" I denied any involvement and claimed to know nothing about it although it didn't come easy to lie to Eric, one of my best and most trusted friends after all.

The sessions over the next few weeks were excruciating. Liam was clearly upset by the whole situation but still had no idea that I'd done the deed with Katherine and that she was now living in a flat in Tolworth, just down the road from me. As for the music itself, I was really struggling to handle all the vocals without Gary but we were committed so that was that.

On the day of the Christmas gig I went round to Katherine's new flat so that we could pop into Kingston to buy me some new clothes for the gig. I was as nervous as hell and a little snappy to say the least. But Katherine took it all in her stride, tolerating my little foibles, fully aware of what I was going through. As we shopped around town, we both agreed that it would be best if Katherine didn't attend that night, even though I desperately wanted her to be at the gig.

I dropped her back at the flat and went home to collect all my gear and prepare myself for the trauma that was to come. A little over an hour later, Katherine rang – she had decided that she couldn't bear to let me go through the evening alone and wanted to be with me. Already running late, I drove round to the flat, picked her up, and headed for the motorway and the journey up to Berkhamsted.

We concocted a plan together as I went over lyrics in my head. We figured that, as we were now so late, everyone else would already be at the scout hut. So we'd pull up outside, Katherine would sneak into the kitchen, I'd meet up with the band, Katherine would appear later claiming she came up by herself and no-one would be any the wiser.

Right?

Wrong.

I could not believe how unlucky we were.

As we pulled into the road outside the scout hut, the exact moment, the very *second* that we arrived, a car pulled up behind us – it was the rest of the band: Eric, Steve and Liam. I was later to learn from Eric that the conversation in the car went something like this:

Eric: Oh look. There's Mart.

Steve: (Desperately practicing 'Space Oddity" on guitar in the back seat) Yeah – and he's got someone with him.

Eric: (Squinting) It looks like a girl.

Liam: It is...it's Katherine?

Steve: I wonder what she's doing with him?

Liam: (Suspiciously) Yeah...I wonder?

Eric: (Under his breath, realising what's going on) Oh, Fook!

I was speechless as I got out of the car. Katherine ran straight inside without saying a word. We all started unpacking the cars and hauling the gear into the scout hut. I was very aware that Liam was glaring angrily at me. He caught me a little bit later on in the hall as we were setting up for the rehearsal.

"I thought Katherine wasn't coming?" he spat.

"Yeah, well...I...er...she changed her mind," I replied, a gibbering wreck.

He straightened up and stormed into the kitchen to confront Katherine.

Muffled voices could be heard through the shutters as I sat there, tucked away in the corner on my amp, feeling just awful. A few minutes later he came out and cornered Eric by the door while Katherine left with Barbara. Steve Hughes ambled by in front of me – I grabbed him.

"Eh? Wha'? Gerroff! Wha's goin' on?!'" he chirped in his Liverpudlian accent.

"Just stay there and DON'T MOVE! Just talk to me!" I commanded, manoeuvring him in front of me.

Over his shoulder I could see Liam away in the other corner talking to Eric – he did not look happy, not in the least tiny bit. As I watched them, I told Steve the whole story – a brief, edited version because I thought at any minute Liam was going to come over and beat the shit out of me.

"Oh, fook!" said Steve as my world crumbled. A moment later, Liam and Eric left the hut too. Tony wandered by with an armful of cables.

"Here, did you know Eric and Liam have just gone down the pub?"

I breathed a short-lived sigh of relief. I then told Tony the story, who was stunned, and Barbara, who was not surprised at all. She had escorted Katherine outside to her car and now knew the whole thing too.

"Anyone with a pair of eyes could have seen the way she felt about you," she said as I sat there feeling wretched. At that point I didn't even know if we were going to still play that evening or not – I thought it most unlikely. The thought of letting all the people down who'd paid money to see us made me feel worse.

"I'm taking Katherine home with me now," she continued and patted my arm. I felt a little better.

After a couple of hours, Liam and Eric returned, Liam with several pints sloshing round his head. Eric took me aside and filled me in.

"Look," he said, "we've talked it through and he understands what's goin' on. He sees now she was never goin' to stay with him and that they should never have got together. He'll have a talk with ya later but the main thing is we're still playing." I mumbled an apology to Eric – I felt I'd let him down the most.

With that sorted, for now at least, we started the afternoon rehearsal with not much spoken between any of us. I couldn't even look at Liam. Midway through the rehearsal, who should turn up but Gary? Everyone realised (but me) that he wanted to play that night but I was too preoccupied. Pat also turned up so Gary spent the remainder of the afternoon with him.

At about 5.30pm, the band trooped over to the pub opposite for some Dutch courage. Eric was in surprisingly good spirits while Liam sat and necked more beer. If I felt bad, I couldn't imagine what he was going through. To change the subject, Eric and Tony suggested that, as Gary had been to a lot of sessions and had also bought a stake in the PA, maybe he could sing on a few numbers. A few days earlier I would have said absolutely no fucking way. But I was numb, nervous and nauseous – I said OK.

It was a clear and frosty night as we walked back to the hut. I was quite surprised at how many people were there – easily 60. We milled around our instruments and tuned up while Eric went and 'persuaded' Gary to sing on a few numbers. And then we were on! 'We Can Work It Out", 'That's Entertainment', 'Space Oddity', 'Jealous Guy'...I cocked up words, couldn't remember chords but as my guitar was far quieter than everyone else it didn't really matter.

Despite all that, we went down quite well. If you listen to the tape now (or even watch the video!) you'll hear some howlers but, on the whole, it was a workman-like performance.

We played for about an hour I suppose but it seemed far longer. People came up and congratulated us but I was just wondering what on earth I was going to say to Liam. Sure enough he came over to me but instead of administering a savage beating he shook my hand. I was stunned.

"It's all right – I understand," he said as I stood there hapless and hopeless. I mumbled an apology and he left with two of his donkey jacket-wearing mates who, throughout the entire set, had stood unsmiling and with arms crossed at the front of the crowd, glaring at me. I genuinely believed they were going to take me outside after the gig and give me a good kicking. I suspect Gary might have joined in if the opportunity had presented itself!

Life with Katherine was idyllic for a while and she quickly moved in with me at Princes Avenue. Dad didn't mind at all. And after being on my own for a couple of years, it was such a relief, such an absolute pleasure, to be with someone who totally enjoyed being with me. I really thought that she might have been 'The One' and I naively thought that nothing could possibly go wrong this time. It was doomed to failure.

CHAPTER 28

The final days at BT. Ahead…the great unknown

Rumours started to circulate at work during the spring of 1992 that the BT Board of Directors were planning a round of far-reaching redundancies across the company. After a few company briefings, these redundancies were confirmed as BT had decided that there were far too many middle-managers and were looking to trim the workforce significantly, ideally through voluntary redundancies. Details of the redundancy package, entitled 'Release: 92', were communicated to those affected. Eric called it "Fuck Off: 92"!

I duly received my invitation to volunteer, with what turned out to be a very generous package indeed. Katherine and I talked about whether I should stay at BT, but with the Prestel product winding down I faced the prospect of moving back into mainstream BT if I didn't take the money and run. Gary had applied and his redundancy request had been approved. Eric, quickly realising that his team was about to dwindle to nothing, constantly asked the management about his own future. They repeatedly failed to offer anything positive so, on the last day he could apply, Eric finally strode across to their offices and had it out with them. We all sang the theme to 'Rocky' to cheer our hero on as he left and he too joined the imminent mass exodus from BT. Ben had by this time left on a long-planned world tour so there didn't seem much point in staying on. Ben had been saving for his trip for a couple years and when the time came I'd said a tearful goodbye to him after a meal and far too many pints in Leicester Square. I could fill an entire book with his shenanigans. He really was a force of nature – the life and soul of the office, barely tolerated by senior management but liked by pretty much everybody else. There are literally dozens of stories I could relate – of nights out, of rambling pub-crawls with our colleagues and tales of escapades from his youth. So here are a few choice and select Tales of Ben...

Tales such as when...

Ben and I worked in separate parts of the building, he at the back, me at the front and in-between there was a kitchen. Following a mass recruitment drive, the place was suddenly full of alluring women, none of whom we knew anything about. As we knew nothing about them, we gave them code-names, such as:

1920s Woman – a young girl but seemed to favour old fashions and with a penchant for seamed stockings.

French Woman – because she drove a Citroen C5. (*She was actually Scottish*).

Purple Woman – because she only ever seemed to wear purple.

Tall Woman – I think you can figure that one out!

Odd Woman – who worked in Personnel and who never seemed to blink.

Mystery Woman – because we knew nothing about her (*that soon changed – see below*).

We ogled them from afar, so when an object of our desire walked past either of our desks, heading for the kitchen to make a cup of tea, we'd ring each other up so we could accidently bump into them as they seductively stirred sugar into their cups of PG Tips and where we could hopefully engage them in casual banter. Ben would leg it from his desk when he got the call from me, the contents of his pockets flying in all directions.

Tales such as when...

I'd phoned him to quickly advise him that Mystery Woman (whose actual name was Elaine) was heading for the kitchen and to get his arse into gear, to casually and accidentally meet up with her to hopefully strike up a conversation, make a coffee and then shag her (although not necessarily at that moment). I left it a few moments then went to make a coffee myself - sure enough there was Mystery Woman and Ben laughing and joking. She turned to make a make a coffee and Ben, having hurriedly made a cup of steaming coffee, struggled to pull the top off a small pot of milk. With one determined tug and an audible grunt, the foil lid popped off squirting the entire contents all over her back. I thought his eyes were going to pop out of his head! She didn't feel a thing but we both watched in horror as the milk droplets trickled down her clothes collecting in small pools at her feet. I left him to it. I had to, because back at my desk I laughed until I was fit to burst.

Tales such as when...

We'd been down to the canteen for lunch and Ben had told me he'd gotten into trouble with one of the senior managers. I can't remember who it was (Tom Baird, I believe), or what Ben had done (I think it was for being noisy and boisterous in the office) but he'd been reprimanded and told to cool it. He was effing and blinding about this shit in a suit that had told him off – I told him not to worry about it but Ben wouldn't be calmed. On the way back to our desks we both needed a leak so we popped into the lavvy. All the bogs at Network House were standard style, i.e. there were no urinals only cubicles, so they could be designated 'Men' or 'Women' as required on each floor. Of the three cubicles that faced us, the one in the middle was engaged so we went to the left and right respectively. As one, we unleashed the accumulation of the morning's tea, coffee and Coke complete with a Morse code barrage of farts that nearly shredded my underpants. I think we even managed to sing a merry tune between us.

From the far cubicle Ben shouted, "Lucky Tom Baird can't hear us!!!"

I was about to agree when there was a cough from the middle cubicle. Ben's flow stopped mid-stream...I heard him flush, zip and exit within about three seconds, the door to the lavvy slamming shut behind him. I continued with my ablutions as normal, zipped up, washed my hands and left to go and find out what was up with Ben. Walking towards his office I glanced over my shoulder and saw a disgruntled Tom Baird emerge from the same lavvy, on the point of apoplexy, looking left and right for Ben. I found Ben cowering behind some filing cabinets, convinced he was about to be sacked on the spot. Poor Ben! He kept out of Baird's way for a few days and thankfully avoided being fired.

Tales such as when...

We had a psycho stalking the corridors of Network House (no, not Ben!). This man (or was it a woman?) with absolute cunning, stealth and bravado, would stalk the corridors in broad daylight, locate an empty thoroughfare and, with impunity bordering on arrogance, smear excrement all over the place! Ben was both horrified and fascinated by this individual who was risking, at the very least, instant dismissal as well as imminent capture and quite public humiliation. Network House was a busy, buzzing place after-all and the chances of being caught were high.

I remember Ben bounding over to my desk one morning announcing, with almost uncontainable excitement and glee, that 'The Phantom Crapper' (as named by Ben) had struck again! In another time he would have been an urchin on a Victorian Whitechapel street corner selling newspapers declaring, "Murder! 'Orrible Murder!" As Ben was so well-liked by most people in Network House, he was befriended by everyone from secretaries, clerical staff and lower and middle management, to security guards and maintenance workers. One of the latter had advised him that The Phantom had hit the very coffee room where we used to meet up with our many objects of desire. However, instead of the smearing technique so favoured in previous attacks, this time he or she had set a time bomb. The Phantom, whoever it was, had brought in a small cling-film parcel of excrement and placed it in the bottom of the tea-caddie and piled the PG Tips on top of it. No-one had been any the wiser, cheerfully pulling tea bags from the caddie, making cup of tea after tea, oblivious to the festering horror that nestled within, shrouded in bags of India's finest. It was only when the last tea bag had been removed and some unsuspecting soul had thrust their hand in to the caddie that the full horror was revealed. The victim was sent home in shock, the coffee room was sealed off with black and yellow hazard tape and security were brought in.

Ben reported over the next few weeks with mounting excitement how the net was closing in on The Phantom because, as we all used 'swipe' cards to gain access to various parts of the building, it was just a matter of time before the 'swipe' records were matched to the attacks. But, like his Victorian 'Ripper' counterpart, The Phantom was never caught, disappearing forever into the labyrinth of corridors at Network House, the attacks stopping and then making way for rumour, gossip and supposition. Popular theorists suspected that it was 'someone in Accounts'...but we shall never know!

Tales such as when...

I'd been selected to attend the week-long residential BT Practical Management course in Brighton with Gary and Anna. Ben had been told he had to go as well but amazingly always managed to avoid attending. With my last Friday in the office before heading off for the weekend, I slouched by Ben's desk as he busied himself with work. I told him he was missing, if nothing else, an all-expenses paid week out of the office but he was not impressed. As we chatted, Odd Woman from Personnel walked by and settled her thin but athletic frame on Ben's desk. She had overheard us talking about the course and asked if we were both going.

"I am, he's not." I replied.

"That's a shame – it's fully booked and it should be good fun! There's lots of people going," and she proceeded to reel off a list of our colleagues, ending with, "...and Elaine who works with me in Personnel."

Ben, tilting his chair back as we talked, nearly crashed to the floor.

"Elaine you say?" I asked mischievously. "I'm not sure I know her – works in Personnel?"

"Oh, you'd know her – a bit mad, red hair, likes a laugh!"

I looked at Ben – he did not look remotely happy.

"Are you sure," he whimpered in a small voice, "that the course is fully booked?"

"Yep, 'fraid so," Odd Woman replied, ejecting herself from Ben's desk and going on her way.

The moment she was out of earshot, I burst out laughing.

"You bastard," Ben wailed. "You *bastard!* A whole week in Brighton in a hotel with Elaine?"

"I said you should have come!" I crowed. He was inconsolable.

Before I returned to my desk, Ben made me sign a hastily-written declaration that during the coming week, I was not to lay a finger on her, not even if she forced her way into my room, ripped her clothes off and demanded sex with me (however unlikely that may have been).

Tales such as when...

We had some high-ranking BT executive VIP visiting Network House to find out, I imagine, why amongst other things, we never made any money and all our products were crap. He was being escorted around the top floor, another vast open-plan work space, by some sycophantic suit that was fawning over every detail of the visit, insisting none of the staff had clutter on their desks, just the all-important work. The VIP and the suit loitered by the collection of desks where Eric, Gary and I worked and were feigning interest in what we did just as the double doors connecting to the offices at the back of the building crashed open. I looked across in horror as Ingrid Goldman, who ordinarily was all professionalism, empire building and power dressing, hurtled shrieking into our open-plan office, closely followed by a gibbering and frothing Ben, chasing her with a 12-inch plastic ruler, desperately trying to flick up her skirt to reveal her shapely buns (and hopefully) no underwear. They ran the

20 yards between the offices, oblivious to the undivided attention of the staff and the VIP visitor and disappeared into the office next door, where Ben's deep guttural gibbering and Ingrid's high-pitched squeals gradually faded into the distance. I looked at Eric, Eric looked at me, and the VIP paused, coughed slightly and carried on with the visit. Why Ben wasn't sacked remains a mystery!

Tales such as when...

I'd had to give Ben the bad news that, after my week-long course in Brighton, Elaine already had a boyfriend. When the course had finished, Elaine stayed on for a couple of nights with him and we'd been introduced as we packed up to leave. He had no redeeming qualities that I could determine and I wondered what Elaine saw in him.

"What's he like?" Ben asked, dismayed.

"Well, if you had her boyfriend here...and a plank of wood here... you wouldn't be able to tell them apart."

He was referred to as "The Plank" thereafter.

Months later, we had a sort of course reunion drink in an upstairs bar just outside Euston Station to which Elaine was going, along with The Plank.

Ben, whose infatuation with Elaine had continued unabated, was invited but faced a dilemma – did he really want to see The Plank for himself? He asked for directions to the bar and said he'd think about it.

Came the night of the course reunion, we assembled in the bar and Elaine arrived with The Plank. Sat at a table in an alcove, he was utterly obnoxious. Currently employed as a cycling courier delivering packages around London, he'd come straight from his last delivery, still decked-out in his Lycra cycling suit, long hair tied back in a pony-tail, one leg up on the table, droning on about how far he'd cycled that day. He claimed he was degree-educated, came from wealthy stock, was an accomplished musician and had released albums. But it was all bull-shit. It threatened to be a very dull evening until I espied Ben at the doorway, myopically scanning the dark bar for us.

"Oh, look!" I said, completely cutting off The Plank mid-bull-shit, "there's Ben!"

He sauntered over to our table, wearing a smart, buttoned down white mackintosh, a neatly-folded newspaper in his gloved hand, all in all the perfect example of a young executive. Clearly he was out to make an impression. The brief introductions over with, Ben proceeded to demolish The Plank with his wit, sarcasm and utter irreverence. The Plank was no match for him

After a couple of pints, Ben rose from the table, his mark made and claim staked and said goodnight. And here the story should end, with Ben, sadly without the girl but with his integrity intact, striding manfully towards the door. However, as he disappeared into the night, we heard the muffled thump and scream as Ben fell down the stairs leading out onto the Euston Station concourse.

Tales such as when...

Ben and I, along with a girl I've elected to keep anonymous, went to St. Albans for lunch, an occasion that was never repeated again by just we three. We both fancied our lunchtime companion and, after a couple of pints, squeezed round a tiny table in the pub, we couldn't help leering intently at her bodily-particles. She'd had a large gin and tonic and announced, as the alcohol took effect, that she genuinely believed she was fat. Ben and I were shaken from our reverie.

"You're not fat!!" we chorused, ogling her fine, warm and luscious body.

"Oh, I am! I am!" she wailed.

"You're not, you're NOT!" we countered but she was adamant.

"Sometimes I go into the ladies toilets at work," she said, "and take off all my clothes just to check in the mirror to see how fat I've got!"

We were both stunned into slack-jawed silence, the mental image of her in the powder room, taking off each item of clothing to stand naked from the toes up, appearing vividly in 70mm Technicolor in our minds. We both squirmed in our seats, unable to shed this image of her, uncomfortable with the 'effect' it was having on us, both planning to follow her at some time in the future to try and catch her naked. We never did though!

Yes, it was going to be a VERY sad place without Ben, which was one of the main factors in my final decision. After due consideration, I decided that the lure of a year's salary, plus a sweetener for leaving the company, was just too much to resist and I agreed to a final leaving date of 31st July 1992.

The last few weeks were spent winding down along with regular visits to the local pubs. The last couple of days were spent clearing out our desks, filing stuff that you hoped would be used in the future but you knew damn-well would never be read again, clearing out cupboards of accumulated rubbish and nicking as much stationery as possible.

The very last day of my near 10-years at BT dawned. It was strangely chilly but with the prospect of a beautiful summer's day ahead. I caught the bus, train, tube and train to work for the final time as we were planning a massive pub-crawl in London after work to celebrate our new-found liberation from the nine to five. Expectation was high, with the promise of new and exciting opportunities just round the corner.

The morning flashed by, visiting desk after desk saying goodbye to various people, posing for numerous silly photographs. Then we trooped out en masse to the Cart and Horses pub a few miles away. All my soon-to-be former colleagues were assembled in the beer garden, the sun blazing down and I honestly felt so optimistic.

Dad thought I was mad to voluntarily leave BT after nearly ten years and demanded to know what I was going to do now.

"Jobs don't come easy these days, son," he warned when I'd told him of my intentions to accept redundancy. I was back in the same position I'd been in back in 1979 when I'd left school – no plans, no real idea of what to do next, no real aspirations. I knew, after taking a few months off, I'd get a job in no time. No problem, right?

Here in the beer garden, with my friends Eric, Tony, Gary and Sue and so many others around me, laughing, joking and raising glasses, telling tall tales about the last 10 years, the future looked very bright indeed.

Eric elected to lead a few colleagues back to the office as the advance party for collecting our redundancy cheques. The management had decided that the cheques would be issued in the afternoon in the misguided belief they could extract one more working day out of us. I stayed on in the pub with Tony for a while and then finally returned to the office where my boss Ray was still working away. The stability of his job and regular salary, compared to a one-off lump sum, meant he was staying put.

Back at my desk, I noticed that most of the advance party were missing. I presumed they were signing documents elsewhere before getting their hands on the readies. Then Pat, the official band photographer, wandered back, anxiously fingering his cheque, his eyes twinkling with greed and avarice.

But there was no sign of Eric. I asked Pat where he was. He reluctantly took his eyes off all the zeroes on his cheque and mumbled a reply.

"He's gone home," he murmured vaguely, his eyes drawn back to the zeroes – so many zeroes.

"What do you mean, gone home?" I asked incredulously and not a little bit angry. Another colleague chipped in.

"When we got back from the pub, Eric ripped his trousers getting out of the car. He doesn't want to go round London with ripped trousers, so he's gone home."

"But coming back though, right?" I ventured cautiously.

"No, just gone home," replied Pat. "I'm off home too in a minute."

I was deflated…the big evening celebration that we had planned, the big 'farewell to all' pub crawl, the jubilation of our new found wealth and freedom was gone.

I went to collect my cheque too, numb that this really was it. I pocketed it without really checking how much it was for. Returning to my desk, the phone was ringing. One of our clients, who I had been nurse-maiding over the past few years, had a major problem and wanted me to sort it out.

"No", I answered absently, "you'll have to speak to Ray now, I guess." I didn't really know or care, the angry voice on the phone tinny and hissing as I replaced the receiver.

I looked about the place one last time. All my friends had gone, the fun and laughter we had shared within these walls silenced forever, my future with BT wiped out by the board of directors, with my role reduced to a mere number in a vast cost-cutting exercise. All the work we had produced was for nothing, a complete waste of time, effort and energy with little encouragement from the senior management but criticism by the bucket-load.

I looked at the desks, vacant now, and saw bare noticeboards that had, until a few days before, held pictures of family, friends, humorous clippings, cartoons and band pictures and the like - all to make the days at work a little more bearable. Now they were as empty as I felt inside. Upset that it had all come to this, I turned away from the ghosts and left Network House with a small bag of belongings and made the journey home on my own.

When I got back to Tolworth, Katherine was already there. I went upstairs to my room, now a jumble of books, clothes and belongings - a mixture of bedroom, dressing room and living room since she'd moved in. I collapsed on the bed. Katherine cautiously entered the room, gently easing herself next to me. I pulled her close, completely defeated.

CHAPTER 29

What day is it?

After leaving BT I took a few months off, made a few half-hearted attempts at applying for jobs, spent days up at Eric's house jamming, rehearsed with the band for occasional gigs and spent money like I had millions. Everything on the face of it seemed fine. My debts were cleared, I paid off all of Katherine's quite significant debts, I bought a new car and a new synth, which added a new dimension to the band's sound, so all I needed was a job, right? I imagined I would have got one by Christmas 1992 but nothing materialised and 1993 arrived with no job, no prospects and a slowly dwindling amount of cash in the bank. Before I knew it, July 1993 rolled past, the first anniversary of leaving BT, and I still hadn't found employment. Meanwhile, Katherine was doing really well in a new job (haven't we heard this somewhere before?) but was starting to get just a little bit impatient that we weren't able to make any plans. She had moved in with me at Princes Avenue in order to save money on paying rent at her nearby flat. We had an idea that we'd put all my remaining redundancy towards a deposit for a house but property prices were rapidly spiralling out of our range. Without a job we couldn't get a mortgage, so that idea was quietly forgotten.

Then things started to go wrong (*again*). I applied for job after job, scoured the papers for suitable vacancies and joined countless agencies, desperate for that one chance, that one opportunity, with Dad's words constantly ringing in my ears. But nothing came my way.

My relationship with Katherine started to deteriorate and I spiralled ever downwards, starting to become a recluse in my room once more, only venturing out to band rehearsals and to post replies to Ben's letters from around the world. I looked forward to each of Ben's letters immensely and I was dismayed to read that he himself was having troubles of his own, predominantly financial, as he travelled from country to country.

Eric was as supportive as ever but reluctantly went back to BT as a freelancer as he was having as much trouble getting a permanent job as I was. With every penny of my redundancy money nearly spent and with spiralling debts, Dad helped out and my brother Peter helped where he could but I was difficult to live with and very difficult to deal with, being totally sensitive about my abject failure to get another job.

When 1993 slipped into 1994 my life was in a complete mess. I was eating and drinking like a pig. I became almost nocturnal, rarely rising before 1.00pm, shuffling downstairs to find the latest round of rejection letters on the doormat – and by this time, I had quite a file of them. Dad was in despair but elected not to get heavily involved or to give me a 'a good talking to' as I probably would have told him exactly where to go and then stayed in my room for a week, sulking.

Katherine, to her credit, had bought me a limited-edition John Lennon series Rickenbacker 325 guitar for Christmas, as a thank-you for sorting out her finances with part of my redundancy and for bank-rolling all our nights out, weekends away and other extravagances I'd paid for when she hadn't been working. It was also a last-ditch attempt on her part to repair the rapidly-widening cracks in our relationship but it was just about too late. While the money lasted, everything was fine. With the money nearly all gone, things got very bitter, very quickly.

The band became a chore and a burden and I lost control of it. I wasn't happy with the latest guitarist, Andy, who'd joined our ranks replacing Liam and who insisted we play lots of blues numbers. The Rumble Brothers played their last on Monday 1st February 1994 when I could no longer stand to be in the same room as Andy nor, I'm ashamed to say, Gary. The final straw was when Andy introduced yet another old deep-south blues number into the set which I was really struggling to get a handle on.

"Just imagine you're a fat, black, unemployed c**t," he said, then muttering under his breath, "Well, three out of four ain't bad." I was driving an 80-mile round trip to the studio for these sessions, when I had barely any money left, to spend a few hours in a room doing things I didn't remotely enjoy any more, with some people whom I didn't like. I was completely incapable of taking charge or making any decisions. I looked for people to blame for my miserable misfortune and everyone was a target, regardless of whether they deserved it or not and regardless of whether they were guilty of contributing to my despair. Even though not *entirely* blameless, Gary bore the brunt of my neuroses, which was unfair and unforgiveable.

And down and down I went. I didn't really know what day of the week it was, although if sport was on the TV, I knew it was probably a Saturday. I was consumed by bleak, black, suffocating, debilitating bouts of depression, which seemed to run into each other as the disappointments mounted, each rejection letter a kick in the head. Everything became a chore, an unbearable burden. Even getting up in the morning or, as was more the case these days, early afternoon, became an almost insurmountable task. All the things that I enjoyed, all my pastimes and hobbies, became irritating and inessential. The room I shared with Katherine that I had kept impeccably tidy became an awkward, uninhabitable, untidy mess of living room and bedroom, where I spent most of my days, brooding. Apart from letters to Ben and very occasional phone calls to Eric, I cut off all contact with other friends and family and gave up looking for anything to actually look forward to. There was nothing. The light at the end of the tunnel had well and truly been turned off. If this wasn't a nervous breakdown, I don't really want to know what one is.

No wonder then that Katherine decided she'd finally had enough and left after a memorable, blazing row one Sunday night in May 1994, never to be seen again.

The day after our massive melt-down, I packed up all her stuff and stacked it in the spare bedroom, then made myself scarce that night when she came round with a van and a man to collect it all (possibly the very man she soon shacked up with, and had possibly been secretly 'shacking' for the past few months). I went down the pub and came back a little worse for wear. Dad was in the backroom, reading the paper.

"How did it go, Dad?" I slurred, trying to tot-up how many pints I'd had. The answer was *lots*.

"Oh, about as well as can be expected," Dad replied, wearily.

He paused.

"She's a left a few bits up in the spare room that she doesn't want."

"I'll chuck them in the bin!" I replied, bitterly.

Dad paused again.

"She wanted the Lennon guitar back."

I nearly coughed-up the evening's consumption of beer and crisps.

"What?!! You're bloody joking?!" I spluttered.

"Yes, she said she wanted the guitar back," Dad continued calmly.

"What happened?"

"Well, she said it was hers and that she was still paying for it, so she wanted it back."

"The fucking bitch!!" I stammered, scarcely able to believe what I was hearing. She'd bought that guitar as a thank-you, for all the money I'd sent her way. Whatever the cost of the guitar had been, it didn't match, by any stretch of the imagination, how much I'd spent on her. Dad knew this and had been glad to have seen the back of her the day before. Life at Princes Avenue over the past few months had been pretty unbearable. Dad was angry that she hadn't exactly been that sympathetic regarding my worsening situation either.

"I said she couldn't have it and that was that."

"Oh, cheers, Dad," I said, calming down.

"Besides, I suspected she was going to make a play for it so I locked it in the boot of my car after you went out."

I could have hugged him.

"Thanks, Dad," I said tearfully, the stress of the past few weeks finally taking its toll.

"Don't worry, son, she was never going to get it back. Anyway, I may look daft sometimes, but I'm not stupid!"

Just when I needed a mate – *really* needed one – Ben returned to these green and pleasant lands after being virtually deported from New Zealand. We immediately hitched up and it was like he hadn't been away. We laughed, almost shed a few tears, we reminisced, we drank and on the first night I caught up with him, we effortlessly sank 20 pints between us. The only thing that stopped us having more was that the pub shut. Over the following weeks, it was hearing Ben's often-unintentional tales of woe from his trip round the globe that helped me out of my depression. He helped me realise that I had reached absolute rock bottom and that the only way, as that bloody fidget Yazz used to sing in the late 1980s, was "up".

CHAPTER 30

Two years of crushing disappointment finally come to an end

All the money had finally gone and I was absolutely broke. Dad helped me pay some of the huge credit card debts I'd accrued but I felt I had to make some gesture and so, with big wet tears in my eyes, reluctantly sold my synth, along with a good portion of my precious comic collection to generate some cash. Despite all this I was a man reborn. I got up at 7.00am each day, showered, shaved, read the print off the paper for possible jobs and badgered the agencies for any job that was suitable. I had my suit dry-cleaned and on permanent stand-by in case of interviews and thought, what the hell, let's lose some weight as well.

After the last, bitter band session in February 1994, Eric had kept a low profile but he'd got wind that Katherine had buggered off so he gave me a call. I was delighted to hear from Eric, as he and I hadn't fallen out at all. He was very sorry to hear the news but, after hearing me tell the whole sorry tale, rapidly revised his opinion of Katherine. He asked what I was doing that Saturday. I said nothing that I knew of.

"How about we have a little session up here? Just you, me, Tone and Hughes?" he suggested. "Then you can come back to our gaff and we can break out the gins as well?"

"Alright then, as long as Gary's not invited,'" I replied, shuddering at just how bad things had got during the last days of The Rumble Brothers.

"If you don't want him there, he's not coming," replied Eric and promised to ring me back. He did soon after – I think he'd already planned a session with Hughes and Tone anyway and just checked with them if it was all right if I came along too. It was, and it was all arranged.

The following Saturday I loaded up the car, said goodbye to Dad and headed north and trooped over to Hughes' house and set up the gear. As we set up, Tony also said how sorry he was that Katherine had left me.

"Do you know what, Tony? Don't be," I replied. "When I was younger and my first real girlfriend left me, it took me about eight months to get over her. The next one took about six months and the next about a month. To be honest my three years with her have been reduced to a level of 'I went shopping on Monday, cleared the cat's litter tray out Wednesday, paid my Visa bill yesterday, had a good shit this morning – and, oh yeah, went out with Katherine for three years'. It doesn't matter – we had good times and they're over."

I'm not sure if Tony got the message, but I had very quickly expunged all traces of affection for her. We did have good times, true, but they were a long time ago. I was sad, very sad, that the girl I had originally fallen in love with had gone, but not sad that I was no longer with the girl who had stormed out that Sunday evening – because, at the end, they were completely different people.

We had a pleasant enough afternoon sessioning and drank lots of beer. We even had a go at writing some songs based on riffs that Hughes had put together. But it wasn't enough to make me want to start driving up to the studio every week again.

Back at Eric's that night I was fed to bursting point and then, after Ros had retired, drank myself into a stupor with Eric at my side – old band rehearsal tapes playing in the background, talking music, the band, the old days at BT, women loved and lost…

My new, rejuvenated regime continued: searching the job ads, registering with endless agencies and just looking for that one opportunity to get me back on my feet. My diet was working a treat – essentially starving myself during the week, then drinking heavily with Ben at the weekend. He and I became inseparable for a few months as we were both in the same situation - he having come back from his world tour penniless and moved back into his parents' house with no prospects of work. We were both pot-less, both single and the prospect of any female company anywhere in the near future seemed remote. "I'm just busting for a shag!" kind of became our mantra, especially after six or seven pints. Oh well... think positive, Martin! Positive!

June 1994 saw my mate Andrew Burton moving into his new house in Kingston with his girlfriend Gill. She had been (and still is I'm very glad to say) a great influence on Andy and he'd mellowed a lot in the few years that they'd been together. The bachelor flat that Andy had was too small for them both now and they were moving to a very smart house. I, of course, offered to help them move (it's not as if I had anything else to do, right?) and on a very hot Thursday 30th June 1994, I arrived at their flat, helped shift everything down three flights of stairs and into the van and then moved onto the new house. Having a well-deserved cup of tea, Gill remarked that I'd lost weight. I was flattered that someone had actually noticed that my diet of starving during the week and drinking copious amounts of beer at the weekend seemed to be working! My enduring memory of the day however is one of deep envy. As all the boxes and furniture were finally in their new house I stood and thought, "How the hell can I ever afford something like this?" I had no job, no money, no prospects, no hope and no woman to love and be loved by. I had nothing. There was absolutely no way I could even contemplate owning a house and I'm afraid I went home quite depressed – only briefly – but I hope it didn't show and spoil their day.

My new regime of searching for a job became a full-time job in itself – I applied for everything that looked even remotely suitable, still hoping for some kind of management position. I saw Ben whenever I could as the summer of 1994 wore on and during this time we were pretty much joined at the hip, spending Friday or Saturday evening, sometimes both (usually financed by Dad), drinking and mourning our lot. But bloody hell, he made me laugh to the point where I could almost lose consciousness from convulsive laughter.

On Monday 15th August 1994 with Dad away on his holidays, I joined a Job Club in Sutton. And what a boost for my confidence - the whole attitude of the people there was totally positive; there were the latest newspapers and trade magazines and journals and, hurrah, a PC and laser printer in the corner ready to send off CVs and applications. I spent the day with other people joining for the first time and looked with growing encouragement at the numbers of letters on the wall from people who had found jobs via the club. This was looking good! Equipped with a better CV than I had before, I started sending speculative letters from home as well as the Job Club. I was also applying for vacancies that, at the Job Club's suggestion, I may not have been wholly suitable for. But their philosophy was, if you had at least one of the advertised requirements, then you should give it a go.

One such ad was from a company based in Vauxhall who were looking for excellent customer service skills and a thorough knowledge of Windows and Windows products. I applied even though I didn't have the faintest idea what Windows was! My job application file looked very healthy.

On Sunday 28th August 1994 after a fine dinner cooked by Dad, fresh back from his holiday, I suggested that as it was such a lovely evening we went for a walk. As we emerged into the late afternoon sun and headed for Tolworth Recreation Ground, the sun caught the leaves on the trees, turning the few noticeable brown autumn leaves into vibrant gold. We walked and talked about the last couple of years and I tried to apologise for all the things I had put him through. Dad told me not to worry and said that I should concentrate now on getting a job. I promised that I would.

We walked and talked some more and eventually found our way to Britannia Road where he used to live. All the old terraced houses had long since been demolished back in the early 1970s to be replaced by modern monstrosities but we were still able to just about find where his tiny childhood home used to be. Looking back to The Castle pub on the corner, Dad remarked that when he was very young, the journey down to the corner had seemed like miles. I knew exactly what he meant. When we lived in the flat over Dad's shoe shop, Peter and I were tasked with going to get the Sunday papers each weekend and if we went to the newsagent by the roundabout on the A3, virtually the last shop on Tolworth Broadway, it took us forever. In actual fact, the newsagent was probably no more than 200 yards away, if that, but we'd eventually return to the flat clutching *The News of The World*, plus, if we were really lucky, a block of ice cream and a bottle of Tizer, to be greeted by the smell of Mum and Dad's possibly *post-coitus* coffee brewing.

But on that Summer's evening in 1994, walking back through the park, the sun was just starting to set, illuminating a huge bank of clouds, spiralling seemingly to Heaven, glowing gold, white and pink. It was breath-taking. Returning home, I knew that things were going to be all right.

Tuesday 30th August 1994 I returned home from a fruitful few hours at the Job Club but as I approached the door, Dad - already there - beckoned me in with a huge smile on his face.

"What's up?" I asked.

"Call this number straight away," he answered excitedly. "They called you earlier on and they want you to go for an interview!"

I glanced at the telephone number – I didn't have a clue who it was. I went upstairs and checked all the jobs I'd applied for recently and married-up the telephone number with an application. Blimey, it was the job that wanted Windows experience. Oh well – it looked promising.

On September 1st 1994, Dad's birthday, I made my way up to Vauxhall for the interview. I was suited and booted and looked, with my recent weight-loss, the dog's bollocks! I hopped off the train at

Vauxhall station and followed the directions to The L&R Group at 70, South Lambeth Road, Vauxhall, London. They explained more about the role – HP were outsourcing their pre-sales operation and The L&R Group had won the tender. They were recruiting a new team to advise potential customers on Hewlett-Packard PC and printer products. Long story short, I got the job. When I got the news and had signed the contract, Peter and Susan came round and we opened a bottle of champagne with Dad to celebrate. Everyone was delighted – I had sold myself at the interview and my two years of crushing disappointment were coming to a close. I wrote a letter of thanks to the Job Club and advised the Jobcentre, with great delight, that I was stopping my unemployment benefit claim. I was overjoyed. Dad was pleased for me because it was going to be a whole new team of people meeting for the first time. There'd be no cliques, no pre-formed friendships – everyone from the manager down to the admin staff would all be starting on the first day.

Monday 3rd October 1994 was a significant date: my first day back at work since July 1992. I'd spent the previous Sunday night making sure the suit was OK, polishing my shoes until you could see the future in them, and Dad, good old Dad, pressed my best shirt to ensure I made a good impression. It was a grey, windy, day with rain in the air. I tried not to think of the day ahead on the train up to Vauxhall but failed miserably. What was the job really going to entail? What would my new boss be like? What would the other people be like? Would I get on with them? Oh, shit, I was nervous.

I arrived at 70 South Lambeth Road again, this time as an employee of The L&R Group, took a very deep breath and entered. I was told to wait in the coffee room and was ushered in to meet all my new colleagues who were waiting to start training for the job. My first impression was that the room was full of men - not a single woman in sight. I'd been led to believe that it was going to be a kind of a mixed group – but clearly this was not the case. I looked about and took it all in. There were a couple of guys laughing and joking whom

I thought already knew each other; another looked very dapper in his suit, casually dragging on a cigarette, while another, who had lots of hair, was working the room. He caught my eye.

"Hi," he said in clipped tones, extending his hand, "my name is Drew – what's yours?"

"Martin," I answered shaking his hand.

"Where have you come from?" he asked.

"Tolworth…"

"No," he scoffed, "what job have you come from?"

"Oh…ah, BT I guess…"

"I've come from Harrods," he said and went back to talking to the person next to him.

The door opened and a few more new entrants came in, one of whom was a girl. She looked round the room and looked stunned. We all sort of nodded hello to her and she sat at a table next to a very tall, blonde-haired guy. He spoke very quietly and started talking to the girl.

The door opened again and in came another new entrant. She was short, with short brown hair and was wearing a grey raincoat and carrying a briefcase.

"Hello, everyone!" she said brightly and we all said hello back.

"I'm Drew," said Drew and he went into his routine again.

Eventually, two of the L&R consultants came in and welcomed everyone to the company. We filed into one of the training rooms and squeezed round a table. I sat next to the dapper guy and the woman with the short brown hair sat opposite me. We were welcomed again to The L&R Group and were told what the next few weeks would entail – basically we would be dividing our time between Vauxhall and Bracknell in Berkshire where HP's main offices were. We'd be trained on the products we would be covering in the call centre, so that we could confidently answer any enquiries. At L&R we'd be taught best customer-service practice and the HP call studio would go live on the 1st November 1994 when the calls, at 9.00am prompt, would be switched from HP to L&R in Vauxhall. We had a month to get up to speed on everything.

We were all introduced to each other and Vicki Collins, sitting opposite me, was introduced to us all as the new manager of the group.

"So you're in charge then?" I asked.

"Yes, it's great to meet you all," she replied and was just ever so nice.

The day concluded with one of the consultants cheerfully announcing that the following day, as part of a team-building exercise, we were all going down to an army assault course near Brighton and that we should wear our tracksuits (what bloody tracksuit?). Dad was convulsed with laughter when I told him that evening what was planned for the following day.

I arrived at the office the following morning on what was a beautiful, cold, crisp, autumn day, having left Dad still laughing over his cornflakes. I don't think he'd stopped laughing since I'd told him about the assault course the previous evening.

The sky was crystal clear blue but it was freezing outside as people hurried down streets wrapped in coats and scarves. I joined my new colleagues as we all bundled onto the coach like excited school kids going on a trip.

Arriving at the encampment, we assembled in an office and were told to sign a form that basically said, if you break anything or kill yourself on this course, don't blame us. We were then split into two teams. My team would start at the beginning of the course and work forwards, while the other team would go to the end and work backwards. I was delighted that my new boss, Vicki, was on my team.

We were walked round the course by some muscle-bound, vest-wearing ex-soldier with a whistle round his neck and clutching a stop-watch and a clipboard, shouting instructions as we anxiously surveyed each challenge. Make no mistake, this was a formidable army assault course. We familiarised ourselves with the hurdles, hoops, planks and pulleys that we were expected to go over, up, through, down and round in this timed event. I feared every one of them.

Assembled at the first event, I viewed what was ahead of me – thin poles of rounded wood zigzagging across a stagnant green pond. I was the first to make the attempt and Vicki cheered me on.

"Do you know what? I'm probably going to fall in," I said, viewing the swamp that lay before me.

"Of course you're not going to fall in! Have a little faith!" she said, doing her best to boost my confidence.

The whistle went and I broke into a jog for the poles as my teammates, including Vicki, shouted encouragement behind me.

"Come on, Martin!" they shouted.

I reached the poles and made my wary way across one, then had to turn 90 degrees to walk along the next. I made it across the second, turned for the third, the other side of the pond in sight.

"I'm going to make it! I'm going to make it!" I thought to myself, just as the rubber soles on my trainers started to slip on the wet wood. I tried to regain my balance, my arms windmilled round, first backwards, then forwards, trying to find something to hold onto. With a yawning howl, I spectacularly parted company with the planks of wood and splashed into the cold dank water, submerged up to my navel. My new colleagues' laughter echoed around the grounds. I waded to the side and hauled my carcass out of the water, leaving my soaked tracksuit bottoms and scum-encrusted pants behind me, the pale autumn sunlight glinting gently off my lily-white arse. They howled even louder as I pulled my undergarments back up. I stood at the side of the pond, steaming slightly from the ankles up, as all my team crossed with no problem. Vicki ran past me – I called after her.

"I said I was going to fall in. Didn't I say? Didn't I say that?"

Vicki laughed good-naturedly as we moved onto the next course, she running sprightly along in her bright tracksuit, me squelching along, water and mud oozing out of the lace holes of my trainers.

The rest of the morning passed without incident but was the most exercise I'd done since I'd left school, oh, so many years ago. I climbed 11-foot walls, hauled my new colleagues over piles of wood, ran through tyres, climbed 30-foot rock faces, and ran myself to the point of exhaustion, squelching all the while. A memorable start to my career at L&R!

Once the training schedule finished and the job started in earnest, it rapidly became very hard work indeed. Each long day comprised of endless phone calls and endless grief from the L&R directors who wanted to know why we were all struggling to meet the agreed in-bound call targets. It really wasn't much fun at all and I was knackered most nights, most weeks, slipping beneath my duvet of an evening, plummeting into a deep sleep...snoring, farting and dribbling, often all at once.

Having been on my own since May and with December approaching, I arranged an ill-advised date with an old Prestel colleague, Chrissie, just for something to do as I was so fed-up. I arranged to meet my date on Saturday 17th December 1994 and met Chrissie mid-morning at Euston Station. She didn't look that pleased to see me. We headed south towards Oxford Street to wander aimlessly around the shops. Sadly, it was not the ideal day for shopping as it was cold, grey and overcast with the prospect of rain. As we emerged from the Virgin Megastore it started to drizzle which dampened our spirits somewhat. After a few hours, we went for lunch in some restaurant down Argyll Street. Over the course of a very average meal and warm, flat lager we chatted about nothing in particular and I felt that it was all a bit of a struggle. And then, quite without warning, Chrissie said she had to be heading home. I glanced at my watch and saw that it was only 2.30pm. However, the thought of spending any more time with her, desperately struggling to think of something to say, did not appeal so I escorted her back to Euston Station and saw her off on the train back to Hemel Hempstead, never to be seen again.

I had been looking forward to the date. When we worked together at Network House, I thought we'd had a bit of a connection and had engaged in some innocent flirting. Dismayed, I headed off on my own, not in the best of moods. I didn't want to go home so decided to go to Putney to a comic shop that I knew and spend some of my hard-earned cash on me. After a convoluted journey, in truly depressing weather, I finally arrived at Putney Bridge Station and began to walk what seemed like miles to the shop. As I trudged on, the bells of a nearby church suddenly started to peal a joyous fanfare as two newly-weds emerged into a storm of confetti, which briefly showered the happy couple before being swept away in the bitter wind. I watched for a few moments and wondered, not for the first time, what the hell was going to happen to me. Would I ever get married? God knows I'd tried but each attempt to find 'The One' had ended in disaster: Dawn, Debbie and all the others during my mostly monogamous courting, plus, most recently, Katherine. I looked back at the newly-weds, the church bells rang, the small crowd of well-wishers cheered, the wind blew, the clouds swirled dark and oppressive above and, thoroughly depressed, I turned and carried on my way.

Christmas 1994 brought an easing off of our workload. Inevitably there were frequent trips to the pub. On Friday 23rd December, with calls into the HP Call-Centre finally petering out, Vicki elected to close the phone lines down for the Christmas break. In shifts, we headed out to our local boozer where I arrived to find one of my colleagues, Seamus Boyd, halfway through a pint of Kronenbourg. Judging by the empties on the table, it wasn't his first. It was surprising as he could have only been there for about 15 minutes before I arrived. What was more surprising was that, at the induction day at The L&R

Group only a few, short months before, Seamus had declared himself to be completely teetotal.

I got a beer and sat down with him. He was clearly not happy.

"What's up?" I asked.

"It's this fucking job!" he spat, angry beyond belief, with none of the Christmas cheer in the pub able to cast any sparkle on his dark mood. "I take call after call after call after fucking CALL, all from dealers wanting to know about HP products!"

This was true. Dealers should have been contacting their wholesalers for advice. We should have just been dealing with home-based customers, asking questions about printers and PCs and fielding questions about this new-fangled thing called "The Internet".

"HP lied! They fucking lied!!" he raged, bitterly.

On and on he went about how he felt betrayed and that the job, as sold to him, was not the job he was doing. I tried to assuage his anger, saying at least in this day and age a job was a job, surely? I knew I was grateful to be working again after two years on the scrapheap. But he wouldn't be swayed. It was a feeble argument on my part anyway, as it really was hard-going and not what any of us had expected.

I looked at the empties on the table and thought carefully before voicing the obvious question.

"Aren't you supposed to be teetotal?"

Seamus drained his beer, then snatched my barely empty glass.

"Yeah, well, fuck it," he said and headed back to the bar to get another round in.

CHAPTER 31

"Ladies and gentlemen... We Fear Change!"

The brand new year of 1995 arrived without ceremony. Even though I, at long last, had a job (albeit earning a salary that was barely half of what I had been earning at BT), I was quite low. I still saw my friends as and when I could, but something was missing. However, I didn't have much time to dwell on my lot, as working at L&R was exhausting.

I could write a book about my time at The L&R Group, about the weird and wonderful characters I met there (some *very* weird) but I'll summarise the life-changing events that happened over the next couple of years. Easily the most important character in all this was Vicki, the manager I got on well with: she was capable, well-respected, firm but fair, took no nonsense from anyone – all this tempered by a great sense of humour. She was also pretty damn attractive and that was no bad thing, believe me! We didn't always see eye to eye and often had some major differences of opinion but we always worked through them. I liked her a lot and she liked me. Sadly, on top of the challenges of running the team and dealing with the histrionics from one of the directors, Vicki was having problems at home with her marriage. She confided in Drew and me, who were probably the most senior members of the team, if not in management aspirations then certainly in maturity. We were always happy to provide a sympathetic ear.

Meanwhile, the band was resurrected! I'd gone up to Eric and Steve's houses over the summer for the occasional jam, sometimes joined by Tony, and there would inevitably be copious amounts of booze drunk afterwards. Steve mentioned that a guitarist mate of his, Martin Barranes, fancied joining us for a session. He was between groups at the minute as his previous band, Red 57, were on a kind of hiatus.

We booked some rehearsal time at Farm Factory Studios in London Colney and Martin Barranes turned up with his kit, which included a classic Vox AC30 Amp. We were all introduced, he plugged in, we said we'd try a few old Cream numbers and, fucking hell, he blew me away. Steve was a good guitarist – a *very* good guitarist – but Marty B was in another league. I always maintain he should have been in touring bands for solo artists, he was that good. When we said we were going to do 'One' by U2, he said, quite without a trace of arrogance, "Oh, I've been practising that one," and proceeded to outplay The Edge! As I wrote in my diary that night, 'full potential achieved'. We even managed to finish some of our own songs we'd been playing around with, and added to our set – 'Last Night (We Can Fly)' and 'Love Let Me Down' (written by Eric, me and an old Prestel colleague, Sue Crawford), 'Albury Days' (music by Steve Hughes and lyrics by me) plus the short-lived 'Born Again'.

We started to rehearse regularly and I was in my element. The band became my focus from 1995. We even started gigging again, including the memorable St.Valentine's Day Gig, February 1995 at The White Horse pub, in Baldock. By then we had a new name – 'We Fear Change' – as suggested by Steve during one Saturday lunchtime band-meet in the pub, a quote from the film, *Wayne's World*.

I even managed to get a Gary Numan track into our live set, by tacking 'Bombers' onto the end of 'Hey Joe' by Jimi Hendrix, leaping from the final "Hey Joe, where you gonna run to now?" straight into, "Look up! I hear! The scream…of sirens on the wall." Same chords, more or less the same bass line and it worked. It used to be our last number before the obligatory encores then, all being well, £50.00 quid straight in the old back pocket!

Not many people recognised this 'Hey Joe/Bombers' mash-up, except on one occasion. In 1995, we played in Eric's massive back-garden at one of his semi-annual "Watstock" summer barbeques. The objective of these events was to entertain friends, family and neighbours and get spectacularly drunk. The band had finished the set and I headed straight for a beer when one of Eric's neighbours stopped me.

"That was a really good show," she said, cradling a half-empty wine glass. I don't think it had been her first glass, either!

"Oh, cheers," I said. "Do you really think so?"

"Oh, yes…I loved it. Especially loved the Jimi Hendrix number," she purred and, blimey, she was a bit of a sort.

"That wasn't Hendrix at the end though, was it?" she asked.

"Ah, no…no, it wasn't," I had to admit.

"That was Tubeway Army, wasn't it"?

I was gobsmacked.

"Yes! Yes, it was!! How did you know?" I demanded.

"I *LOVE* Tubeway Army," she enthused, taking another sip of wine from her glass.

"Really? That must be just you and me then these days!" I joked.

"No, no…Gary Numan is…just…brilliant! I've got all his albums at home," she replied, seductively running her finger round the rim of her glass.

So we nipped back to her house, put *Replicas* on, sank a bottle of wine, she ripped her clothes off, we had a bit of 'How's Your Father' then I headed back, sweaty and red-faced, for the evening encore.

(I didn't, of course, but it would have made a nice end to that particular story!).

Back at work, one of Vicki's great qualities as a manager was that, whenever it was someone's birthday, she'd go out and buy a cake. Everyone would down tools (if briefly, because the calls into the pre-sales call centre *never* stopped) have a slice of cake, sing "Happy

Birthday" and the recipient would have the ritual humiliation of opening their card and making a speech. On one such occasion, the cake was handed out, the card was given but Vicki, strangely, left the office. I went down to the otherwise empty coffee room and she was in there alone, still wearing her green paper party hat, still holding her paper plate with a bit of cake on but was crying her eyes out.

"What's the matter?" I asked gently.

She sobbed and sobbed but eventually managed to say, "I just want someone to look after me."

And I knew then, at that very moment, at that *very* second, that *the someone* she needed to look after her, was me.

I also knew, without any doubt, that Vicki was, definitely and without any question, THE ONE.

CHAPTER 32

The One

The moment that I realised that I was the one Vicki needed to look after her, I mounted a yearlong campaign to woo her and I slowly made my feelings known. To her credit again, she continued to try and make her marriage work but to no avail. We cautiously, nervously, like two teenagers starting a romance, got closer and closer to 'the line'. I recognised then, without a doubt, that all my previous relationships, every single one of them, had just been a rehearsal, a mere precursor to this. I absolutely knew it was going to be big. It was just a matter of time.

Nevertheless, Vicki and I tried our best to keep our new-found love a secret, especially as she was my direct line-manager. Email was in its infancy so we used the old-fashioned method of writing each other letters and secretly depositing them in our respective coat-pockets in the office wardrobe so that we could read them in private later.

Far more mundanely, the task of trying to persuade prospective customers to buy Hewlett-Packard products went on, day in day out, and eventually it began to take its toll on the team. Seamus finally cracked one lunchtime when, after a particularly harrowing morning, he headed down to the pub. Here, he managed to sink five pints of Kronie in an hour, staggered back to work red-faced and belligerent with his tie round his head like a headband. Seamus started taking calls and, one by one, just as they started to speak, told every single customer to "fuck off." Our call abandonment rate was pretty good for about 20 minutes until someone realised what he was doing and he was sacked on the spot. Several other original members of the team also fell by the way-side, which led to an influx of brand new recruits.

One of the new entrants was a guy named David Okomah. He

was very stylish, half Irish/half Nigerian. He would talk in a voice only marginally less deep than Barry White's about his "mammy" from Ireland. As the original group were such a close-knit team, I didn't immediately click with him. Yet when I did, that was it – a true, lifelong friend, there for me through thick and thin. I feel privileged to have met him. With some people you take ages to forge any kind of friendship, but in other rare instances, once you're mates it's like you've known each other for ever. Very soon, we started socialising and over many lunches down The Wheatsheaf, he'd regale me with stories about bands he'd seen, such as meeting Ultravox back stage at one early gig, or being enthralled by The Jam at a very early gig, an event captured on film and shown occasionally on TV. It shows Weller, Foxton and Buckler giving it large, rows of angry young men twitching and gobbing at the front of the stage and in their midst, a little kid with an afro, completely incongruous but having the time of his life. That was Dave.

Eventually, Vicki and I got to 'the line'. Having made one last attempt to repair her marriage, which ultimately failed, she finally gave up on that relationship and gave in to me. It was the most exciting, not to mention frustrating, time of my life.

I remember, during the first giddy days of our new relationship, we went to see Gary Numan in concert at a warm-up gig in Battersea's Adrenalin Village, a very small venue. He was over an hour late arriving on stage and when he did, he played none of the hits and less…he played some obscure tracks and some new stuff, none of which Vicki would recognise. The only redeeming feature for me was that he played "Me! I Disconnect From You".

"They all sound a bit the same," Vicki said sweetly and, gosh, on this night, they did.

Once Vicki's house was sold, we bought a house not far from Dad's and moved in during December 1996. In September 1997 The Hewlett-Packard contract came to an end after three years but we'd already decided it was best that we had separate jobs as we didn't want to spend all our time together! Vicki went to another branch of the company and I stayed on with The L&R Group for another year as a research executive.

Meanwhile, the band was in full-swing with regular rehearsals and occasional gigs. However, we all agreed that we needed a second singer as sometimes I struggled on my own. In quick succession, we went through a few girlie singers, as Eric fancied a bit of eye-candy in the group. They were good but none of them lasted long. Tony decided enough was enough and arranged for a band meet at The Bell, Fleet Street and secretly invited Gary Smith along, who I had not seen since the last Rumble Brothers rehearsal back in February 1994.

Thursday 24th September 1998 was the date. I sat with my band mates in my spiritual home getting drunk and then, later in the evening, espied my old, estranged band-mate nonchalantly drinking at the bar.

"It's Gary!" I hissed, trying my best to look inconspicuous.

"Why, so it is!" said Tony, innocently.

"Wass he doin' here?" I demanded.

"Why don't you go and ask him?" Tony helpfully suggested.

I staggered up to the bar and Gary feigned surprise to see me. I was drunk and belligerent and we had a 'colourful' conversation about things. And do you know what? We cleared the air, right there and then. Joining us at the table, pints in hand, we sat and reminisced and I realised what a miserable, self-centred fuck I'd been. One of my former Prestel colleagues once commented that I could hold a grudge as long as the half-life of plutonium and he was probably right. But Gary was back in the band and all was well with the world. Vocal harmonies were restored and it was just like the good old days of The Rumble Brothers – fun, plenty of laughs and plenty of beers.

After L&R, I eventually found a new job working for *The Guinness*

Book of Records. They were advertising for multi-lingual researchers and Vick suggested I send a speculative letter seeing if they had any other jobs. I argued that it was probably a waste of time but, grumbling, agreed to send off my CV. Which I did and, in this instance, it arrived on the right day on the right desk in front of the right person who, looking for a customer service manager was astonished that my CV, with just the skills and experience he was looking for, materialized in his In-Tray. I got a phone call and was invited in for a preliminary interview just before Christmas 1998.

Suited and booted as ever, I headed off with plenty of time to spare for the 11.00am interview but decided that, regardless of it being overcast, I didn't need a coat or umbrella. I also neglected to have my customary pre-interview crap, which I regretted very soon after. I arrived at Waterloo Station feeling decidedly uncomfortable. I checked my watch and decided that, despite the worrying intestinal gurgling in my stomach and twitching in my large bowel, I didn't have time to use the toilet facilities and headed instead for the Northern Line. Guinness was then based at prestigious offices on the Euston Road and by the time I got to Warren Street I was in agony. Bent double, I sprinted off the train as best I could and headed for the nearest McDonald's and their toilets, dodging the huge wet raindrops that were starting to fall out of the now cement-grey sky. I literally dived into the first cubicle available and, with scant seconds to spare, explosively evacuated my bowels, with images flashing round my head of Elvis in August 1977 breathing his last on the toilet. With a mixture of relief and part delirium, I rested for a few minutes and then realised that I was going to be late for the interview if I didn't get a move on. The delirium turned to hysteria when I reached round to the toilet roll holder to be greeted by the sight of a scant inch of toilet paper hanging forlornly from the otherwise empty brown cardboard tube. I was horrified. What the hell was I going to do? I hoisted up my trousers and pants as far as I dared then started to head for the adjacent cubicle when I heard the door to the toilets opening. I darted back into my cubicle, then spent the next ten minutes waddling like a penguin back and forth to the adjacent bog when I thought it was safe, only to be stymied each and every time by the constant stream of people coming in to use the facilities. It was like a coach load of people had suddenly arrived, all desperate for a McDonald's quarter pounder and a crap. I finally managed to sort myself out without turning either cubicle into a scene of a dirty protest and emerged about a stone lighter onto Tottenham Court Road. By this time, the weather was truly horrendous and I was still faced with a ten-minute walk to the Guinness offices. I got soaked.

Arriving on the eighth floor, I was greeted by a pretty young blonde girl on the reception desk who asked if I needed anything while I waited. I was tempted to say a towel and a clean pair of pants but made do with a cup of tea. As I waited to be summoned for the interview, various members of staff stopped by reception and it became clear that this was the morning after their office Christmas party as there were some major hangovers in evidence. I strained to hear some of their whispered conversations, with snippets such as, "I tried to get her dressed in the girls' toilet but she was too drunk,", "I hid behind one of the curtains to avoid him," and "Any idea what happened to my red shoes?" before I was called for the interview. It sounded like it had been a memorable party!

The initial interview went well and I was called back for a second one in February 1999 and then offered the job of Head of Records Research Services – a prestigious role. I started in March 1999 and if I could write a book about The L&R Group, then I could write a multi-volume series of books about my time at Guinness during a period when the style of the book was moving away from the staid, old, fact-based publication to a much more dynamic, more visual one. It was a very strange place, full of very different people. Some were young, creative types who actively embraced this new direction, while others were very much from the old-school who'd been employed when Norris McWhirter had still been at the helm and who resisted any suggestion of change to the traditional, fact-driven book. It didn't help that the senior managers (very senior managers), citing personal differences about the direction the product was going in, refused to speak to each other.

I became the manager of the admin team and some of the researchers, one of whom very much retained the 'old-school' mentality. He was a bloody menace and singularly failed to do any allocated tasks on time or to-plan and was the most miserable, dour, put upon person you could possibly imagine who, after a day of reading the paper, probably went home to his wife to collapse exhausted on the sofa, accepting a large Martini and a scented hankie from his wife, uttering, "You wouldn't believe the day I've had, darling!" Starting at bang on 9.00am and leaving on the dot at 5.00pm, he never once contemplated the possibility of doing a bit of overtime to help clear the burgeoning backlog of work that we had. He wouldn't have known the concept of 'busy' even if it had bitten him on the arse. He thought he knew it all and thought he was untouchable when redundancies were announced a few years later, but having survived the first round of redundancies, nearly fell off his chair in surprise when he got the heave-ho during the second round.

The Guinness Book of Records had been re-branded as I joined, by someone no doubt earning an obscene salary, and became the *Guinness World Records* book. It is still referred to by much of the media today by its original title, indicating what a ridiculous idea it was in the first place! Aside from the world's best-selling copyright book there was another publication, *The Guinness Book of British Hit Singles*. This was compiled and edited with panache and perspicacity (plus perspiration when the printing deadline loomed) by David Roberts. David was a veteran of Guinness and music was (and still is) his passion. I got to know him over time and, once he knew of my own passion for music, drafted me in to do some database fact-checking for artists that I knew about. I immediately set about correcting the book's entries for Gary Numan and Tubeway Army (Nick Beggs from Kajagoogoo played bass in Numan's touring band? I think not!). This would have been the ideal job for me but, alas, it never came to pass.

Vicki and I had spent a few idyllic years together, travelling to San Diego, New York, New England in The Fall and eventually our thoughts turned to marriage. It wasn't really a difficult decision; in fact it was the easiest decision I have ever made in my life. I proposed on Christmas Day 1996 and Vicki, tearfully overjoyed, accepted. We took our time making plans for the wedding itself. Eventually, the date was set for August 1999 and it was the happiest day of my life. Family, friends and colleagues old and new, joined us for a very special day. My Dad gave Vicki away – sadly she'd lost her step-Dad a few months before the wedding. Peter was my Best Man and I remember, as we sat in front of the Registrar with our back to the assembled group of family and friends, turning round to see my wife-to-be for the first time. Both Vicki and Dad were holding onto each other for dear life and she looked like a princess. As this was a Register Office wedding, we couldn't have anything remotely religious in our chosen music to play when the bride arrived and when the register was being signed. So I asked Gary Smith to make up a CD of songs for us, which included 'Down in The Park (Piano Version)'. Only one person amongst the gathered guests twigged it was a Gary Numan song.

The day went by in a blur and countless photographs were taken. I was delighted that most of the band made it and I had the photographer take one of just me, Eric, Martin Barranes and Gary Smith. When presented with the wedding album a month or two later, we leafed through the pages of so many people so happy, so full of joy, so full of life. When we look back over it now, it's sad to see how many of them are no longer with us, never suspecting who was going to be the first to go, only a few short years later.

Our first son was born in June 2002 after an emergency caesarian. Leaving the birth as long as possible, the doctors, worried for the baby's health, opted for the caesarian option and, within half an hour, I was a Dad. While Vicki was in the post-op room, I cradled my precious gift, still wrapped in a little blue blanket and pink knitted hat to keep him warm. Nothing could prepare me for this truly wonderful event as I sat there, tears in my eyes, still wearing the protective gown I'd worn in the delivery room.

We were inundated with cards from family and friends, all wishing us well. One card was from Eric, in which he'd cheerfully written, "Welcome to the 'No Sleep' Club!" Eric had become a father himself a few years before, quite unexpectedly as, after years of trying, he and Ros thought they just weren't destined to be parents.

My Dad, like my wonderful mother-in-law, Emily, was absolutely beside himself with joy when he was presented with his third grandchild – Dad loved Vicki as if she were his own daughter.

Our second son was born in June 2004, another bundle of sheer joy. When he finally made his way into the world, after the initial crying, he was as quiet as a mouse, wrapped up in my arms. I sat next to the bed while Vicki recovered, the moon outside bathing the silent room, and I just gazed at our second son, amazed that we had another little man in our life.

We'd struggled as neither Vicki nor I were prepared for being a parent. You can read all the books you like about it, go to all the ante-natal classes and watch as many parenting DVDs but, until that bundle is yours and you're at home from the hospital with no nurses or support or 24-hour panic buttons and you're wondering what you can do stop the incessant crying, then you have no idea what's involved. But we coped because we had to and that's when your life changes – I would emphasise for the better – between the time "before kids" and your life "after kids".

The band obviously took a back seat but I still saw Eric as regularly

as I could for a beer in town. Eric was having difficulties of his own. I
know he loved his son but I don't necessarily think cozy domesticity
was what Eric really wanted. He was still a rock'n'roll rebel and the
scars in his ears where he had numerous studs from when he was a
teenager were still visible. But here he was, the managing director
of a technology media company, living in a leafy suburban close in
Stevenage, earning a small fortune affording him a very comfortable
life-style.

But something was missing and his marriage was beginning to
suffer. He loved being in the band as much as I did and if there had
ever been a realistic offer of two months on the continent touring
round bars and clubs, he would have been packed in an instant.

A fortnight before our second addition to the family was due, he
rang and asked whether I fancied a beer at our spiritual home, The
Bell on Fleet Street. Vick said it was OK as there was no guarantee I'd
be able to meet him any time soon after the new baby was born, so I
said yes. I asked whether he wanted a full band turn out so we could
relive old glories and discuss songs that we should try and have a
go at.

"Nah, Mart, just me and thee," he said and we agreed to meet the
following night.

We drank far too many beers and discussed all our woes, all our
problems and had a lengthy wander down memory and mammary
lane, revisiting the early days of the band, our time at Prestel, life in
general, wine, women and song.

Very late into the night, we staggered out onto Fleet Street and we
hugged each other good-bye.

"Hope all goes well with the baby!" he called as he headed to the
train station, leaving me at the bus-top, watching him stagger off into
the night at an angle of about 60 degrees like an old ship on the sea.

"Cheers, Eric!" I called after him and he waved without looking
back.

That was the last time I saw him.

Two weeks later, on the day that our second baby was due, I got the phone call from Steve Hughes to say that Eric had died of a massive heart attack the previous evening.

CHAPTER 33

Loss

And then, bloody hell, poor old Dad died a few years later in November 2006, alone at home, unexpectedly and without warning, aged 78. He was recuperating from a hip-replacement operation and, even though he was in some discomfort, we had no idea it was life threatening. I saw him the night before he died and he looked very tired. I should have guessed that something was wrong when he asked whether I would mind seeing myself out which was totally out of character. He got up the next morning and, irony of ironies, died of the same thing that had killed Mum all those years ago, a blood clot that had been lurking undetected in his bloodstream since the hip operation. He was in the bathroom about to clean his teeth and he dropped like a stone, dead before he hit the carpet. My poor Daddy.

I didn't even get to say goodbye.

Dad passing away was just the saddest thing, made worse by the fact that Peter was in Dubai when it happened. He flew back the moment he heard and when I met him the next day, we just cried and cried. We faced the unbearable task of sorting out the funeral arrangements and making sure that we gave Dad a good send off. And we did. We elected to have the wake at Princes Avenue and the house had never seen so many people. It was packed. Peter had the brilliant idea of scanning hundreds of family photos and creating a slideshow on his laptop PC that we set up on Dad's sideboard in the front room. People gathered round and reminisced about Dad, the family, and just what a huge part of our life, and so many others, he'd been. He's missed so much and has missed so much. I remember when our roles were reversed and Dad went from being the towering presence in the family to someone that we needed to look after. This began on Tuesday 23rd September 1997. Dad wanted to go and see his brother Reg and sister-in-law Olive in Plymouth but didn't fancy the drive so elected to go by train. I knew he'd be worried about getting up to Paddington so accompanied him on the journey up from Tolworth to make sure he caught his train on time. Arriving at Paddington, I carried his case and found the right train and located his pre-booked seat.

"Have you got everything?" I asked as he settled himself in, if a little nervously.

"Yep, I think so, son."

"Sandwiches?"

He checked a small carrier bag on his lap.

"Yep."

"Have you got your wallet?"

"Yep," he replied, patting the inside pocket of his coat.

"Have you got a clean hankie?"

He patted the other pocket.

"Yep."

There was a loud whistle-blast from the platform, signaling the train was about to leave.

"OK then, have a safe journey and I'll pick you up on Friday."

"OK, son, see you then. I'll send everyone your love."

I kissed him on the top of his head, said good-bye then waited out on the platform for the train to depart. He waved as the train pulled out and as I watched him I thought how small and vulnerable he looked, like a little boy off on a big adventure somewhere. I was barely able to stop myself from crying.

And now he was gone. A few days before he died, I'd driven past Princes Avenue and thought, "One day, he's not going to be there," but didn't realise, had no way of knowing, that it would be just a matter of hours before that came to pass. As grief-stricken as I was, one small part of me, one tiny, tiny, *tiny* percentage, was relieved that he'd passed away. Sounds callous, right? But consider that for *every single day of my life* since Mum had died in 1977, I'd worried about Dad, and the fact that one day I'd have to face the fact that he was going to die as well and that it might be me that found him. In many ways, it was the best way for Dad to go – quick, painless. He never wanted to be a burden and had a morbid dread of becoming frail and infirm. Dementia was his biggest fear and he extracted a promise from me that if ever his quality of life got to the point where he didn't have a clue what was going and needed 24-hour home care, I'd do the right thing for him and put him out of his misery.

And yet, despite the fact that we were so desperately sad, Peter and I couldn't help but remember a night round at Dad's a few years before. We were there with Susan and Vicki, along with Peter's sons, James and Eliot, sat in the backroom drinking tea. Susan glanced at a vase and said, jokingly, that she was going to start putting little round coloured stickers on the things she fancied keeping when Dad passed away. Dad spluttered with faux indignation.

"You're joking, right? The first thing you'll do when I pop my clogs is get a bloody skip!"

There was a pause before Peter, with perfect comic timing, replied, "No, don't worry Dad, we'll get you a coffin." We all laughed until we all had tears rolling down our cheeks.

I've always thought that when someone dies, it's like those black hole diagrams you see in text books with concentric circles around a hole that falls into the beyond; it's like there are strings attached to all the friends and family, with the deceased falling through the hole into the next life, and the friends and family facing two choices, either be dragged together as the string bunches with the passing, or drift apart if the string breaks. I'm glad to say that the strings that bind my family are stronger than ever.

And I needed them all when, two years later in August 2009 I was diagnosed with Lymphoma, a blood cancer, resulting in 6-months of chemotherapy. I had the joy of being given the all-clear in spring 2010, then the sheer devastation of relapsing a month later. There followed three months of near-fatal levels of chemotherapy, then a month in hospital for more chemotherapy and a stem-cell transplant. I'd kept my hair during the first round of treatment but lost it all, literally overnight, in hospital; I had a full head of hair when I went to bed, I didn't in the morning – that's how virulent the chemotherapy was.

During the months that followed I recuperated from the transplant with the loving support of Vicki, Peter and the rest of the family, along with the unconditional love of my two young sons. Sadly, we lost my lovely mother-in-law, Emily, to cancer during this time and I really didn't know her as long as I would've liked.

I had regular texts and cards from David Okomah, and various insane emails and cartoons from Ben. As I gradually regained my strength, I had the time and opportunity to reflect on the past as, when the dreaded word "cancer" is mentioned and diagnosed, you start to think of your own mortality. I was signed off from work for six months, as, during the first few months of the recuperation, I'd struggle to climb the stairs and, if I'd left something downstairs, I'd struggle – really struggle – to find the strength to go back down and retrieve it. That's not to say I was the worst off by any means. It broke my heart during the month I was in hospital to see little kids, without a hair on their heads, walking round attached to drips, desperately clutching their teddy-bears. Why does the great Almighty allow children to suffer? Maybe there isn't one and we are, after all, alone in the universe and we're nothing more than loud, destructive apes, all intent on destroying the planet and everything on it. If that's the case, then we're making a bloody good job of it.

I had left *Guinness World Records* in 2001 and David Roberts left a few years later, both victims of a sequence of ill-advised sales of the Guinness publishing brand by the parent company, Diageo. Undaunted, David set up his own company, PopPublishing, and over a very drunken lunch in 2007, we batted ideas back and forth about what books he could possibly write or edit. David suggested that we release a book of essays titled *The Song That Changed My Life*, comprising possibly 12 to 15 chapters, written by fans of, perhaps, Bowie, The Police, Blondie, Queen and the like. I volunteered to write the first chapter about Gary Numan, Tubeway Army and 'Are 'friends' electric?' which David could tout round his many contacts within the publishing industry to give potential publishers an idea of what we were hoping to achieve. We received some very positive feedback, some from publishers that David thought would be very critical and dismissive, but none were prepared at that time to commission our book. A key question that they all asked was "would all the essays be as entertaining as the Gary Numan one", considering for example how notoriously po-faced Queen fans could be? We couldn't make that guarantee of course, so the project was kind of put on the backburner, especially as I got ill soon after.

However, the essay buzzed in the back of my mind like an itch I couldn't scratch so, with some time on my hands, I started adding bits and pieces when the mood and muse took me. With the advent of eBooks, David encouraged me to turn my initial chapter into a full book, as it was his belief that it had never been easier to self-publish, planning this as just an e-book. But then David got me a deal with a proper honest to God book publisher and we produced the book you now hold in your hand.

CHAPTER 34

Now

I sit and watch my boys growing up with each passing day, with so many of the things that were part of our daily routines – nightly bath times, a story before they went to sleep – all slipping away. They're getting bigger and more confident and will grow up in a world that will change beyond all recognition in the coming decades. I turned 50 in 2013 and I know that I'm far younger than my Dad was at 50. Dad had lived through the war, through the austerity of the post-war years and everything was a lot more serious and more of a struggle. I can't imagine what life was like in the 1940s and 1950s so I count my blessings that we live in an age of convenience, medical wonder and scientific breakthrough. I doubt Dad could have comprehended that on my iPod, barely thicker than a credit card, I have several hundred songs available at the press of a single button.

Inevitably, my boys are attached to devices nearly every hour of the day, whether at school where an iPad appears to be the default resource in the classroom, or on their own iPods at home, where they have hundreds of songs, which they play in heavy rotation. I listen to some of these songs and it makes me sad that there is so little variation in their style, rhythm and soul. They're all seemingly placed under the banner of rap and R&B but, freely acknowledging that I've turned into my Dad, they all sound the bloody same to me. Where's the danger? Where are the innovative artists? Where's the variety? Where are the songs that will change your life? Where is a cackling Johnny Rotten-like character, rubbing his hands together off in the shadows, preparing to leap into view and upset everyone? Songs these days seem to be anodyne, manufactured, formulaic, synthesized, pitch-corrected, comp-tracks which, on occasion, when my boys have played them for the 10th time, I have uttered my Dad's oft-used phrase, "Oh, Christ, not him again." At least my boys don't like Robbie Williams. Frankly, they'd be confined to the shed if they did.

We were sitting having Sunday dinner the other day and I had some old music playing on my iPod. One track I had sourced from vinyl, as it wasn't available on iTunes. It was an obscure 12-inch B-side remix which I'd imported onto my PC and tidied up the track, taking out the scratches, clicks and hiss.

"You'd never guess this was taken from vinyl!" I boasted, very proud of the several hours of work it had taken to make the song as clean as possible.

My boys looked blankly at each other.

"What's vinyl, Dad?"

"What's a B-Side?"

I nearly cried. Then I asked them what was currently No.1 in the charts but they both shrugged indifferently, having no idea who was A-No.1, King of The Hill, Top of the Heap etc. Not only did they have no idea, they didn't remotely care. It's not that they don't like music, it just that it doesn't matter anymore. There's no big chart run-down on TV, the joy and despair at seeing the climbers and fallers. At their age, I would have probably known each week's Top Ten as a matter of course, anxiously awaiting the chart run down to see who had claimed the top spot. There doesn't seem to be one, definitive, chart of charts these days, so the achievement of getting to No.1 appears to me to have been completely diluted. It barely makes any kind of dent in the media anyway. Where's the celebration? Where's the public acknowledgement? Do gold discs even get presented anymore, or do the artists just get an email saying, "Dear Sir/Madam. Please find attached a generic certificate acknowledging your twelve minutes at No.1 last Tuesday afternoon. Well done!"

My boys live in a society where everything is instant. Music is available to download in seconds. There's no waiting for the shops to open to go to a record store and buy the 7-inch, 12-inch or album. There is no longer any need to anxiously protect your valuable purchase on the crowded bus home, a purchase that no doubt features lavish, lovingly prepared cover artwork, plus, maybe, a gatefold sleeve and, if you're lucky, a free poster. Everything now is on-demand and the sales of physical media such as CDs, DVDs and Blu-Ray are in freefall. In a few short years' time, they'll be considered as outdated as VHS and C-90 cassette tapes.

I take a photo on my phone or camera and they say, "Can I see it?" There's no waiting for the 36-exposure film to be finished, then taking it into the chemist and waiting a few days for it be developed. With the advent of digital photography and the trend for endless selfies, we have literally thousands of photographs of us with the boys, taken almost daily, all documenting how they're growing up and showing us as the happy family that we truly are. It's telling to note that I don't think I have more than one photo of my Mum, Dad, Peter and me together as a family, as someone was always missing to take the picture. The only one that I can recall is one of us gathered round the dinner table at Pontin's in Bracklesham Bay, Sussex, from about 1967, none of us looking particularly happy as Peter reliably informs me that Mum and Dad had just had a blazing row. Other than that, all I have are a few black and white photos of Mum, Peter and me, or Dad, Peter and me, or Mum, Dad and me.

My life has returned to some semblance of normality, although the shadow of the cancer returning in one form or another hangs over me daily. But with Vicki and my boys, looking after me, I'm pretty upbeat about things. And my brother, Peter, and I are pretty damn steady.

And on that note, it seems a pretty good point to finish. But, before we go, here's a somehow appropriate final word, taking us back to 2004. We had just been blessed with our first son and Dad was a regular visitor once Vicki was out of hospital and home with our precious baby boy. The house had become a post-natal unit, filled with baby-wipes, nappies, baby-grows, sterilization equipment, bottles and even stair-gates for when he started crawling. But that was a long way off yet so, in these first tentative days of being new parents, all we had was this exquisite gift. Dad and Emily were just amazing, helping wherever and whenever they could, even if it was just doing the washing up while I fed Vicki her dinner as she'd finally got our first born to sleep, tucked up in her arms, wrapped in the blanket that Emily had crotched and didn't want to disturb him by putting him in his Moses basket.

On one early visit, as Dad cradled our new born baby in his arms, I said, somewhat mischievously, "Here, Dad, guess what's No.1 at the moment?"

"No idea, son," he replied. I doubt Dad had had the remotest interest in the charts and popular music for over thirty years!

I put on The Sugarbabe's 'Freak Like Me' which heavily sampled Numan's 'Are 'friends' electric?'. It was the "We Don't Give a Damn" mix, which initially slightly distorted the sample. The vocals started then – bang – the riff from Numan's 1979 classic – that unmistakable, timeless, evocative, innovative riff that Dad had heard a thousand times or more – roared in. Dad winced.

"Oh, Christ, not him again?"

And we all laughed.

END BIT

And that was my story

Everything I've related in the preceding chapters actually happened *as I remember it* but, to quote Eric Morecambe, not *necessarily* in the right order. I've moved a couple of bits around and combined a few events to further the narrative a bit. I *might* have exaggerated a few incidences (my Poetic Licence Number is: 399-0844) but other than that, it's a pretty accurate memoir of a child born in the UK in the 1960s and growing up in the 1970s and beyond.

I've elected to change nearly all the names of my old school-friends at the hallowed halls of Ivywood School and the staff at Fine Fare and the MoD so as to avoid upsetting anyone and to protect the innocent (and the guilty!). Ivywood itself is a pseudonym and I daresay the real school is now a jewel in the crown of Surrey's Secondary Modern Educational System and no doubt has Ofsted plaudits by the truckload. But back in the dim-dark days of the mid-1970s, it was a pretty miserable place with wanton bullying, violence, and vandalism, plus inherent racism and victimization.

I also elected to change the name of my first girlfriend and her insidious family as I've made some fairly serious accusations about them, especially her Dad. These accusations, especially about his treatment of Martine, were not exaggerated at all, sadly. All bar Penny, the family was nuts.

Thanks go to Terry Easton, my first musical partner for the joy of our first, stumbling steps together playing in a band. Some of the nights out clubbing were pretty memorable, too!

Most of the remaining names are (all bar one) genuine so it makes a certain amount of sense to do some thanks right about now.

First off, a big thank you to my editor and the chief-supporter of this project, David Roberts of PopPublishing. He and I have collaborated on various projects since our meeting at *Guinness World*

Records back in 1999 and we continue to spend hours visiting and photographing notable music sites and venues, seeking out obscure pubs where The Rolling Stones played in 1963, identifying the locations of album cover photo-shoots and even visiting John and Yoko's flat in Montagu Square in London, standing on the exact spot where they stripped naked for their notorious *Two Virgins* album cover. We elected to keep our clothes on but it was a very, very close call. All this to support David's various PopPublishing publications, including the rather wonderful portfolio of *Rock Atlas* books where I'm very proud of my modest contributions in the form of photos and articles.

By the way, if anyone reading this can suggest a UK location that is intrinsically linked to Numan, let me know – it might make the next edition of *Rock Atlas*!

Big thanks also go to my friends Ben Nicholas, David Okomah and Andrew Burton, all of whom will hopefully realise that my life would be a very sad place without them:

Ben is still the most manic, insane, loud, irreverent lunatic I could ever hope to meet. We have been through tremendous highs and penniless lows together. He was also my chief supporter during my year-long campaign to woo Vicki, so my thanks here seem somehow insufficient. Ben can make me laugh so much that I nearly pass out – we regularly clear several tables around us in the busiest of pubs in London. I fear that one day, after several beers, he will try and reveal his innermost self to his god, a-la the telepathic mutants in *Beneath the Planet of The Apes*. Don't ever change, Ben!

David is a true gent, who regales me with his rock'n'roll tales of his youth, including his escapades bunking off school to go and see bands! He could write a book of his own! I look forward like a kid on Christmas Eve to our 'Dave & Martin Days' up in London, mooching around guitar shops, music shops, comic shops and then spending six to eight hours in a pub, where Dave regularly relates the tale of an L&R colleague who he accompanied to some rock gig, where she ended up in the mosh pit, diving in wearing very little and staggering out wearing even less. With each telling, she wears less and less! (No photos are known to exist, sadly).

Andrew I've known nearly all my life, so that's quite a few years now! In the mid-1980s through to the early 1990s, he accompanied me to several Numan concerts, always a keen concert-goer. Given his metal roots, I'm not sure he totally 'got' Numan but was impressed by the axe-wielding Kipper and his extended, not to mention loud, guitar solos at some of those shows (others weren't so keen!). Andrew has helped me out on numerous occasions where his DIY, plumbing and electrical skills far outweighed mine and ensured that I didn't end up in A&E or hosing down the few remaining cinders of my house. I've lost count of the number of car-alarms and car-radios he's installed in the various jalopies I've owned. While he is a forward-thinking man, when he comes round for dinner with his wife, Gill, I drag him back into the past and make him reminisce, usually after several beers, numerous bottles of wine and a good meal. We'll go out for that drink one of these days!

Further thanks go to the boys in the band, Gary Smith, Tony Sweet, Steve Hughes and Martin Barranes – my band of brothers. The best of times, the worst of times they may have been but when We Fear Change were good, we were very, very good. There were times in the rehearsal studios where we were pretty damn tight and I would sometimes step back from the mic and watch them all singing or playing and think, "Do you know what? We ain't bad!" Those were some very good days, indeed. And who knows? Maybe we will play again one day!

RIP Eric Watson, I miss you, old chum.

Thanks to Sue Crawford whose dream-like poetry inspired us to write 'Last Night (we can fly)'.

Thanks to all my old school friends, including Kim Taylor and Ian Ash for reminding me of a few incidents at Tolworth Infants School and Ivywood School. And no thanks, whatsoever, to most of the teachers at Ivywood...there were a few exceptions, such as my art teacher, Miss Gordon, who was simply wonderful and an inspiration. The rest were mostly hopeless.

Thanks to Nick Bendall, Bill Desmond, Hayley Bovey and Katie Czamara for their friendship and support. And thanks to Bill Worman who, like Dr. Frankenstein, helped create my drunken alter-ego, Dr. Hanz!

Thank you Michelle Harris, my specialist nurse at The Royal Marsden Hospital in Sutton. Michelle is a shining example of the NHS at its very best – patient, professional, compassionate – who kept Vicki and I from going insane during my treatment. Michelle went to great lengths, well above and way, way beyond, to make sure that I was OK, translating the diagnosis and endless acronyms so we knew what they really meant and what the implications were. She made sure that Vicki and the boys had all the support they needed as well. I've cried on her shoulder many, many times.

Thanks to the families we've met through school who have become great friends and who have helped us on so many occasions – especially Jeff and Vida Evans, Clive and Rachel Bennett.

Vicki would like to thank Sarah, Jo, Rachel, Claire, Cindy and Caroline for all their help and support during the often difficult times when I was not exactly at my fighting-best.

I'd like to thank all my comrades at TUI who also stood by me during those darker days, particularly Steve Henson, Clive Norton and Jill Punter

Now the biggies!

A heartfelt thank you to my wife, Vicki, and my boys. Vicki, for putting up with me and the boys for keeping me young. Growing up fast, I see in them some of my idiosyncrasies – the way they behave, the way they look, the way they talk. I hope I've been more of a visible father than my Dad was when I was their age. As for Vicki, she is my rock. My soul-mate. My best friend. I only wish I could've met her sooner so I could have loved her longer.

To my brother, Peter, I'll keep it as short as the voice-mail messages he leaves for me from time to time, and say, "I love you loads." He knows this, I'm sure, plus he'd cringe with embarrassment if I said how much he means to me.

Thanks to my cousin, Tim Weaver, who has accompanied me dozens of times to see Numan in concert (we never did get the long-promised backstage passes from Bert Hayter at Guildford Civic Hall, did we?). He's fixed all my jalopies, often up to his armpits in grease and is a workaholic. Despite this, when I've called him down in Guildford to give him news about my health, he's been at my front-door within the hour and not many people can claim to have done that.

Thanks go to the rest of the Clan Downham, my in-laws and outlaws (with our Bermondesy roots, there were bound to be a few rogues!). As long as you have friends and family, everything else is a bonus.

Thanks and love go to the Herring Family – they know why and they know why it would be impossible to go into detail for all the things they've done for us. It would seem totally inadequate anyway.

And, ultimately, this book is dedicated to my Mum and Dad. How would my life have turned out under different circumstances? In some parallel universe, I'm living that life where Mum didn't die and I *DID* go down the path of a destructive adolescent. I wonder what became of me?

Finally, a huge thank you and tip of the hat to Gary Numan. What is absolutely beyond question, beyond any doubt and impossible to underestimate, is the impact that 'Are 'friends' electric?' and his other classic songs and albums had on me. He will always be 'The Man'.

Martin Downham

Ewell Court, Surrey

August 2016

Gary Numan:
an appraisal

Martin Downham may have finished his own story, but here he delves into Gary Numan's, with a career appraisal of the man who is a constant presence in Remind Me To Smile.

I said earlier in this book that it was very difficult to be a Numan fan in the late 1980s, 1990s and beyond. It was a period when he made some increasingly poor decisions. These ranged from setting up the well-intended, altruistic but ultimately doomed Numa Records, to some of his more questionable and down-right God-awful releases. Songs his subsequent record labels convinced him would be winners? What about the covers of Prince's '1999' and 'U Got The Look' for starters. Worse still was his appearance on BBC-TV with Leo Sayer in a musical comedy sketch pretending to be drunk and performing 'Warriors' on *Crackerjack*. Although some fans mocked his occasional but strangely profitable late 1980s collaboration with Bill Sharpe from Shakatak, with the singles 'Change Your Mind', 'New Thing from London Town' and 'No More Lies', they all made quite healthy and possibly unexpected returns to the charts for Numan. The collaboration with the group Radio Heart and the resultant 'Radio Heart' single was pretty good but the follow-ups, 'London Times' and 'All Across The Nation' were dreadful.

Numan toured nearly every single year and I religiously bought every album, CD and single. But even I cringed when I heard the truly awful *Machine & Soul* album, which was his absolute nadir as a recording artist. Numan recognized this too and retreated to the sanctity of his home with his bride-to-be, Gemma, to lick his wounds and decide what to do next. His next release was the awesome *Sacrifice*, a sinister, bleak, stripped-back, eerie album on which he played nearly every instrument. Dispensing with lavish and incongruous heavy-metal guitar solos, prevalent on his last couple of albums and tours, this release was a haunting, menacing, claustrophobic album, which showed a man who had regained control of his life, his music and musical direction. It could almost be called *Tubeway Army Volume II* as it was virtually a new start for Numan.

The fiercely patriotic Numan decamped to LA a few years ago, causing some derision and contempt within his fan base. The more narrow-minded took to the message boards in disgust, declaring that if he was so fucking proud to British, why did he fuck off to America? But consider this. He's a family man, he's got a wife and three kids, and he made the decision there were more opportunities in the US than in the UK, where he is still regarded here by some as a novelty, 'one-hit' wonder. In the US, he is championed as a pioneering artist and regularly name-checked and endorsed by the likes of Beck, Marilyn Manson, The Foo Fighters, Afrika Bambaataa, Queens of the Stone Age, Lady Gaga and, perhaps most significantly, Nine Inch Nails, who go out of their way to declare their respect for Numan and his undeniable influence on their music.

And let's take another minute here. What influence did Gary Numan *really* have on British music? The stock answer from the naysayers would be none, but the question bears further analysis. His contemporaries, The Human League, OMD and the pre-Midge Ultravox, were, in 1978 and 1979, penning songs similar to those found on *Replicas* but it took the breakthrough hit of 'Are 'friends' electric?', at the forefront of the synth movement, to enable them to have chart success of their own. I wonder, for example, if John Foxx with his brilliant, menacing 'Underpass' single would have made the charts without the groundswell of interest in synth music? Would his album, *Metamatic*, arguably a bookend to Numan's *The Pleasure Principle* album, have also made the charts? This groundswell showed other musicians, some who had previously been in more traditional bands, exactly what could be achieved with the sound of the clinical, efficient and industrial notes of a Roland synthesizer or Yamaha CS-80. So, I'll go out on a limb here and say that the following, for example, arguably – *possibly* – owe their livelihood to Gary Numan:

Tears for Fears.

Depeche Mode

A Flock of Seagulls

Japan

Soft Cell

The Midge-fronted Ultravox (ergo, Midge Ure's solo career)

Eurythmics – their first album, In The Garden was a million-miles from the synth-heavy follow-up, *Sweet Dreams (are made of this)* (ergo, Annie Lennox's solo career)

Thompson Twins

Thomas Dolby

Howard Jones

Nik Kershaw

Pet Shops Boys

I'm not dismissing their talent or ability or their multi-million selling records, but it was Gary Numan, who made synth music popular and allowed other synth bands to finally crack the charts. Nevertheless, I'd almost bet my house-keys that, if challenged, these artists would inevitably, predictably, cite Bowie, Kraftwerk and Roxy Music as their influences.

Actors, authors and presenters now have the confidence to publicly, openly declare, "I like Gary Numan!" whereas once upon a time they would rather have declared their support for the reintroduction of prohibition. And why shouldn't they? Gary Numan is great – I've known it for years, as have some of my fellow Numanoids.

I solicited a few comments via the various Numan Facebook groups:

Jill Booth

I first became hooked on Gary Numan and his music in 1979 when I saw him on TOTP singing 'Are 'friends' electric?', but I was a young married mum with three young children and so time and money was tight, therefore travelling around and going to his concerts was out of the question. But I always followed his career as much as possible. In more recent years I saw him on an old TOTP again and the magic returned and now I enjoy collecting all his records and CDs and even going to some of his concerts with my grown children and grandchildren! Now that Gary has the symptoms of Asperger's Syndrome (but not clinically diagnosed as far as I know) I understand why he always seemed self-conscious, awkward and shy in his youth, but he has done amazingly well to overcome it and get where he is today even though the press also treated him abominably.

I had VIP Meet & Greet tickets for his concert in Manchester in 2015. My eldest daughter, Jennifer, accompanied me who was only two years old when AFE was No 1. I thought that I would be a nervous wreck as we queued up but I was very calm indeed! When it was my turn to see Gary I gave him a hug which was 36 years overdue! My daughter and Dave the tour manager took some photos of us. Dave used my device and he took a little while so I took advantage and gave Gary some extra cuddles (bliss)! He was laughing and squeezed me too! Then he signed some items for me, of which one was my copy of his book 'Praying to the Aliens'. I asked him if he was writing a sequel and he said that he was...a continuation from 1997/98. I told him that his three little girls were lovely and [his wife] Gemma was too. We talked a bit about the ups and downs in his career and I told him not to be so hard on himself about some of the lows. He came across as the very gentle, shy and inoffensive man that I always knew that he was and I felt very humbled to have met him at last. I am eternally grateful to my daughter too for making it happen. A little later we watched the sound check and took photos and short films and then it was almost time for the concert which was brilliant and I'm now looking forward to meeting him again (hopefully).

Chris Smith

As a 15-year-old kid in May 1979, a very shy and quiet kid, I kept myself to myself but so wanted to be part of the gang at school. During the lunch break one day, one of the teachers had the radio on and 'Are 'friends' electric?' was playing. I couldn't believe what I was hearing! When I got home I searched the radio for it but when I saw Numan for the first time, I knew then that I'd found what I was looking for; his look, his sound, everything about him is what I wanted to be. The following week, I went to school with a different attitude, a different look and was a lot more confident and all because of that song and Gary Numan's look. I opened up more, got involved in talks about him and, without doubt, he changed my life for the better. And now, 36 years later, I still feel exactly the same.

Dan Ciappi

In 1979 I was 14 when Gary Numan/Tubeway Army first appeared on The Old Grey Whistle Test performing 'Down in the Park' and 'Are 'friends' electric?' It was different to anything else I'd ever heard. It was dreary, it was slow, it was depressing. It was fantastic! I'd never felt so related to a song or tune before, but this was it. Nobody else liked his music except me and one other kid in the whole school. One album after another came out, as brilliant as the last: Tubeway Army, Replicas, The Pleasure Principle, Telekon. I ran home from school to listen to an interview with Kid Jensen. Jensen introduced 'This Wreckage' by asking about the Japanese writing, with Numan replying, "It means, 'I leave you.'" He went on to say he was making four more albums and that was it. I was devastated. I saw him perform at the Odeon, Birmingham, and it was brilliant. I saw him at Wembley for the farewell concert in 1981 and I hated him for making my sister cry. My mate said he wouldn't like to meet him just in case it spoilt his idea of him. However, I met Gary when he did a book signing around 1997. He was great. I still enjoy his early tracks as well as the new. I believe everything happens for a reason. Bands split up now only to reform years later; maybe Numan was a genius in retiring so early only to comeback reinvented? Thanks GN!

Steve Eveleigh

Well, where to start? On Christmas Day 1979, I opened a square, flat package wondering what was inside. As I slid the cover out, I instantly recognised the picture; it was The Pleasure Principle album. My Mum then came in with her little mono record player. I had heard 'Cars' on the radio and loved it! I'd previously heard 'Are 'friends' electric?' by Tubeway Army but at nine-years-old, I didn't realise it was the same singer. My Step-Dad suggested to my Mum that they got me an album for Christmas, so The Pleasure Principle it was! The first album I ever owned. I played it until it wouldn't play anymore! I've since had three copies on vinyl and still have nearly all my Numan vinyl records. Gary's move into new styles of music has kept me a Numanoid right up to the present day. Long may he reign – the king of electronic music!

Ian Meikle

I was blown away by the synth sound of 'Are 'friends' electric?' and was fortunately given both Replicas and The Pleasure Principle for birthday and Christmas, both now regarded as classic albums. However, it wasn't until I saw Numan live on the Teletour in 1980 that I realised just how good he was. It was my first concert, at the age of 14. I was hooked and there was no turning back after that. Despite his temporary decision to retire in 1981, followed by some wilderness years where his musical direction changed and he had clearly lost his way, this made me even more determined to follow his every move. For a while it was unfashionable to be a Numan fan, which often resulted in some ridicule from friends. However, the change in musical direction again, and critical acclaim for his most recent albums has made this all worthwhile. And it's so richly deserved! The culmination for me was a VIP meeting with Numan during his Dead Son Rising tour in Glasgow. I've never met such a nice guy, and his commitment to always include at least one

Scottish date on his tours is refreshing and very much welcome. He has, without doubt, had a major impact on my life story so far.

Brian Dale

I was a bit lost musically, bit of punk, bit of disco, plus a smattering of, dare I say it, a bit of Abba. I'd just enjoyed watching a documentary on Toyah, when one Thursday evening in 1979 I tuned into Top of the Pops as usual. I saw an almost androgynous, semi-human, flanked by synths, delivering a cold, dystopian diatribe, in a shrill emotionless voice. My hair stood on end......'Are 'friends' electric?' changed my life for good.

Mark Moran

I went to Kent with my best friend in the summer of 1979, during early May. We were there to pick the crops and work on the farm, aged just 16. On the weekend we used to travel to Canterbury and go to a restaurant and have a really big blow out and gorge ourselves. I'll never forget the third time we went there to eat. Just as our main course was brought out, this synthesizer riff started playing on the restaurant radio and it was mesmerising. Then this voice started to sing and it was weird, odd, different, amazing: "It's cold outside, and the paints peeling off of my walls…". I was stuck in a time warp, staring at the radio and listening to this song. From the instant that synthesizer started the song I was hooked, I was a Gary Numan fan. Bear in mind that he used synthesizers to create magic: Eerie, jaunty, happy, creepy and dark melodic songs using those old Korg keyboards with the cables and a patch board to make the sounds. They used Mini Moogs too, which frankly were from the Ark. Amps, PA systems, mixing desks and the like used by Numan back then would be laughed at and ridiculed now, yet Gary Numan managed perfectly well using them. He changed the course of music right from May 1979 with 'Are 'friends' electric?' right up until the present day.

Numan is and always will be unique. He's not afraid to be 'out there' experimenting and trying new things, sometimes putting his own reputation on the line. Gary Numan is one of those people who knows what the next trend will be, then goes and does it himself without waiting. A pioneer, a ground-breaker, a massive presence on stage, a burning desire to please his fans which was shown when he used to spend EVERY penny he made on the stage sets he used. Despite all this, he remains a humble man, willing to mix with his fans and attend parties they throw for him. You won't meet a nicer guy or a kinder guy and you sure as hell won't meet anyone with as much talent and drive as Gary Numan. Somebody hit the play button; let's listen to 'Joe The Waiter' again!

David Okomah

Occasionally, you hear a song that moves into your head, unpacks its bags and makes itself at home. One such tune was by a punk band I once saw called Mean Street. A ragged assortment of miscreants and undesirables, the type of also-rans who regularly appeared at the foot of the bill at clubs like the Marquee in London, back in 1977. They opened their set with a song called 'Bunch of Stiffs' - an unremarkable punk-by-numbers ditty that I've heard just once, over thirty years ago. Even now, I could sing you the chorus. They never achieved much, apart from the song featuring on the compilation album Live at the Vortex, by which time they'd unceremoniously sacked their frontman and songwriter, a young man named Gary Webb. I didn't realise it at the time, but 'Bunch of Stiffs' was to be the first of many Webb compositions that would take up permanent residence in my brain.

Shortly after being thrown out of the band, "Webb" became "Numan". I guess you know what happened next...

On Numan's Facebook page, there is the following quote:
Malcolm McLaren, the Sex Pistols Svengali.
"I remember hearing Gary Numan's 'Cars' and looking at this madly volatile black crowd in the middle of the South Bronx - my first visit to witness a party that I was invited to by Afrika Bambaataa. I, a naive

white honky, thought that it was in some apartment building, but it turned out to be this massive debris site and there in the middle of it was these guys telling their stories, freestyle, to Gary Numan's 'Cars'. My thoughts were interrupted when waves parted in the crowd like the Red Sea and there, in a pool of light on the floor, came characters who started to spin and breakdance. I'd never seen anything quite like it, I thought it was amazing."

A cursory check of the 'net reveals the following comments from Numan's peers:

DJ Carl Cox on 'Cars'

"All of the sound on this is electronic – the only thing that's human is Numan. It's still one of the most powerful songs you can hear today and it still sends chills down my spine."

Tricky

"Listen: I know without doubt that I am the best artist in the world and have been for the last seven years. Not because my music is the best, but because there's never been any compromise. The only artists who've done that are old school: Bob Dylan, James Brown, Public Enemy and Gary Numan."

Prince

"You know, his album Replicas never left my turntable...there are people still trying to work out what a genius he was."

Kanye West

"I was listening to Gary Numan. I ended up becoming more polished as a designer. I designed my tracks."

Lady Gaga

"Gary Numan proves music has always been really inventive for the masses."

THE CONTEMPORARIES HAVE THEIR SAY...

Recent well-produced documentaries on BBC-4 and the Sky Arts channel, revealed some interesting comments from Numan's contemporaries:

Andy McClusky/OMD

"People like ourselves and Cabaret Voltaire and The Human League had all just got used to the fact that we existed and that [we were] sharing our space. And then along comes someone we thought at the time was some Johnny-Come-Lately...and we thought, "Who the hell is this guy from London, who's on telly and having a massive hit record"? I'd never heard of him!"

Trent Reznor / Nine Inch Nails

"I was always impressed by the way that it was unmistakably him, that it was notably him. I see me doing now what I've learned from him."

Phil Oakey / The Human League

"Gary is fantastically influential in a way that he just has not had credit for. I think there were three [synth] No.1 hits – certainly Dave Stewart and Barbara Gaskin, Gary Numan and The Flying Lizards, and I actually stood there, after I think we'd done a couple of LPs and I thought, "We've blown it. We now look like the also-rans and everyone has taken the idea and done a lot better than us."

John Foxx/Ultravox! and the Godfather of Modern Synth

"I really liked Gary's music. I think he made the best records, at that time. I think he, if anyone, really condensed it into a form that was perfect at that point."

Suzanne Sulley/The Human League

"When Gary was first on Top of the Pops, I phoned Joanne Catherall and

said, "Are you watching this? Have you seen this man? He's fantastic!"
The look and the sound were so different, sort of alien."

Martyn Ware/Heaven 17
"I was gutted when 'Cars' came out. I thought it was really good. All
this time we were convinced it was just a matter of time before we had a
No.1 record. Then someone comes out of the blue and does it!"

Andy McClusky/OMD
[(Numan's music] wasn't rock'n'roll. It wasn't honest, it wasn't working
class, it wasn't worthy. It wasn't earthy, it wasn't real, it wasn't
sweaty, it wasn't manly. It was pretentious, pseudo-intellectual and
I am absolutely convinced that Numan's career was shortened by
nasty, nasty vitriolic journalism. I think Gary has now got some of the
recognition and the kudos that he deserved a long time ago." (You're
forgiven for not mentioning Numan in that recent magazine article! –
Martin Downham)

Martin Mills, founder of Beggars Banquet Records
"His use of electronic sounds was way ahead of its time. He was one
of those artists that created a new way of making music. 'Are 'friends'
electric?' was an extraordinarily different-sounding record. It was as
different as 'Good Vibrations' by The Beach Boys was, or 'A Whiter
Shade of Pale' by Procul Harum when they were No.1. It just came out
of nowhere. I think it's one of the greatest No.1s ever because it's so
completely original."

MORE FAN WORSHIP FROM ON HIGH...

The respected actor Michael Sheen was on *The Late Late Show* in the
US recently, then hosted by Craig Ferguson. Both enthused about
Numan and his music, both stating they'd seen him on a recent US
tour. Ferguson was genuinely jealous when Sheen revealed he'd had
Numan on a one-off radio show he'd hosted for the BBC. They then
discussed what a great record 'Down in The Park' was – no argument
from me there!

Bill Bailey, the actor, comedian, musician and presenter, frequently
includes a version of 'Cars' in his live shows, sung entirely in French
with the synth hook replaced by car horns. It's quite an authentic
version but, tellingly, Bill always states, quite seriously, that it
represents his tribute to the genius of Gary Numan and one of the
greatest songs of all time.

There was a double album of cover versions released in 1997,
Random, which featured some faithful versions of Numan's songs,
along with some interesting interpretations, by artists that included
Saint Etienne, Damon Albarn, EMF, Jesus Jones, Republica, The Orb,
Pop Will Eat Itself, Moloko, Magnetic Fields and Dave Clarke.

Foo Fighters covered 'Down in The Park', an outstanding version
showcasing Dave Grohl's iconic power drumming, (goddammit, the
man is a machine!). The track was featured on 1996's *The Songs in the
Key of X* album, featuring songs influenced by *The X-Files* TV series
and was highlighted by Sandy Masuo of *The Los Angeles Times* as the
best track on the album.

Basement Jaxx heavily sampled 'M.E.' from *The Pleasure Principle*
for their 2001 hit 'Where's Your Head At". As I've already mentioned,
The Sugababes, with their No.1 hit 'Freak Like Me', featured the main
riff from 'Are 'friends' electric?'

In 2014 a remastered and expanded edition of the *Nightclubbing*
album by the much-maligned Grace Jones (blimey, you punch one
TV presenter and no-one forgets!) was released. This new version

of the original 1981 album featured a disc of bonus material which included a version of 'Me! I Disconnect From You', which proved to be a popular download on iTunes.

Neil Finn, the powerhouse behind Crowded House, launched a side-project in 2011, The Pajama Club, who, at their live concerts, performed The Finn Brothers' 'Suffer Never' which segued into a blinding version of 'Are 'friends' electric?', complete with a few Bob Dylan lyrics thrown in for good measure.

If you want to know what Led Zeppelin's version of 'Are 'friends' electric?' might have sounded like had they ever covered it, seek out Generator's version from the early 1990s.

And, of course, the late David Bowie never had a kind word to say about Numan, apart from what I can't believe were anything other than sarcastic comments about him writing two of the finest records in British pop music.

I made compilation CDs of some of these tracks for friends and associates, taking great delight in pointing out that they were Numan songs. The *Random* album resides on a four-foot wide shelf in my Man Cave that houses all my Numan CD albums and CD singles. All my Numan vinyl – 12-inch singles, albums and picture discs – are lovingly stored on another shelf. On another, I have my Numan magazines, articles and books, including the indispensable *Electric Pioneer* by Paul Goodwin which details every UK Numan single, LP, and CD, every song played on tour, every notable TV appearance and every video and DVD.

I have the *Warriors Tour Book*, which I proudly and excitedly brought home in 1984 after a shopping trip to London, only to have my Dad say, "Was it in the bargain bin?" I even have the notorious *Numan by Computer* book from 1980, which, as with every copy ever printed, instantly fell apart the moment I got it home. I have all the tour programmes, from 1979 to 1997, plus a couple of souvenir tour CDs. Alas, my 'Numan File' of original press cuttings vanished in a house move a couple of years ago.

As healthy as my collection is, it pales into utter insignificance compared to the lavish collections assembled by other Numan fans who have every album, single and CD from around the world, including obscure foreign imports, miss-pressed picture discs and every subtle variation of the coloured vinyl releases of 'We Are Glass'. There are websites that studiously describe in loving detail every Numan release. And, my God, there are even touring tribute bands now, such as the spot-on, note-perfect but recently defunct Nuway Army (sorry I got so drunk at the March 2014 gig at Bar XL in Epsom, lads – I hope that's not the reason why you called it a day?), and Pat Martin who brings the distinctive Numan-sound to venues across the UK.

Numan is a warrior, a survivor, and disarmingly honest. He's human and fallible. He has been through every conceivable high and unimaginable low in his career, from Punk wannabe, to global star, to a despised, Tory-loving has-been.

With every setback, he has dusted himself down and come back, often only to be knocked back down again. Some of his friends, colleagues and recording associates have not survived the journey:

Paul Gardiner: Tubeway Army stalwart and original bassist

Ced Sharpley: The inimitable drummer – a great loss.

Nash The Slash: The wildly eccentric artist that played a pivotal role in Numan's 1981 farewell shows: manic, dressed in white undertaker's outfit and top hat with face covered in bandages like a mummy, his violin solo on 'The Joy Circuit' was unforgettable.

Robert Palmer: Numan collaborated on a couple of tracks on Palmer's 1980 album, Clues which included a magnificent cover of Numan's 'I Dream of Wires'. Palmer also played "Cars" and "Me! I Disconnect From You" live at his concerts.

Mick Karn: Who provided the silky, exotic and I believe largely improvised bass lines to 'Slowcar to China' and others on Dance.

Dick Morrissey: The go-to sax player who worked on several Numan albums.

Gary Numan has made a fortune and lost a fortune. He has overcome virtual bankruptcy by selling his house, his flash cars and even old stage and recording equipment: all this in an effort to keep afloat, and retain, his status as a recording artist, even if the UK music press and, indeed, some of his so-called loyal fans derided every release.

Despite financial pressure and battling overwhelming odds, I have never seen Numan put on a bad show. Even on club tours, he's put 100% into his performance, from the lighting to the sound to the band. I've even seen him in concert when he could barely sing due to a bout of laryngitis. But whereas other artists might have cancelled, he followed the adage 'the show must go on' and still played a blinder. Throughout his entire career, I doubt he's ever cancelled more than half a dozen gigs.

I have never, ever come out of a Numan live show and thought, "That was a bit bland..." I'll admit some of the songs played have been average on some occasions. Starting to doubt his own abilities and musical direction, he listened to questionable advice from the so-called experts within the industry and released songs he wasn't entirely sure were in his best interests, trusting the record label knew what they were doing.

He never wanted to be famous and would have, perhaps, settled for just being a cult-artist back in 1979. In many ways, he has become that cult-artist now and toured across several continents in 2014, getting his new music live in front of as many people as he could even if the venues were far, far smaller than his Wembley Arena 'final tour' shows from 1981. I think it's commendable. Numan had undertaken the tour to support his then recently-released *Splinter (Songs from a broken mind)* album. Amid great critical acclaim it attracted fans who weren't even born when Tubeway Army started. The album continues his new direction as a credible artist – angry, industrial, sinister, eerie and God-baiting. How many of his contemporaries from 1979 are still releasing new albums and touring with new material? His new fans love it and I wonder what opportunities he will find next in America.

In 2006, he undertook an innovative tour where he played the 1980 *Telekon* album in its entirety, with associated singles and B-sides. I went with David Okomah and it was a memorable night, hearing songs I'd never heard live and some I thought I'd never hear live again. As we stood in the cramped auditorium at The Forum in Kentish Town, Numan played a version of 'Sleep By Windows', with the refrain:

"And we are just sound, and we are just noise, and we are all here to lie,"

This line was repeated in this live version like a mantra. As I stood mesmerized in the darkness, I noticed a huge man next to me, built like the proverbial brick shit-house, taller than me, covered in tattoos, large veiny arms, muscles rippling beneath his white vest, ears pierced...with tears streaming down his cheeks. He looked at me, tipped his shaven head towards the stage and just nodded. It was that kind of evening.

A further series of concerts took place in October 2015 where Numan played at sold-out venues in the UK, performing over three nights, the *Replicas*, *The Pleasure Principle* and *Telekon* albums. Fans have said they were probably among the best gigs he's done. I would sleep overnight on a wet pavement to queue for tickets to see a performance of the *Dance* album in its entirety. It's doubtful it'll to come to pass though, as I think it unlikely that anyone could even come anywhere close to emulating the peerless Mick Karn on bass.

At the Q Music Awards 2015, Jean Michel Jarre presented Numan with the award for Innovation in Sound, finally, publicly recognizing just how important he has been in steering music and music technology to where it is now.

Even though Numan is generally reluctant to dwell too much on the past, annoyingly answering many questions about his rise to fame with the stock answer, "I can't really remember," his catalogue of music has touched thousands and thousands of people over the years.

I truly hope that some might read this and think, "Yeah, I can relate to that," whip out their iPods and listen to not only the well-known songs but also some of the wonderful innovative album tracks as well.

Someone asked the question in a recent magazine article about whether you should ever meet your heroes. I think the answer is, no. You have anidealised image of them – tall, invincible, and mesmerizing – but to meet them in real life…is that wise? In the mid-1990s, Numan, in a valiant effort to keep in touch with his dwindling fan base, organized meet and greet events where winners of callers to his 0898 fan club competition line, could actually meet him at events such as outdoor go-karting. I never entered the competitions, as I didn't want to meet him. Your heroes should be aloof, elusive and mysterious. I don't want to race them in go-karts.

My editor, David Roberts, suggested a fictitious final chapter where I actually got to meet Numan – what would I say? How would I react? What questions would I ask? But I said no. That's not to say I didn't have one, solitary contact with him.

When I was at Guinness World Records, I arrived at my desk one morning and there was a stiff card-backed brown envelope on my desk with David's name and our work address written on it in a very distinct hand. I recognized it but couldn't immediately place the writing. A note attached to the front read, "This is for you! DR". I slit open the envelope and inside there was a glossy B&W photo of Numan, personally inscribed:

"For Martin, Best wishes, Gary Numan"

David, when editor of *The Guinness Book of Hit Singles*, had the good fortune to meet Numan and, contacting the fan club, arranged for an autographed photo to be sent to me. I was taken completely by surprise and was absolutely thrilled. I demanded David give me Gary's personal contact email so that I could thank him for the photo, which he did, but I never got a reply. I didn't really expect to get one to be honest.

Whether Numan ever stops to think about how his music may have affected people – in my case 'Are 'friends' electric?' which literally changed my life, saving me from my inarticulate mourning – is debatable. A song composed on an out-of-tune piano and recorded using a synth in a studio that had been left behind by the previous band, it is actually two songs merged together, part science fiction story/part dig at an ex-girlfriend. Music academics cheerfully point out that the main riff features 'the wrong note'. It has no soaring, sing along chorus; you can't dance to it, and, as the notorious, lisping music impresario Eric Hall once commented about one of Marc Bolan's poems, it doesn't even rhyme.

It's odd, it's quirky, it's clumsy, it's too long for commercial radio but I will never grow tired of hearing it.

You see, it meant everything to me.

Further reading and information sources

FURTHER READING

www.garynuman.co.uk
   The official Numan website for up to date information regarding tours and releases, plus Numan's Twitter updates.

www.beggars.com
   Home of Beggars Banquet Records, Numan's first record-label.

www.nureference.co.uk
   Everything you ever wanted to know about ANY Gary Numan release, tour, single, album...you name it.   Every variation, re-release, promo, coloured vinyl, all lovingly detailed with scans of just about every album and single cover from around the world. Always a work in progress as a rare hitherto unknown Guatemalan pressing of 'We Are Glass" on 12-inch picture-disc may well be out there somewhere.

Rock Atlas (ISBN-13: 9781905959570)
   David Roberts' recently-published labour of love is now onto its well-deserved second edition. It features details of famous music landmarks, events, locations, album-cover photo locations and everything in between. Not sure the picture of me on the Ian Dury memorial bench located at Poet's Corner in Richmond Park is the most flattering? As I've said, if anyone knows of a location intrinsically linked to Numan, let me know!

www.facebook.com/TheSoloNumanExperience

Pat Martin's Facebook page, with details of his Numan tribute shows and forthcoming appearances.

INFORMATION SOURCES

My Diaries: 1975 to date

These are the key sources for my life events. From 1975 to 1987, they're a bit sketchy but from 1988 onwards, they are full and complete. Useful when compiling this book as I'm sure I've lost about ten million brain-cells following the chemotherapy! It still saddens me even now to see that Friday 15th April 1977 just has a big black cross through it.

Praying to The Aliens (ISBN-10: 0233992057)

Numan's autobiography, covering birth, childhood, adolescence, Punk, Bowie, the mania of 1979 and 1980, through the lean years and up to 1997. I wonder if he really did audition for The Jam!

Gary Numan – The Authorised Biography (ISBN-10: 0-283-98876-2)

Ray Coleman's excellent in-depth biography, again, from birth, childhood, adolescence, superstardom, through to 1982. Long out of print, but worth tracking down for, if nothing else, the superb front cover photograph from the *Dance* album cover photo sessions.

Electric Pioneer Redux (ISBN-10: 1495278085)

Paul Goodwin's labour of love, detailing every release plus commentary, plus tour dates, tour set-lists, scans of albums, covers and memorabilia.

Numan By Computer (no ISBN)

The curious oddity by Fred and Judy Vermorel, this was released in the early 1980s, and featured some great photographs, along with brief Numan quotes, augmented by a computer program from the Department of Statistics at University College, London which randomised the text!

Smash Hits, Sounds, Record Mirror
Long-defunct weekly and bi-weekly music newspapers and magazines, which covered Numan's career; some were quite hostile while others gave Numan fair coverage.

The Guinness Book of Hit Singles and Albums (ISBN-10: 1904994105)
Edited by David Roberts, this was the pinnacle of music chart data, produced annually until 2006 with the publication of the final 19th edition. Much missed, often imitated, never equalled.

Official Fan-Club Magazines
Originally run by Gary's Mum, Beryl, who sadly passed away earlier this year. Beryl WAS the fan-club for so many of us and her often hand-written letters and notes included with membership renewals and answers to the endless fan questions was a nice, personal and always appreciated touch. The fan-club was, in those innocent pre-internet days, the only source of official Numan news from the Numan camp. The fan-club magazines included rare photographs, news, competitions, all worth tracking down on eBay.

Official Fan-Club Year Books
Provided a year-in-review of Numan activity, releases, tours, flights and, again, featured some quite lovely photographs, mostly exclusive to the club.

Official Tour Brochures
I have most from 1979 to 1997, an essential purchase at each gig (my heart sank when I found out the 1984 Berserker Tour brochure had sold out on the night!). Great souvenirs from great concerts!

The Author

Martin Downham has spent all his life in sweet suburbia on the fringes of South West London, where his passion, naturally, is music. He has been a member of several ramshackle bands over the years, most recently We Fear Change, where he has sung, played guitar and even co-written a few toe-tappers. Martin has also contributed photos and articles to various music publications, including the rather wonderful *Rock Atlas* series of books. He is blissfully married to Vicki and has two young sons, along with a huge collection of vinyl and CDs, an attic full of vintage Marvel and DC Comics and a garden full of stray – but very well fed – cats.

Also from Hornet Books

The Sword That Saves

The Sword That Saves, by Ambrose Merrell, is the first in a series of
young adult novels introducing orphan Sam Stone.
Separated from his younger sisters Zoe and Sophie when his
parents are killed in a road accident, Sam's miserable and lonely
existence is transformed when he is introduced to the ancient
martial art, aikido. The extraordinary powers he discovers during
one very special day enable him to travel back in time from his
home in Vancouver to 16 th -century Japan. A mysterious sword
that Sam is taught to use is both his protection, and his only hope, in
a journey that will see him drawn into a
battle against the evil powers of Darkness who seek to steal it.

Sing to Silent Stones

Sing to Silent Stones: Violet's War is the first volume in David
Snell's family saga chronicling the tale of unmarried mother Violet
and her son Frank. After surviving many moving and harrowing
experiences as a nurse in World War I Violet is reunited with
Frank, whose childhood friendships are tested with dramatic and
unexpected results as he grows up in the Loire Valley during World
War II. Providing new insight into the lives of those who endured
and survived both World Wars, *Sing to Silent Stones* is based around
the dramatic stories from his own family.

The Chant

The Chant, by Carl Mason, is a powerful legal thriller with erotic undertones. The arrival of a new member of staff sees the ordinary private life of college lecturer Will Taylor thrown into turmoil. Usually it is Will's friend Dominic who catches the eye of the ladies but the newly arrived Lisa makes it known it is Will that interests her. But a dangerous game ensues when Will is dragged, at first willingly, into a red hot relationship where the sex is not safe, sane or consensual. Attempting to end the relationship only leads to more misery when a violent incident sets off a harrowing prosecution process and an excruciating trial. A supercharged climax reveals where the true power rests.

Muddy Water

Muddy Water is the extraordinary tale of revenge and unexpected love, from Neil Watson.

Leslie Markland hasn't a clue what the word entailment means, but when his father's will is read he soon finds out – and it's not good news. Cruelly denied his inheritance – the Markland Estate in York-shire – Leslie sets out to gain revenge on the father who betrayed him. Living on a barge on the river estuary at Wivenhoe in Essex, he plots his retribution. The unforeseen train of events this unleashes backfires spectacularly when he winds up in prison. *Muddy Water* is the dramatic story he has plenty of time to write during his stay at Her Majesty's pleasure.

BanGk!

BanGk!, by former Radio Luxembourg DJ Mark Wesley, is a crime caper where three first-time bank robbers come up with a crazy plan to steal gold bullion from the Bank of England. *BanGk!*'s leading man is James Stack, ex-Captain Special Forces, a tough, intelligent risk taker, who figures that if you want to rob the Bank of England you don't go through the front door guns blazing, tunnel up through the floor, climb through windows, lower yourself on a harness, screw around with the computers, fix security cameras, or play Twister with invisible Laser beams. You don't do any of that stuff because it won't work. In *BanGk!* it's easy to see why gold has never been stolen from the vaults of the Bank of England. They've got every angle covered apparently: Except one.

www.hornetbooks.com